Caring For Your Miniature Donkey

Second Edition

By Bonnie R. Gross

DISCLAIMER: The suggestions, recommendations and advice in this book are written in the hope that readers will accept the information as a guide and apply them accordingly. Although every effort has been made to present accurate, up-to-date information, it should be understood that the results of medical treatments depend upon many factors, including proper diagnosis and individual conditions. Therefore, neither the Author nor the Publisher assumes responsibility for and makes no warranty with respect to results that may be obtained from the procedures herein. Neither the Author nor the Publisher shall be liable to any person for damage resulting from reliance on any information contained in this book. To ensure the reader's understanding of some technical descriptions offered in this book, brand names have been used as examples of particular substances or equipment. However, the use of a particular brand name is not intended to imply an endorsement of any particular product. Each reader should contact their own veterinarian and follow their advice.

*Dedicated to and in honor of
donkeys around the world*

CONTENTS

Chapter 1: Introduction

A Bit of History...9
Miniature Donkey Facts 10
Breed Standards 13
Conformation Charts.. 17
Points of the Donkey Drawing 21
Skeletal Drawing 22
Internal Organs Drawing... 23

Chapter 2: Purchasing and New Owners

But what do you DO with 'em? 25
In The Beginning.. 27
    What potential buyers need to know
Marketing Miniature Donkeys...................................... 30
Long Distance Shipping.. 38
Integrating the new Donkey 46
When You Get Your New Weanling Home..................... 49
Know What's Normal For Your Donkey.......................... 51

Chapter 3: Feeding and Bedding

Feeding Donkeys Hay 54
Blister Beetle Poisoning.. 58
What is Your Feed Tag Telling You? 59
Salt: Don't Sell Them Short 61
Fences for Horses/Donkeys 62
Stall Bedding 72
    Types of bedding and disposal of
Manure Management... 77
Cold Weather Care 79
Cold Weather Care of Weanlings.................................. 81
The Battle Against Flies.. 84

Bot Fly Season...86

Chapter 4: Hoof Care

Handling the Legs and Hooves 89
Rasping and Trimming Donkey Hooves 92
Hoof Abscesses 98
Thrush or Abscess? 101
Seedy Toe..103
Keratoma..107
Scratches 109

Chapter 5: Disease, Illness, Skin

Choosing a Veterinarian 113
Hematology Testing...117
  Blood work counts
Household First Aid..119
The Killing Fields...121
  Poisonous Plants, Grasses, Weeds, Ornamentals
Hyperlipaemia and Obese Donkeys.............................130
Plugged Tear Ducts 134
Treating Eye Problems 135
Allergies and Their Treatment 138
Lyme Disease 140
Equine Sarcoid: Frequently Asked Questions 143
Asinine Herpesvirus 3 149
New Discoveries on Rhino Virus 151
Dryland Distemper 153
  Pigeon Fever
Strangles – Equine Distemper......................................156
Diarrhea...161
Foal Diarrhea...164
Does My Donkey Have Arthritis? 166
Equine Infectious Anemia 167
So Your Pet Has Cancer 170
Choke 173
Hypothyroidism 175
Heaves - Emphysema 177

Hot Weather Hauling and Heat Stress 181
Upward Fixation of the Patella...183
Misconceptions About Salmonella Infection 187
Selenium Deficiency...190
    White Muscle Disease
Selenium Intoxication 198
Tetanus..200
Bladder Stone Removal in Miniature Donkey...............................203
End Stage Liver Disease 206
Treating the Open Wound 210
Identifying the Cause of Weight Loss..212
    Donkey weight condition charts
Laminitis (Founder)...215
Skin Problems 218
    Treating skin ailments
Ringworm..222
Skin Disease Charts..224
Botulism...227
The Obese Donkey..229
Death and Euthanasia 232

Chapter 6: Vaccinations and Medication

The Ins & Outs of Antibiotics...237
Do Mini Donkeys Get Mini Vaccinations?....................................243
The facts about Vaccine Products 244
Miniature Donkey Vaccinations 246
What Vaccinations Do I Really Need? 249
Respiratory Infections..251
Injections: What You Should Know..256
Injection Sites 257
Vaccination Chart..262
Important Notes About Administering Medications! 263
Most Commonly Used Medicines...265

Chapter 7: Worms and Parasites

The Worm War..270
Should you *Really* be using Ivomec® on your Donkeys? 272

Types of Worms...275
Worming Methods..277

Chapter 8: Reproduction, Breeding, Foaling

Prostaglandins 280
Cryptorchidism 282
Castration 285
Rectal Palpation..291
Udder Edema in the Miniature Jennet..............................293
Early Embryo Loss...295
Causes of Abortion..297
Helping To Avoid Foal Rejection 301
Navel or Joint ILL 306
Foal Septicemia 307

Chapter 9: Behavior, Psychology and Training

Wood Chewing...310
Twitching 314
Donkey *ill-Manners*: The Biter.......................................317
The Elderly Donkey..320
A Little About Jacks...324
The Donkey Guardian...326
How to become Confident with your Donkey.....................330
Hard to Catch Donkey 333
Teaching a Young Donkey to Lead....................................336
How to teach a donkey to lead...... Quick 341
The Beginners Guide to Driving 343

Chapter 10: Miscellaneous

Most Common Newbie Questions on Donkeys....................358
Miniature Donkey Talk 361
Foaling Manual..362
International Miniature Donkey Registry 363
Index..364

Chapter 1

Introduction

A Bit of History

The miniature donkey is a native to the Mediterranean islands of Sicily and Sardinia where they were generally used as working animals. A handful of people imported them and began breeding them. One of the largest original breeders was August Busch of Busch Beer fame. He gave many young donkeys away to his friends as gifts. Another large breeder was Danby Farms in Nebraska who later established the original registry in 1958. In the past the donkeys have been referred to as "Sicilian donkeys", "Sardinian donkeys", "Miniature Mediterranean donkeys" but today are simply called "Miniature donkeys". The great majority of the donkeys originally imported and bred were between the sizes of 32" and 38". Breeders, thankfully, have not been overly concerned about breeding down in size, but have concentrated more on breeding for correct conformation, which has maintained the donkey's natural tendency to be healthy and also stay in the average size range of 32" to 35". It has been suggested that all the original miniature donkeys were gray but due to some out-crossing with larger standard size donkeys today we have a variety of colors.

Miniature Donkey Facts
A Quick Overview

Life Span: With proper lifelong care, 25-45 years
Height: 36" or under (IMDR Class A Registry)
    38" or under (IMDR Class B Registry)
Weight: 200 to 450 pounds
Average Gestation: 11 months, 3 weeks, 5 days.
    (Unlike other animals, donkeys can have a normal pregnancy
of 11 months to 13 months.)

Color: As with most animals, donkeys can range in color from black to white and everything in between. The most common - and predominant color - is "gray-dun." This is mouse gray with a dark gray or brown cross on the back. There are variations of this gray-dun from dark to light. True blacks are extremely rare with black/browns (not quite black) being more common. There are chestnut/sorrels which are various shades of reddish brown. There are also white donkeys and "spotted" donkeys. Some people refer to spotted as "pinto" and this really boils down to semantics. Spotted or pintos are generally gray or brown and white. There are also various colors of roans. Roan coloring is black, brown, gray hairs intermingled with white hairs. Donkeys do not breed true to color. Since gray-dun is by far the predominant gene, you can breed black to black and get gray-dun, spotted to spotted and get gray-dun, etc. Never knowing what color foal will be produced is part of the excitement of having foals.

Reproduction: Jennets (females) can become fertile at one year of age but if bred, make very poor mothers and usually reject their foals. Jennets can be considered for breeding after the age of two years depending on their overall physical and mental maturity. Jacks (males) can be fertile at one year of age but generally wait until 16 to 18 months. Jacks inherit much of their overall fertility and libido from their sires. It is important to remember that you cannot purchase a weanling jack and a weanling jennet and raise them together, as the jack will breed the jennet before she is ready to be bred. They would need to be separated at 10-11 months of age or you could buy a two year old jennet and a weanling jack and raise them together so that when the jack is fertile, the jennet will be old enough to be bred. Twinning in Miniature Donkeys is rare. Birth weights are generally between 18 and 25 pounds. Jennets between the size of 33" and 38" usually have an easy time foaling. Smaller jennets may need human intervention.

Health Care: Miniature Donkeys are very healthy animals. They require the same yearly vaccinations as horses. They should also be dewormed, with an equine dewormer, at a minimum of three times per year, preferably six times per year. They require the same hoof care as equine and should be trimmed at least three times per year.

Feeding: Donkeys can survive on good quality hay alone. A good hay to feed donkeys is a mixture of alfalfa and grass, if a donkey needs to put on some weight, or quality grass hay if the donkey is already in good weight. Pure alfalfa is too rich a feed for Miniature Donkeys and does not set well with their digestive systems. They can also become extremely fat on alfalfa hay. With severe droughts often occurring in different parts of the country, sometimes only poor quality hay is available and in this case, donkeys should be supplemented with a 10%-12% protein equine sweet feed. Adult donkeys are termed as "easy keepers" meaning they utilize their feed very efficiently and you must be careful that they do not get fat. Fat donkeys will develop a "crest" - or fat roll - on their necks that will be there for life once it develops.

Personality: The first and foremost attraction to Miniature Donkeys is their loving personalities. They demand attention! They form close attachments to their owners and to other donkeys. Donkeys are herd animals and one *lone* donkey is a very *lonely* donkey. Because of their laid-back, easy going personalities, they make wonderful pets for children, the handicapped and the elderly.

Donkey Communication: Donkeys communicate with their human owners and with other donkeys by "braying", also more commonly known as a *hee-haw*. Every donkey has his or her own style of braying with some sounding quite comical. They range from barely being audible to a loud thunderous bray. Donkeys develop schedules and if you are late in feeding, you will *hear* about it! Jacks pastured apart from their jennets, will *call* to them several times a day. On the whole, donkeys are very quiet animals.

Investment: Miniature Donkeys can be a mid to high level income producing investment depending on the quality of the animal you want to raise. The better quality animal you purchase the better quality foals you have. We see many retirees raising Miniature Donkeys as a second income and also buying them for Grandchildren to help pay for their educations.

Carlton Standish of Texas

Breed Standards

Miniature Donkeys come in all shapes, sizes, and colors. The breed standard for any animal must be based on proper proportion and balance whether it be of the light boned, slender build or heavy boned and draft build. Regardless of bone structure, the original Miniature Donkeys from Sicily and Sardinia, along with a few other parts of the world, were of heights up to 38" which is why the original Miniature Donkey Registry established by Mrs. Bea Langfeld registered up to this size. The *International Miniature Donkey Registry* therefore recognizes foundation donkeys up to 38" as registerable in the I.M.D.R., as many of these "Sicilian" donkeys are still in production.

The overall appearance of a Miniature Donkey should be attractive, well balanced, and nicely coupled with an attentive expression. Jennets should look more feminine with jacks having a more masculine appearance.

Overall bone structure should appear strong and sound and in proportion to the body size and muscular development of the body. The bone structure should not be too heavy nor too fine.

Head

The head should be pleasing to look at and in proportion to the body. The side view of the head should have a straight profile or one that is slightly dished. The forehead should be broad with sufficient width between the eyes. Nostrils should not be too small to allow sufficient air to enter the lungs. Ears, no matter the length, should be in proportion to the head but not overly long or short. Ears should be firm, alert and not loose or floppy. Eyes should not be too small (pig eyes) nor overly large and bulging. Jowls should be well defined being somewhat larger on Jacks and more refined on Jennets. Lips should meet evenly or the top lip can protrude slightly. Lips should not hang loose and open.

Faults: Roman nosed and thick muzzled; Too small nostrils; Too small eyes; Ears that flop to sides of head; Head too large and/or too long.

Teeth

The ideal mouth structure would enable the teeth to meet evenly. A 1/8" overbite or underbite is very common in Miniature Donkeys and should rot be considered a bad fault. The *International Miniature Donkey* Registry allows up to a 1/4" differential.

Faults: In excess of 1/4" Overbite (Parrot Mouth) or Underbite (Monkey Mouth)

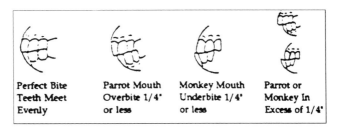

| Perfect Bite Teeth Meet Evenly | Parrot Mouth Overbite 1/4" or less | Monkey Mouth Underbite 1/4" or less | Parrot or Monkey In Excess of 1/4" |

Neck

The ideal neck is in proportion to the rest of the donkey's body. It should be firm and in good flesh. It should not be overly thin and long nor short and thick. The top of the neck and bottom of the neck should show straight lines as they connect to the shoulder and chest areas. Fat crest (fat build up on the top of the neck) is more of a management problem than a conformation defect however, can be unsightly.

Faults: Ewe necks (top line shows a depression between withers and ears) and necks are usually too thin; Short thick neck (makes it difficult to graze and turn and bend necks).

Body

The topline (back) of the donkey should be straight or slightly dipped. (Older Brood jennets should be given consideration in the top line area due to births.) Withers should be somewhat noticeable but should not protrude. The back should be fairly short and give a strong appearance and not swayed or too long and also should not be roached (humped up). Jennets may be a little longer in this area than jacks allowing sufficient room to carry a foal. The croup may be just slightly higher than the withers. Chest should be wide from front view and donkey should have adequate heart girth.

Faults: Sway back; Excessively long or short; Roach back; Croup much higher than withers; chest too narrow.

Hindquarters

Donkeys have a sharper sloping croup because of higher pelvic bones, so should not be compared to horses. The rump should be strong, wide and nicely rounded. It should be in good flesh and have good length between the point of the hip and point of the buttock. Good tail set.

Faults: Narrow hips, Pointed hips, too high tail set, Croup set too high.

Legs

Front legs should be straight. From a side view, drawing a straight line down from the middle of the upper forearm, the line would go through the middle of the knee and pass directly behind the heel. Any derivative of this would be a crooked limb. From the front view, drawing a straight line down from the point of the shoulder, the line would go through the middle of the knee, the middle of the forearm and the middle of the hoof. Back legs should be straight. From a side view, a straight line drawn from the point of the buttock would go just behind the point of the hock and hind cannon. From the back view, a straight line drawn from the point of the buttock would touch the middle of the hock, cannon and fetlocks. Most donkeys tend to stand with hocks slightly turned out and this is perfectly acceptable to the I.M.D.R. Cannon bones should be shorter than the forearm.

Faults: Any serious deviation from straight legged both in front and back; excessively toed out or toed in, cowhocked; forearm longer than cannon.

Feet

Donkeys stand higher in the heel than horses and should not be compared with horses. From a side view, the front foot, when drawing a straight line from the toe to the fetlock, would be at a 55 degree angle. The hind foot, would be at a 60 degree angle. Regardless of the build of the foot, it should be trimmed to follow a straight line to the fetlock if possible. When drawing a straight line from the front view, the line would go through the middle of the fetlock joint to the middle of the hoof.

Faults: Hooves too upright or slacking backwards, long upright pastern, short upright pastern, club foot.

Ungelded Jacks - Ungelded jacks used for breeding purposes should possess excellent conformation, have no mouth deformities and have both testicles descended. Jacks who have one or both testicles retained will only be permitted "pet quality" registration papers.

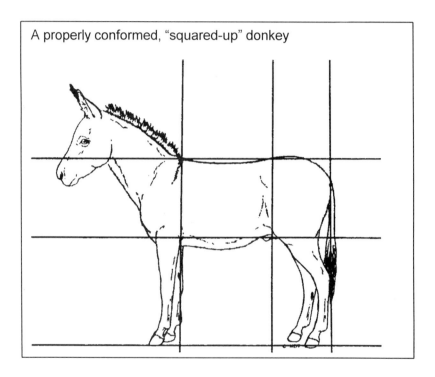

A properly conformed, "squared-up" donkey

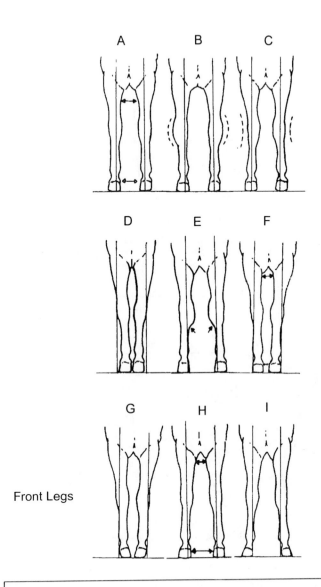

Front Legs

(A) Idea l   (B) Bow Leg   (C) Knock Kneed
(D) Stands too close   (E) Bench Knees
(F) Feet too close together   (G) Toes In
(H) Distance between feet further than distance between
forearm   (I) Toes out

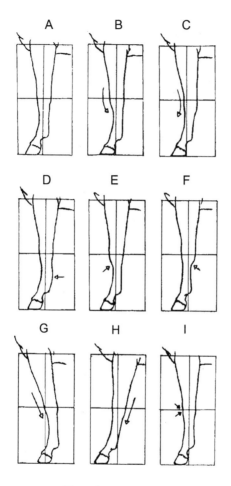

Front Legs, Side View

(A) Ideal (B) Buck Kneed (C) Calf Kneed
(D) Bowed Tendon   (E) Weak cannon
(F) Tied in at knee   (G) Standing under in front
(H) Camped out in front   (I) Open Knee

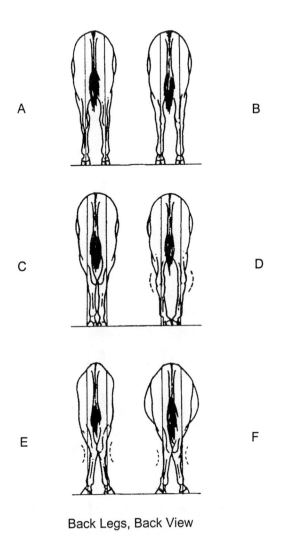

Back Legs, Back View

(A) Ideal   (B) Acceptable - hock is slightly turned out.
(C) Standing too close behind (D) Bow Legs, Pigeon Toes
(E) Cow hocks, toes out (F) Narrow hips

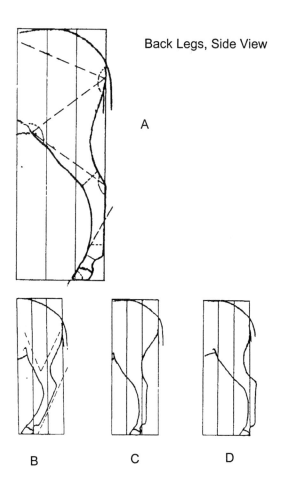

Back Legs, Side View

A

B   C   D

(A) Ideal - Draw a line from the point of the buttock
down and the line will touch the back of the leg
(B) Sickle hocks - Stands in and under
(C) Standing under body
(D) Camped Behind - Legs set too far back

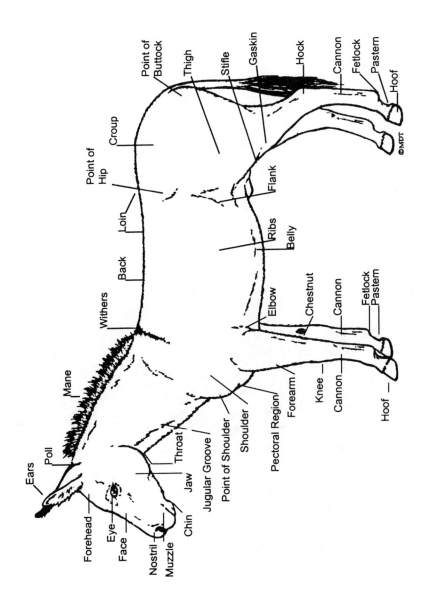

Point of Buttock
Thigh
Stifle
Gaskin
Hock
Cannon
Fetlock
Pastern
Hoof
Croup
Point of Hip
Flank
Loin
Ribs
Belly
Back
Elbow
Chestnut
Cannon
Fetlock
Pastern
Withers
Mane
Poll
Ears
Forehead
Eye
Face
Nostril
Muzzle
Chin
Jaw
Throat
Jugular Groove
Point of Shoulder
Shoulder
Pectoral Region
Forearm
Knee
Cannon
Hoof

©MDT

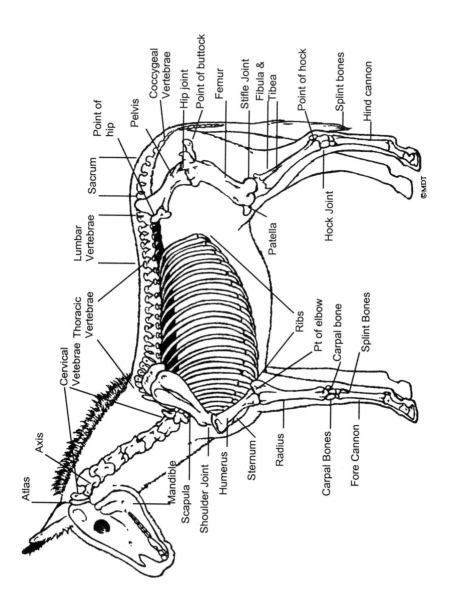

Atlas

Axis

Cervical Vetebrae

Thoracic Vertebrae

Lumbar Vertebrae

Sacrum

Point of hip

Pelvis

Coccygeal Vertebrae

Hip joint

Point of buttock

Femur

Stifle Joint

Fibula & Tibea

Point of hock

Splint bones

Hind cannon

Patella

Hock Joint

©MDT

Mandible

Scapula

Shoulder Joint

Humerus

Sternum

Radius

Ribs

Pt of elbow

Carpal bone

Splint Bones

Carpal Bones

Fore Cannon

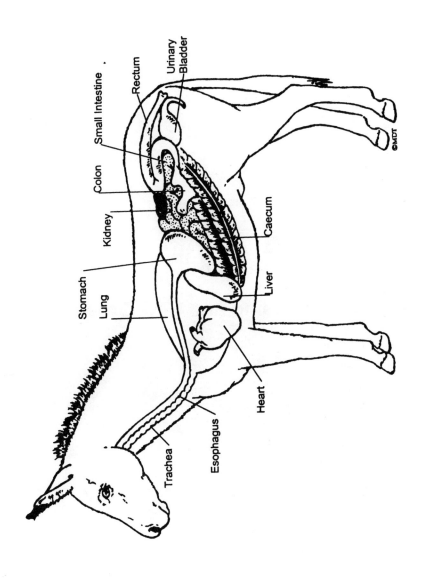

Rectum

Urinary
Bladder

Small Intestine .

Colon

Kidney

Stomach

Lung

Caecum

Liver

Heart

Trachea

Esophagus

©MDT

Chapter 2

Purchasing and New Owners

But what do you DO with 'em?

Donkeys are very entertaining. They're fun to watch. Foals love to run and play with each other. Adults often get into the act trying to catch up with their kids and eventually give up and stand still while their babies run by them in circles. Mothers continuously discipline their foals and it is very interesting to observe. Jack foals love to jump on their mother's neck and bite them with the mother quickly moving their heads downward to bite their foals back on the front legs as a form of discipline.

Donkeys are good for the soul

You often hear lately "...donkeys are good for the soul". Unlike others in the equine family, if you go out in a pasture of donkeys, they will quickly surround you, rubbing up against your legs, begging for attention. Their owner's love is very important to them. If you chose to ignore them, they'll let you know their dissatisfaction by grabbing your pants leg in their mouth and pulling. Come home from a hard day's work schedule, walk out to your donkeys, and be surrounded by love.

Donkeys are fantastic pets for the elderly, handicapped and small children. Small children not only learn responsibility for caring for an animal but can also ride donkeys, as larger miniatures can hold up to 100 pounds on their back. They are much easier to train than ponies and most willingly accept a child on their backs. Donkeys are generally much smarter than other equine. Most people, who are experienced with horses, can train a donkey to pull a cart in a matter of hours. If they come across a situation that they fear may hurt them or that they are unsure of, they will stop and look everything over before proceeding. The old wives tale of donkeys being *stubborn*, is actually their sign of intelligence.

It is a rarity indeed for a donkey to kick their handler. The only time I have ever seen a donkey kick at a human is out of intense fear of a stranger in a confined area. Donkeys are more apt to run when in doubt of a situation. It is also extremely rare for a donkey to show anger at a human.

Probably the most enjoyment people get out of their donkeys is driving them. Donkeys are fast learners and it's fun!

Many, many people take their donkeys to nursing homes and elementary schools, petting zoos and farm shows. They are such a quiet, laid-back, rare animal that these functions welcome donkeys with open arms. With the rising interest in keeping physically fit, many donkeys are used as pack animals. You can buy packing outfits for your donkeys, or make your own, and have them carry a picnic lunch for you or camping supplies for overnight adventures.

So you see, putting aside the nice investments Miniature Donkeys are, they are also a versatile pet that you can do almost anything with!

In The Beginning...

What potential donkeys buyers need to know

If you are considering purchasing one Miniature Donkey or a whole herd, there are basic questions that most potential buyers have. This is the only book available solely covering Miniature Donkeys and the most reliable informational source along with *Miniature Donkey Talk Magazine*. Our phones constantly ring from potential buyers asking, "where do I begin?" Some of these callers have never even seen a Miniature Donkey before while others have picked up a copy of *Miniature Donkey Talk* and their curiosity has gotten the best of them. Still others have visited a local breeder however do not know if they should trust that person to sell them a quality animal or even an animal for a pet. *The International Miniature Donkey Registry* has a list of breeders that raise IMDR donkeys. Call them and ask them for some names of breeders in your area.

Just by the mere fact that you are reading this book, says that donkeys have captured your heart and you want some. Before you begin, you must first decide what you want to do with them. Do you want some donkeys in a pasture, just to look at? Do you want to show? Do you want to hook them to a cart and drive them? Do you want to breed and sell their offspring? Do you want to do all of the above?

We cannot stress the importance of doing your homework before you start writing out checks for thousands of dollars. The most important part of doing your homework is visiting breeders in your area. Call these people up, make an appointment, and start making the rounds. Have a list of questions to ask. Most breeders who advertise are more than willing to *talk donkey* and answer questions. Ask what they like the most about having donkeys. If you think you are interested in showing, ask breeders in your area if there are shows nearby. Ask about the prices of donkeys that they have for sale. If one is cheaper than others, ask why.

Beauty is in the eye of the beholder! What one person may think is a beautiful donkey, may not appeal to you at all.

Also, if you are only looking for pets, beauty probably will have very little to do with what you are interested in. If one of the breeders you are visiting picks out a jennet and says how much they like her, ask them why. If it's because of conformation, ask them to tell you specifically why they like the way the animal is built. If you do this with everyone you visit, you will end up learning a great deal about conformation.

Check out the facilities closely. This will accomplish two purposes. One, if their barns are filthy, their water supply is filthy, and it looks like a farrier hasn't been there in years, chances are the donkeys have not been vaccinated or dewormed. Ask about health care information. Does the breeder have records on each individual animal? If the donkeys haven't been dewormed regularly, parasite damage may not show up until several months later and you would be in for a lot of heartbreak and veterinarian bills. Will the donkeys freely walk up to you or do they appear to be frightened of people? Do all animals have adequate shelter in both summer and winter? Secondly, well-kept facilities and nicely arranged pastures and stalls will give you lots of ideas on how to arrange your own facilities to best suit your needs.

If you are purchasing a pregnant jennet, can the breeder show you a blood test confirming her pregnant? If not, are they willing to have a blood test done to confirm pregnancy at the time of sale? Remember, just because a jennet was "bred to" a jack, does not mean she is pregnant. If for some reason the seller is not willing to have a pregnancy test done, maybe it is wise for you to spend $40.00 to have a veterinarian go to the farm and do the test before the sale. Never let a veterinarian do a rectal palpation! Always get either a blood test or an outside-the-belly ultra sound.

Donkeys do not require elaborate fencing. Unlike other animals, they are not constantly trying to find a way out. Once they realize that where they are being kept is to be considered home, they are quite willing to stay put.

When you are considering buying from a breeder, is the seller the type of person who wouldn't mind answering questions *after* the sale? You may need to know about past health care, feeding, breeding, etc., for that particular donkey.

So now that we've *really* sparked your interest, don't let go of that wallet yet. If at all possible, you should never buy just one donkey. Donkeys are extremely social animals and are very herd-oriented. You certainly may put one in with a horse, or some other livestock, but they will not develop a friendship the same way they will with another donkey. Even if put in with other animals, you will often see them in another part of the pasture alone. You will very seldom see this if you have two donkeys. They will almost always be together. Buying a young ungelded jack to put in with goats or sheep almost never works out. Young jacks are very playful and get too rough with goats or sheep.

Donkeys do not require special grooming equipment. In fact, if they are not going to a show or fair, and are not in the process of shedding a winter coat, most prefer little grooming. They will roll three or four times a day in soft dirt or sand if available. This helps insulate their coats in winter and helps keep flies off them in summer.

Is the donkey registered? If so, what do you know about the animals on the pedigree? What does the seller know about the animals on the pedigree? Extended pedigrees are great, I suppose, but the only problem is, if the breeder cannot tell you what size, color and the conformation of all the animals on the pedigree, then what good are they? If a donkey has been rated© by the *International Miniature Donkey Registry* (in Maryland) and has a two, three or four star rating, you can be assured that the donkey's conformation was evaluated by professionals and is a quality animal. You can also have more confidence in your choice of foals if their parents have both been rated by I.M.D.R.

Another great learning tool before buying your first Miniature Donkeys is ordering the *Back Issue Package* of *Miniature Donkey Talk Magazine.* As advertised, it is a wealth of information! Read and re-read them. Many, many potential buyers are now doing this. We want you to be educated and informed *before* you buy. This makes the chances greater of you buying donkeys that you will be happy with. It's also a sure bet that you won't stop at one or two or......

Marketing Miniature Donkeys

There are probably as many marketing strategies as there are people to market these nice animals. Each seller has to arrive at an individual style of marketing that best suits their philosophical outlook, personality and the financial necessity to make a sale. Marketing is defined as the act of promoting, cultivating a clientele for, and selling any good or service.

Who Buys Miniature Donkeys

It seems important that we determine who is buying what we are selling. Essentially there appears to be two broad types of buyers for Miniature Donkeys. The first are people interested in deriving an income from breeding and selling Miniature Donkeys. The second are people interested in purchasing a unique, fairly rare backyard pet or companion. The backgrounds of these buyers are varied as some have owned horses in the past, some have owned other types of livestock and still others have never owned any type of livestock but the diminutive size of the donkey appeals to them more than a 16 hand horse would. The initial purchase is probably the result of simply the desire to own a unique little animal.

Miniature donkeys are not a necessity of life such as housing, food and clothing. They are a luxury item frequently purchased with money from savings accounts. The money may well have been spent on boats, vacations and other luxuries. Prevailing economic attitudes can heavily effect the sale of Miniature Donkeys. It is important that the seller be aware of current trends in the economy in order to determine the direction of emphasis for his or her marketing strategy.

It would be interesting to know how often buyers sell close to home and how often they sell outside their area. We at *Pheasant Meadow Farm* rarely sell close to home as the majority of our buyers are other breeders in the midwest or west coast as there are few breeders on the east coast. However, from all the people we talk to and correspond with, we feel that at this time, most sales take place between breeders and first time buyers and not breeders to breeders. If this assumption is correct, the market is healthy due to this new interest. There are buyers for every Miniature Donkey. The key is to bring the buyer and donkey together.

A highly positive aspect of marketing Miniature Donkeys is their appeal. Most people are genuinely taken with their small size, the cute fuzzy look of weanlings and overly friendly personalities.

Establishing a Price

Probably the biggest determiner as to whether a buyer is going to seriously consider your donkey is your asking price. Any price you put on a donkey can be the right price if you have a buyer who is willing to pay it. Potential buyers of donkeys are no different than buyers of other items. The educated buyer is going to do some comparison shopping. Each buyer has criteria that must be met before they purchase and a sale depends on whether your donkey meets this criteria. The *first time buyer* may have some of these factors in mind: By the way, these are not listed in any priority.

1. Personality - Another breeder may just be looking for good breeding stock and not be overly interested in how friendly the donkey is. Personality is almost always at the top of the list for first time buyers because in donkeys, this is what has attracted them in the first place.
2. Height - We often find this to be at the bottom of the list. First time buyers looking for pets are generally not concerned with height.
3. Sex - On average, jennets command higher prices than jacks unless the jack is outstanding in some way.
4. Pedigree - We find that donkeys sired by well-known, advertised herd sires command higher prices.
5. Conformation - Although extremely important for breeding stock, we find that many first time buyers do not learn about conformation strengths and weaknesses until after they purchase their first donkeys. This is unfortunate as we often get calls from these people saying, "The first donkeys I bought did not have very good conformation and now I'm looking for good stock."
6. Show record - With the limited number of shows around, we find this to be a non-issue with new buyers.
7. Age - New buyers generally have their minds made up as to whether they are looking for weanlings, adults or older breeder stock. We are fortunate that donkeys have a long life span so even those in their teens are still marketable.

Other factors affecting the price of the donkey can be the sellers' personal situation. How anxious are you to sell? The higher the price, the fewer qualified buyers available. One needs to keep in mind that the price will reflect how fast the donkey sells. The lower the price the more buyers there are available.

The sellers emotional bond to the donkey will also reflect on the price set. Being attached to a donkey doesn't mean that potential buyers will see the same qualities in the donkey as you do.

When setting a price you need to put emotion and biases away and honestly evaluate the animal. A seller can ask as much as he wants for the donkey, but its true worth at any particular time is measured by what a buyer is willing to pay.

Exposure to the public

The more your business and farm is exposed to the public, the more sales you'll have. Most advertisers in *Miniature Donkey Talk Magazine* sell donkeys with ease. Repetitive advertising keeps your name and your farm in plain view and easy to recognize. New buyers feel more comfortable buying from sellers who take the time and expense to promote their donkeys. They feel more at ease in asking questions and feel repeat advertisers will be around if months down the road they have questions. We find that new buyers especially like to have weanlings from well-known herd sires.

Buyers interested in breeding Miniature Donkeys and selling their offspring need to not only spend the money to purchase quality donkeys, they need to have money set aside for advertising on a continual basis. So many first time buyers feel that when its time for them to sell, people will automatically come to their door. If you aren't willing to take the time and effort to promote yourself and your donkeys, then you need to realize you'll have to accept lower prices for your donkeys.

"Twenty percent of the sellers make eighty percent of the sales and the other eighty percent of the sellers divide the remaining twenty percent of the sales." The more often people see your advertising in *Miniature Donkey Talk*, the more name recognition you have. You of course need to base your advertising on what you expect to have in future sales. If you are producing one or two foals a year, then running a full page color ad for a year seems rather silly. On the other hand, if you have high quality stock, producing high quality offspring there is no better way to show off your animals than with a glossy color ad. For smaller breeders producing limited numbers, a business card ad may be all that's needed to keep your name out in public and develop name recognition.

Low Cost Exposure

There are a variety of lost cost ways to promote your animals locally.

Participate in parades
Attend county fairs
Take your donkeys to public facilities like nursing homes, schools.
Contact your chamber of commerce and let them know you may be open for tours.
Shopping mall openings

Making an Impression

Try to remember what it was that impressed you the most with the people you bought your first donkey from. Was it their advertising? The cleanliness of their facilities? Their personalities? The quality of their donkeys? The odd thing about a lot of new buyers is that they are impressed by things that many times do not even reflect on the quality of the animal they are buying.

The first impression of your farm is something that many buyers always remember. Many other buyers are only concerned with the immediate area that the donkeys are in. If buyers are distracted by smell, mud and poor facilities, it will be hard for them to concentrate on evaluating the donkey.

Physical condition of the donkey

Even inexperienced buyers seem to be able to pick up on the fact that a donkey is not healthy. Poor coat quality and thin animals reflect badly on your entire herd and your management practices. If you are selling during wet weather, try to clean the donkey up and keep it clean before the buyer arrives. If you are selling in winter, please think of the welfare of the donkey before you decide to body clip it. Nothing turns new buyers off faster than long untrimmed hooves.

Well kept records

You should be able to tell potential buyers all about vaccinations and dewormings on the donkey you have for sale. If the animal is an adult, you should know in advance all the foals produced and should be able to answer any health questions relating to the animal. Buyers do not like to hear "all the donkeys were vaccinated last year" because they don't believe you. They want dates. They want to know that you are going to give them all health records in writing when they pick the donkey up.

Selling yourself

We all live busy lives these days. Buyers and/or browsers should not show up without appointments and if they do, they need to expect that you may very well not have time for them. On the other hand, if appointments are made, expect to spend as much time with the buyer as the buyer wants. Open yourself up for all the questions that they want to ask and invite those questions. If something rotten is going on in your life, mention a little of it to your visitors or simply tell them that you're having a rotten day. Don't let them walk away feeling like they intruded on you or they were not welcomed when it wasn't that at all. Encourage questions and be forthcoming with information. Ask potential buyers about their farm and try to get a feel of what type of donkeys would best fit their needs.

Written or telephone inquiries

You receive one of those letters asking about your donkeys or what you have for sale. You get a phone call asking if you have information you can send out. Are these people tire-kickers or are they serious buyers. Who knows? That is why you have to take the time to answer their requests. Even if you do not have what they are looking for at the moment, they might not be ready to buy now but are gathering information so when they are ready, they'll come visit you. I have a general information packet covering donkeys in both general terms and also in more detail. It not only covers the glory aspects of owning donkeys but gives buyers details on the work involved properly caring for livestock. I want potential buyers to know in advance that animal ownership is not all fun and games. However you respond to written inquires, you should remember that they are also writing other farms and your written information will be in competition with others.

The FF's - Friendly Foals

Nothing appeals more to potential buyers than fuzzy little foals running up to them begging for attention. What gives the better impression: 1) foals running up, pulling on pant legs, untying shoe laces and rubbing against legs, or, 2) you out there, waving arms, herding up a group into a small corral so you can get near them. It takes very little effort on your part having foals that are overly friendly. Spending time with them, scratching and rubbing, during their first week of life guarantees an appealing very saleable pet.

Your share of the market

No matter what business you are in there is always some form of competition. An important part of marketing is the manner in which the producer cultivates his share of the market. People remain in business because of the strategy they use in attracting buyers. Here are some of the strategies people use in carving out a share of the marketplace.

1. Breeding for a specific color.
2. Breeding for small size.
3. Breeding for conformation, regardless of color
4. Breeding lots of different types of donkeys for good selection.
5. Dealers who do very little breeding but more buying and reselling.

One thing to keep in mind if you get too specialized is that you greatly limit your clientele. Many times your specialty will depend on the size of your herd.

Unfortunately there are a number of highly questionable practices employed to 'get in on the action'. These people are selling donkeys to make money, period. The sad thing is that less than ethical business practices reflects on the rest of us who work so hard. We've heard so many new buyers becoming disenchanted after being sold donkeys that were misrepresented. Educating naïve buyers as to the potential pitfalls in buying can be an excellent marketing tool. Buyers appreciate the guidance.

I highly encourage all potential buyers to visit as many farms as possible before buying. I ask that they become as educated as they possibly can on evaluating conformation. When they are ready to buy, but do not have the money to buy top of the line, at least they know what they are buying and will not feel taken advantage of. Some times buyers simply want back yard pets and have no interest in breeding therefore have no desire or need for top quality breeding stock. Any breeder who tells potential buyers that they always have top quality foals has either not been in business long, has not had many foals, or simply has no understanding of donkey conformation. No matter how great your breeding stock, pet quality foals are going to pop out from time to time. Buyers understand this. Do not insult their intelligence by claiming otherwise.

Word of mouth

One of the most powerful marketing tools is word of mouth recommendation from other breeders or people who have purchased from you. Several breeders can work together so if a buyer comes to one and the breeder doesn't have what they are looking for, they can refer them to another farm. We find that when we refer someone to another breeder and they are treated fairly, the buyer still comes back to us when they are ready to purchase more donkeys. Of course you need to make sure that the seller you are referring the buyer to is reputable or the referring farm can suffer a loss of credibility. A solid reputation, gained by your fairness in doing business is like money in the bank.

Rated Registrations

The *International Miniature Donkey Registry* developed a wonderful conformation rating system. Ratings were designed to help new or inexperienced buyers in determining well-conformed donkeys without having to know a lot about conformation. They can buy with the knowledge that an independent party has reviewed this donkey and has given an evaluation of the animal. Rating reviews also help breeders in their breeding programs. Evaluations help by pointing out certain faults that may be overcome by proper matching of breeding pairs, and producing better-conformed foals. Ratings also help justify your asking price versus someone selling unregistered or non-rated donkeys. Many buyers call IMDR and ask to be referred to breeders who have rated their donkeys which gives buyers a big advantage in purchasing quality animals. Ratings are a wonderful tool for both the buyer and the seller!

Marketing strategies can be very spartan endeavors or can run the gambit all the way to large scale promotional plans. Developing your approach to marketing your donkeys is a very important step and should be well thought out.

John Whiteman and Lone Pine Murphy with Italian Festival Cart

Long Distance Shipping

Whether you're moving to a new home in a new state or selling donkeys long distance, sooner or later you are going to be in need of a professional hauler. There are of course other ways to get your animal to its new location, but oftentimes the easiest is to use a professional equine transportation company. These people load the animal, drive to the new destination and deliver him to your doorstep. If you have a horse trailer, you also have the option of hauling the donkey yourself. Whichever method you choose usually depends on how much money, time and expertise you have or may be what you just feel more comfortable with.

Which ever option you choose, you need to do some research to know what legal requirements each state has, including the states you'll be passing through. Most states require some type of documentation. All states require a coggins test, most states require Interstate Health Certificates and some states require bills of sale, and other certificates. Colorado for example requires proof of ownership when crossing the border or in the case of commercial haulers certificates showing that they are authorized to transport the donkey into the state. Disease outbreaks also can result in severe restrictions on any equine travel. Make sure you are aware of this. i.e. as of this writing, Vesicular Stomatitis has been again diagnosed in areas of New Mexico and Arizona. Texas will not allow any equine into the state originating from these disease outbreak areas. When coming from other parts of New Mexico and Arizona, Texas requires a written permit from the Texas Animal Health Commission to be allowed in, along with special written notations from veterinarians who examine the animals. While commercial haulers may be aware of these special provisions, don't expect them to make sure you, as the owner, have all the appropriate paperwork. That's your job.

Commercial Haulers

You've no doubt seen ads for long distance equine shipping companies in all the major horse publications. You may even have seen their rigs going down the road in your town. Most of the major companies make routine hauls from coast to coast and others concentrate on more specific areas such as up and down the east coast only.

The way it all works is relatively simple. You pay a fee, usually determined by the mile, on how far your donkey has to travel. The shipper gives you a quote on 'stall area' and this usually means one horse takes up one stall. "Miniature" donkeys certainly have their advantages as often two younger donkeys, or a mother and foal, can travel in the same stall area so you get two for the price of one. I can't stress this next statement enough: <u>Be very cautious of cutthroat prices!</u> Rates can vary greatly but there's always a reason for one company quoting a price much lower than their competitors. We have heard, and experienced some real horror stories with commercial shippers. Know who you're dealing with! When it comes to turning over the well being of your donkey to someone else, now is not the time to be skimping on money. We at *Miniature Donkey Talk Magazine* have a listing of commercial haulers that we've had personal experience with and we'd be happy to give you their telephone numbers. We also won't be shy about telling you who to absolutely avoid using at all costs. If you've found a commercial hauler that you'd like to use but know nothing about them, don't be afraid to ask for references. If they haven't hauled miniature donkeys before they've surely hauled miniature horses as there are about 8 times more miniature horses around than donkeys. Call these previous customers and see what they have to say. Just because the hauler gave you their telephone numbers as references, you might be surprised what they end up telling you.

The first time you call a commercial hauler, don't be afraid to ask questions. When can they arrange pickup? Is that a FIRM date? What is the quoted price? Exactly when will the donkey be delivered? How often do you stop and water? Will you call me 24 hours before pickup and will you call either me or the buyer during the trip? Can they pick up at your home and deliver at the exact destination you require or if you are off the main strip, do you need to meet them somewhere with the animal?

You should be aware that if you live in the northern U.S., you may have difficulty getting animals delivered to you or picked up during winter months. For example, many commercial shippers will not travel further north than southern New York during winter months. Everyone living in northern states and/or Canada needs to inquire about what happens if you're hit with a last minute snow storm or what happens if a snow storm arrives mid-trip with your donkey on their van.

Find out if the company is licensed by the Department of Transportation, since this government agency has requirements for safety that apply to both the drivers and the rigs. Specific guidelines for inspection, repair and maintenance of vehicles, along with qualifications for drivers, and driving requirements must be met by a shipper before the Department of

Transportation will license it. Be aware that this still doesn't protect you from the unscrupulous! On the other hand, many smaller operators are not licensed by DOT yet offer excellent service.

Don't wait till the last minute to schedule a trip. Most companies need a minimum of 3 to 4 weeks notice to arrange a pickup in your area. Also remember that you need, at the very least, a coggins test and Interstate Health papers completed by your veterinarian. Commercial transport companies will not accept your animals without these documents. Interstate Health papers simply consist of your veterinarian giving the donkey a complete physical and filling out a paper stating the donkey is in a healthy condition. Shipment must take place within 30 days of the date on the paperwork so if shipment is delayed, they have to be redone. In most states, coggins test results and paperwork can take up to two weeks to get back from your vet depending on which lab your vet uses. In a rush, we can get our coggins results back in a matter of hours if we're really in a spot. We have our vet pull the blood and we take it to our nearest horse race track which has their own lab. In our situation, the nearest race track is a good distance away, however, for $15.00 we can wait and get the results back in two hours or for $7.00 can get it back the next day.

Most shippers have multi-horse vans or trailers and will schedule your pickup with other pickups and deliveries in your area. We have a commercial shipper that we often use who has a more specialized service in that they do not haul our donkeys with other people's horses. Instead, they schedule one trip at a time and our donkeys are the only animals in the trailer. One of the reasons we like using this company is that our donkeys aren't being hauled all over the country. With large commercial shippers, many horses are usually on the truck. This means that instead of our donkeys going directly from say Maryland to Ohio, they first go south to Virginia because the shipper has a drop off there, then they go Kentucky because they have a pick up there, then they go to Indiana because they have a drop off there and then eventually end up in Ohio. So instead of our donkeys being picked up and delivered in one day, it may take 3 days before our donkeys see their new home.

Good shippers stop along the way to give the animals a break, offer water, etc. Some times overnight layovers are required. Several commercial shippers are home based in the Colorado or Texas areas and when shipping an animal from one coast to the other, may unload the animal in their home state at their own farm. I've never heard of a problem with this. It's usually done so that the animal can be loaded on a different truck going from their home base the rest of the way to their final destination. This layover can be anywhere from over night to several days in length.

One big downfall of commercial shippers is that you go by their schedule not yours. If they happen to arrive in your area at 2:00 a.m., whether they're picking up or delivering, guess what time they'll show up at your place. You got it - 2:00 a.m. That's another advantage of using a more specialized company that is only hauling your donkeys and only does a single trip at a time. They'll arrive at your schedule. If they happen to arrive in your area at 2:00 a.m., they'll pull over for the night and deliver in the morning.

If the donkey is being shipped cross-country or far distances, long trips can really tire an animal. The whole time they are riding, they're doing a balancing act with their legs. If you don't think that's stressful and tiring, ride in a horse trailer for an hour sometime and you'll understand what I'm talking about. Find out from the shipper how often they stop. 20 to 45 minutes every five or six hours is preferable. Many of the larger commercial shippers have two drivers and they stop as little as possible. However, you also must remember whenever they stop for a pick up or delivery, it does give your animal time to rest. You'll find that donkeys will drink very little while traveling. Some commercial carriers hang half-full buckets of water inside stalls and others don't.

One thing you need to make absolutely sure of is that your donkeys are up to date on vaccinations, especially influenza and rhino. Putting your donkey in an enclosed van with any number of different horses coming and going, carrying any number of germs or diseases is asking for trouble. It's like a breeding ground for disease. Take that worry off your shoulders and vaccinate the donkey at least 4 weeks before the trip.

* * * * * * * * * * * * * * * * * * * *
When there's stress there's danger
of disease
* * * * * * * * * * * * * * * * * * * *

Traveling is stressful for both horses and donkeys and where there's stress, there's danger of respiratory disease. This is another reason why very current vaccinations are so important.

Shipping stress has long been implicated in the development of respiratory disease in equine. Recently, researchers at the University of Illinois participated in a study.

The first project sought to establish a model of transport stress induced pneumonia in young horses. A total of 131 horses aged three years or younger were loaded onto five tractor-trailer shipments from Michigan to southern Illinois.

Within 14 days of arrival, over 70% of the horses developed signs of pneumonia: fever, cough, nasal discharge, rapid breathing and depression. In addition, they found that animals traveling in the bottom back section of the trailer were at increased risk for respiratory disease. While the reasons are not known, the researchers speculate that horses in the back are exposed to more allergens, straw, hay and other irritants that blow in their faces. Presumably, equine shipped further than the animals in this study would experience even more stress and more exposure to airborne pathogens and other risk factors.

Treatment for Respiratory Disease or Flu-like Symptoms in young Miniature Donkeys

It has already been proven that the stress of any type of travel along with the stress of new surroundings can cause "the snots". Sometimes it requires no treatment, other times if you have a runny nose consisting of a thick discharge along with crusty eyes, it should be treated. We treat with a drug called Tribissen. It's an excellent drug for this problem and must be obtained from your veterinarian. It can be purchased in paste form in a tube (follow instructions for weight) or in tablet form - we give 1/2 tablet every 12 hours for 5 days. We put the tablet in an empty syringe (no needle) and melt with a little hot water. We then mix in a little corn syrup and squeeze into the donkey's mouth. As long as your donkey's temperature remains below 101.5 degrees and he is eating, you have no serious problems. If you have any questions, always consult your veterinarian. The chances are <u>small</u> that a donkey will develop shipping fever, but still you should be prepared.

Having your donkey hauled commercially doesn't mean that every single thing is going to go right and you have to be somewhat understanding about this. We've had deliveries hung up because:

1. During a pickup, a fussy Arabian wasn't about to load on a horse van and it was 4 hours before they got him loaded.
2. Van or pickup engine trouble.
3. A horse became ill during the trip and the drivers stopped to obtain veterinary care.
4. No one was at a drop off point and the drivers had to wait.
5. Bad weather

6. Drivers got a last minute call to pick up a horse in another state and our picked got diverted.

And the list goes on. The more prudent you are in choosing a respectable and reliable hauler, <u>the less chance you have of anything AT ALL going wrong.</u>

Doing it Yourself

If you don't want to worry about what we've just talked about, you have the option of hauling donkeys yourself if you have a horse trailer and something to pull it with. Having an open stock trailer limits your hauling in winter months as the air flow would be much too cold for hauling. If you're hauling in winter, you must have a fully enclosed trailer.

We mainly sell weanlings here at *Pheasant Meadow Farm* and I'm trying to remember the last time someone actually showed up with a horse trailer. There is any number of ways to haul weanlings. Bronco's seem to be everyone's favorite although we did once have some guys show up in a Volkswagon Beetle car with the back seat removed. A local TV station happened to see them in New York on Route 95, pulled them over and did a nice interview with them on the evening news. Bronco's, pick up trucks with caps are all suitable for hauling weanlings as long as you have proper, non-slip flooring for them.

Something we get asked about often is if you should tie your donkey up inside with a lead line. The answer is absolutely not! Donkeys should be left loose to find their own comfort zone in how and where they want to stand while traveling. If you are hauling 5 or 6 donkeys, having a partition to section them off in two parts is helpful so that they aren't stepping on each other. Do your best not to haul a foal under the age of two months. Also try not to put two mothers with two young foals together or the foals will be walking around and the mothers will be fighting with each other over their foals and someone is going to get hurt.

Before you get started you need to do a maintenance check. Tires need to be in great shape, door hinges and latches need to be in good working order to make sure nothing flies open. One of the most important things many people forget is the flooring. Most trailers have rubber mats over top wood flooring. Even if the wood is treated wood, it can still rot through if manure and urine has been sitting in there since the last trip.

Probably the biggest problem are the trailer lights. When's the last time all your trailer lights all worked property. Oh come on, be honest. Seems like every time we use our trailer we have to set aside several hours to play with the lights before the trip.

For Do-It-Yourselfers

The Nationwide Overnight Stabling Directory published by the Equine Travelers of America, Inc., lists hundreds of layover locations throughout the country, ranging from simple accommodations with corrals and pastures to large facilities with amenities for both animals and humans. Most are located close to interstate highways. The 1997 directory is currently available for $26.95 plus $2.50 handling from Equine Travelers of America, PO Box 322, Arkansas City, KS 67005 (316) 442-8131.

When you call the people in the directory, make certain you tell them you have donkeys and not horses. If a horse has never see a donkey before, some of them are scared out of their wits at donkeys for a few minutes and some of these places may simply not accept donkeys.

Remember to take extra halters, lead lines, buckets, hay and spare tires with you.

I personally enjoy having buyers show up here to haul themselves. It's a lot of stress off me knowing that my babies are going to get special care on their whole trip. I think its a lot of stress off the new owner also to not worry about when their donkeys are being picked up and when they're being delivered. If you have the capabilities, hauling yourself can be a rewarding experience.

Mimi Cantwell of Virginia picking up her new donkey

Integrating the new Donkey

Guidelines for introducing a new donkey into your herd

One of the first things you need to know when bringing in a new donkey is their past health care records. You need to know what vaccinations they have had and what deworming program they have been on. If you buy a donkey at a sale, you will seldom receive this information and will have no idea what you are dealing with. This is one very big downfall of buying at sales and one you should be aware of. On the other hand, there are animal dealers who sell donkeys who do not spend the money for vaccinations or deworming because they are in the business of making money and doing a quick turn-around. If you do not know any health care information on the donkey, it is best to wait at least two or three days, until the animal settles down and then vaccinate and deworm the donkey.

It is the custom in the horse industry to quarantine a new animal if the horse is not up-to-date on vaccinations and worming, and/or past health records are unknown or unavailable.

I personally quarantine all new donkeys for a period of at least 10 days. However, if a lone donkey is shipped to me, I always put another donkey in with the new donkey in the quarantine pasture. There is a chance that the donkey that was shipped in may develop a slight respiratory disease due to the stress of shipping. This is extremely common in all animals and goes along with being in the business of having animals under your care. So why would I put another donkey in with the new one? Donkeys, unlike horses, can become extremely stressed if kept by itself. This alone, could cause respiratory disease.

All of my donkeys are up-to-date on their vaccinations and if the companion donkey were to catch an illness from the new donkey, I know it would not become serious due to the high immunities our donkey's have. I try to pick a donkey out of our herd that is in the same age group and one that is not socially attached to any other donkey. You will find the new donkey will quickly develop an attachment to the companion donkey and they may very well become friends forever. This is especially true of weanlings. I am not advocating this practice to anyone else but simply telling you how we handle this situation.

Our quarantine pasture is about 1/4 acre located in the back of our property and has its own stall attached to the back of our barn. I generally find new donkeys to be reluctant to walk up to their new owners, no matter how friendly they were with their previous owners, for the first few days. I don't push it. We make it a point not to bang buckets, wave our arms or make quick movements around the new donkey in order to induce any further undue stress. I also make it a point to lean down when talking to the new donkey. I want to be on their level and it seems to make them more comfortable until they realize that the big bad wolf does not reside here and they have nothing to fear. We do a lot of rubbing and scratching for the first few days.

Feeding The New Donkey

It is also important to know the donkeys previous feeding program. If you purchase a donkey who basically was fed nothing but hay, then you turn the donkey out on lush green pasture, that donkey will surely develop severe diarrhea and possibly colic. Likewise is said for feeding grain. If the donkey has not been fed grain in the past and you feed the donkey a scoop of grain, it could put too much stress on the donkey's system.

If you do not know what the donkey has been fed, limit the grain to only one or two handfuls per day for the first three weeks and avoid feeding hay that has more than 10-15% alfalfa in it. For the first several days, you should set out two piles of hay - one for the new donkey and one for the companion donkey, approximately 10 feet apart. The companion donkey usually establishes themselves as the "head honcho" and may object to the new donkey eating at her/his pile of hay.

And what about water? We have all automatic waterers here. Many donkeys have never seen an automatic waterer before. On the arrival of the new donkey, we keep a full bucket of water right beside the automatic waterer and they soon learn, from their companion, how to drink from an automatic waterer and not be scared of the sound it makes.

When moving bred jennets, you should move them 30 to 45 days before their expected foaling dates to help reduce the amount of stress associated with foaling. This is especially important to establish immunity factors in the milk, and subsequently transfer the immunity to the foals. When jennets are moved from an old environment to a new one, and exposed to the organisms in the new environment, they build up an immune response to them. The jennet then puts those antibodies in her colostrum, so the foal is protected against the organisms of the new place.

After what you feel has been an appropriate quarantine, it is time to turn the new donkey out with the rest of your herd. **Never do this at night!**

A lot of space is needed to introduce the new donkey to the rest of the herd. (The term "herd" is being used for simplicity even though you may only have two or three other donkeys.) If this is done in a small paddock area, someone is going to get hurt. No matter what you do or how you feel about it, you are going to witness some nasty behavior. You are going to see biting, kicking and chasing until they work out their differences and establish what is known in the animal world as their "pecking order." All established donkeys are going to let the new donkey know who is queen, who is willing to accept a new friend - and who isn't - who doesn't mind having a new donkey eat beside them and who will threaten death at the mere thought of it.

If you let your jack run with your jennets, you should never turn out a pregnant jennet with this jack or any other jennet that you do not want bred. This includes yearlings. Even though a jennet may already be pregnant, a jack may very well force himself on the new jennet to establish his dominance over her, thus causing her to abort. You also should never turn a new jennet out with a jack without putting a muzzle on the jack. His instinct is to bite and conquer and a muzzle will help prevent the jennet from getting hurt.

Always turn the new donkey and their companion out with the rest of the herd after the morning feeding. Most donkeys will be too busy munching on hay to be bothered by a new donkey. This gives the new donkey time to do some investigating and see where the fence lines are. Be sure in the evening that the hay is spread out so the new donkey has ample room to get to some hay in case differences have yet to be settled.

The pecking order helps prevent conflict and injuries. Once it's established, the dominance order is pretty matter of fact. It also provides peace and tranquillity and helps prevent a constant chaotic battle every time feed is taken out. It sets the guidelines for the herd.

A little common sense goes a long way in helping your new donkey adjust to his new home.

When You Get Your New Weanling Home

A new halter should be given with the sale of every donkey. This is simply a courtesy that all sellers should extend to the buyer of a donkey, whether it is a foal or an adult. NEVER leave a halter on any age donkey when you put them out to pasture, in their paddock or when you are not specifically handling them and need to control them. There have been numerous reports of people finding their donkeys lying in the pasture with their back leg entangled in the halter when they tried to scratch and got hung up.

We suggest that you spend as much time as you can with your weanling the first several days. Most donkeys are very people and animal oriented and will become very depressed, and possibly ill, if they are totally ignored and kept alone. Of course, purchasing a single donkey is never a good idea to begin with. Your donkey may be a little stand-offish for the first few days until they get to know you. You should pet, scratch and rub them as much as possible for the first few days. Donkeys love to have their lower chest scratched. Some foals are not used to being brushed. If yours isn't, don't brush them for a few days. Start getting them used to being brushed by lightly brushing them on their necks and chests and work back toward the rump after a few days.

Feed

Your weanling should be fed one or two cups of grain (sweet feed) - depending on how old they are and what they have been used to getting - in the evenings. He should be fed this for his first year. After that, if he is in good weight, you can stop the sweet feed or only give them a limited amount as a treat. We feed our weanlings a horse sweet feed (12-13% protein) that can be purchased in any feed store. Weanlings can be fed a hay that contains a mixture of alfalfa and grass. If they have never been fed any alfalfa, you will have to introduce it to them very slowly or the alfalfa will give them diarrhea. (The same is true if they have never had sweet feed.) Alfalfa is delicious to donkeys. Weanling donkeys can generally eat as much hay as they want without getting fat.

Water

Donkeys will not drink stale or dirty water. They must have fresh water daily. If you have automatic waterers in your paddocks, make sure you check them daily for cleanliness. Note: If your weanling did not grow up around automatic waterers, they will be scared of the sound. Set a bucket of water near the automatic waterer for two weeks so the weanling can get used to the sound as other animals drink from it. It is extremely important to keep an eye on weanlings to make sure they are drinking water several times a day.

Training

If you want to teach your new donkey to lead, wait at least two weeks before doing so. Let them become accustomed to you and their new home first. Foals and weanlings have a very short attention span. Your training sessions should never last more than 15 minutes at a time. Weanlings like to play with people the same way they play with other foals - nipping. If your foal nips you, very quickly pinch his nose. You want to show him that biting you - hurts him. (see article on biting later in this book.) Do not slap your donkey in the face as it will make him very head shy and they usually never get over this. It is important that you do not let jack foals get away with nipping. This behavior should be corrected as soon as it starts. Never, ever grab ears or hit ears as a form of discipline.

Know What's Normal For Your Donkey

You can spot trouble before it becomes serious if you know your animals. Knowing what is 'normal' for your donkey can help you decide if you have a medical problem. Some donkeys are extremely laid back and normally stand around a lot. Other donkeys are almost constantly on the go. Knowing the personalities of your donkeys and observing them regularly can help you detect an early illness before it gets out of hand.

The average normal temperature for most Miniature Donkeys is 99.5 to 101.5. You should take the temperature of each of your donkeys when they are feeling *well* and record it on their medical records. If a donkey's normal temperature is 100 and out of suspicious circumstance you take his temperature and it is 102, you will know that you have a problem. If the same donkey's temperature is normally 101.5, and it's a hot summer day, a reading of 102 could be perfectly normal.

Behavior

Your donkeys mental attitude can tell you a lot. Does your normally aggressive jennet, who tries to run you down when she sees you coming with the grain, now stand back in a corner with no interest? A jennet who is normally very laid back may become aggressive during her heat cycle. Jennets in their last month of pregnancy lay down more than they normally would. Is a normally watchful jack now standing in the corner of his pasture with an "I don't care" attitude about the jennets in the other pasture?

Posture

Sick animals often assume unusual positions. A donkey with colic (pains in stomach) often stretches out much like a dog stretches when it gets up from a nap. Shifting weight from leg to leg may indicate soreness in either the leg or shoulder.

Movement

Abnormal movements are often the first sign of injury or disease. Excessive movements such as pawing, shaking the head, yawning or scratching may indicate a problem. Short, choppy steps may indicate soreness in the legs or hooves.

Appetite

How well your donkey is eating is probably the best indicator of his overall health. Feeding time is always the best time to observe your donkeys. Always take an extra two minutes to look each and every donkey over to make sure they are eating normally. If a donkey appears normal in every other way but just seems reluctant to eat, he could have a tooth problem. Sharp edges on teeth can cause sore gums and the teeth need to be floated (rasped). If you have a donkey in a stall that you do not think is feeling well, be sure to also monitor its water intake.

Coat

Compare your donkey's coat to other donkeys. A donkey's summer coat should be shiny and even a long winter coat should have a certain glow to it. A rough coat of hair with no shine can indicate worm infestation or a vitamin deficiency. Scrapes, bites or sores can indicate either internal or external parasites.

Feces

Normal donkey droppings should be fairly well formed. Very hard droppings could indicate that the donkey is not drinking water. Overly soft droppings could indicate an illness or result from stress, a change of diet or too little roughage. Diarrhea is not normal for donkeys and should be cause for alarm. Donkey foals often go through a bout of diarrhea at 7 to 12 days of age and is due to bacteria entering the system. It is extremely important that you keep a close eye on foal diarrhea as tiny donkey foals can dehydrate in a matter of hours.

Owners who *know* their donkeys can often spot the signs of an oncoming illness or recognize a possible injury.

Chapter 3

Feeding and Bedding

Feeding Donkeys Hay

What's the best hay for your donkey? Should you feed grass hay or pure alfalfa? How about grass and alfalfa mix? Are some hays actually bad for your donkeys?

The best hay for your donkeys depends on several things. First are the requirements of your donkeys, second is the hay's nutrient content and third is the price of the hay. If the hay doesn't meet your donkey's nutrient requirements, you will have to supplement it with additional feeds. You must also take in to account availability of pasture.

You want your feeding program to be cost effective. Is it better to feed a lower quality hay and supplement with grain or is it better to feed a high quality hay and not supplement?

First of all, it would be difficult to feed enough supplemental feed to make up for poor quality hay. The poorer the hay, the less your donkey will eat. To try and supplement with grain, you risk colic, founder and your donkeys getting too fat. All donkeys utilize their feed differently. If you feed your donkeys in a group situation, you will always have dominant individuals who will chase away shyer animals.

On the other hand, it's a waste of money to buy and pay for the best quality hay you can get if your donkeys really don't need it. Donkeys are what is termed as "easy keepers". This means, they generally utilize their hay very efficiently and are prone to put on weight easily, especially adults over the age of three years.

How Much Hay?

In winter, two feedings a day is adequate, three a day is better. Each feeding would consist of a 'flake'. A 'flake' of hay is approximately a lump of about 4-5" wide. Hay bales are baled in flakes and some flakes are larger than others depending on how the farmer's machinery was set. How do you know if you're feeding enough or too much? If you are feeding good quality hay, a donkey will generally consume 80-90% of it and 10-20% of it will be wasted. This 10-20% is usually made up of weeds and other ingredients that may actually be harmful to the donkey and he knows not to eat it. This wastage needs to be expected and accepted by you. A donkey that cleans up every flake of hay is not being fed enough and as previously stated, may actually be harmful.

Grass Hay

Grass hays are the choice for donkeys. They have a low incidence of mold, are less dusty and help prevent a donkey from becoming overweight. On the other hand, they are generally low in protein, possibly too low. This basically depends on when the hay was cut.

If cut at an early stage of growth, grass hay can be highly digestible and of good protein value. Mature grass is usually low in both. Timothy, orchard grass and brome are all comparable in nutritional value when cut at similar stage of growth. Timothy is a good clean hay however most farmers wait too late to cut it to maximize the yield.

Bermuda grass is popular in the south and is comparable to timothy in nutrient value.

Oat hay is popular but it must be cut before the grain is ripe. If it's cut after that point, nothing is left but poorly digested straw.

Tall fescue grass, Sudan grass and Johnson grass can sometimes contain harmful amounts of nitrates and Johnson or Sudan grass hays that have not fully cured can cause cyanide toxicity.

Legumes

Legumes used for hay include alfalfa and red clover. If cut properly, it's high in protein and calcium and can be a good hay for horses. Pure alfalfa hay is not good for donkeys and does not set well with their digestive systems. Most donkeys fed pure alfalfa hay have continuous diarrhea. You must remember that donkeys are from desert regions and alfalfa was not part of their diet. Donkeys will also become fat very quickly off of alfalfa hay. Legume hay is much more difficult to cure than grass hay. Unless you grow your own hay, you cannot control curing. If baled too wet, legumes are highly susceptible to mold. Mold can - and has - caused abortions in pregnant donkeys. Dusty hay, when pulled apart, can indicate that the mold has dried, but can cause coughing and heaves (similar to human emphysema).

Legume hays baled too dry are susceptible to leaf shatter and leaves are the most nutritious part of the plant.

The good news is that a mixture of grass hay and alfalfa hay can make excellent hay for your donkeys. Mixed hays are less likely to mold and become dusty like legumes, and have a higher protein and calcium content than grasses. The best mixture for donkeys would be 10/15 percent alfalfa with the remainder being grass.

Composition of Some Common Feeds for Equine

Feed	Dry matter	TDN [b]	Digestible protein	Calcium	Phosphorus	Carotene
	%	%	%	%	%	mg/lb
Roughages						
Alfalfa hay						
All Analyses	88	50	11.0	1.47	0.26	27.7
Early bloom	90	51	12.1	1.25	0.26	57.7
Full bloom	88	48	10.0	1.28	0.30	16.8
Past bloom	91	44	9.9	1.34	0.35	12.2
Clover hay (all analyses)	90	46	10.0	1.41	0.29	24.9
Mixed hay (less than 30% legumes)	89	48	4.8	0.90	0.19	8.0
Oat hay (Dough stage)	90	46	5.3	0.33	0.17	14.6
Timothy hay						
All analyses	88	45	3.1	0.37	0.19	6.2
Early bloom	88	47	4.2	0.60	0.26	9.2
Full bloom	87	43	3.4	0.41	0.19	4.4
Past bloom	87	37	2.9	0.35	0.21	2.8
Concentrates						
Beet pulp	92	70	6.0	0.56	0.08	—
Corn, yellow #2	89	80	6.7	0.02	0.27	5.5
Linseed meal	91	71	29.5	0.40	0.83	—
Oats	90	70	9.4	0.09	0.33	—
Soybean meal	89	77	38.2	0.32	0.32	—
Wheat bran	89	63	13.0	0.14	1.17	—

Which cutting to purchase

In most parts of the country, farmers can get at least three cuttings of hay. Northern states can usually get two with southern states getting sometimes up to eight cuttings.

First cutting hays usually are of lesser quality. They are difficult to cure and most farmers wait way too long to cut. First cutting hay, which occurs in the spring, is usually abundantly filled with weeds and other non-nutritious herbage. Intermediate cuttings tend to be lower in digestibility because higher temperatures during the season promote more stem growth. The last cutting often matures more slowly due to cooler temperatures and has a higher leaf-to-stem ratio.

With severe droughts in different parts of the country each year and then an over abundance of wet weather in other parts, some of you may not have much of a choice in what type of hay you purchase. When buying hay, reject any bales that are exceptionally heavier than the rest, especially if the hay is freshly baled. This often means that the hay was baled wet and will mold. As previously stated, mold can cause abortion, and if enough is ingested, will cause a donkey to become seriously ill. When cleaning up your barn floor, do not give the old droppings of hay to your donkeys. It can contain not only mold, but also mice droppings and surely will be extremely dusty causing lung damage.

There are numerous mixtures of hay for sale. Most hays, cut at the right time and properly baled, will contain sufficient nutritional values. Keep in mind, hay rained on several times before it was baled, can lose up to 40% of its nutritional value. If the hay was cut at the perfect time of growth, rained on only once and then properly cured, it may only lose 15-20% of its nutritional value.

Hay heavily rained on will be brownish in color. Note: Sun shining into the barn can also brown the outside of hay. Most farmers will not mind you asking them to break open a bale of hay for you to take a look at. (Be courteous enough to take that bale with you if you purchase hay!)

You can also purchase "hay cubes" from your feed store. They are normally clean, light in weight and convenient to feed. However, it may be difficult to tell if they were made from poor quality hay or hay that is too weedy. Another disadvantage is that your donkey will consume his meal in about 10 minutes and then stands around the rest of the day rather than taking one or two hours to munch his dinner. This may cause your donkeys to turn into termites, chewing on anything and everything in sight, to satisfy their natural urge to chew.

Blister beetle poisoning

Blister beetle poisoning comes from ingesting alfalfa hay or cubes that are contaminated by the beetle. Blister beetles are a large family occurring throughout the U.S. Generally they are brownish green or yellow bugs with distinct black stripes on their backs. They are around a half inch long. The beetles become trapped in the alfalfa during bailing and die. They remain poisonous indefinitely. The toxin, cantharidin, is a contact irritant that is absorbed by the intestines. Most of the clinical signs are caused by the irritating effects on the bowel, kidney, and heart. As little as a teaspoon of the beetles can be fatal to a horse.

Symptoms include colic, straining to urinate, weakness, depression, red mucous membranes, and diarrhea. There may be lesions on the gums and lips of the animal. The severity of the symptoms are dose dependent. Laboratory findings of decreased calcium and magnesium in the blood, along with elevated muscle enzymes (CPK) are helpful in diagnosing this disease.

Affected donkeys should be treated with repeated doses of mineral oil to help clear the digestive tract of the toxin. Pain should be controlled with Banamine or Xylazine. Dehydration is a frequent problem that needs to be treated promptly. This will also help stimulate urine production and remove the toxin from the body. Diuretics are useful early, if used carefully, but dehydration must first be corrected. Aggressive therapy is essential if the horse is to be saved.

The prognosis in all cases of blister beetle poisoning is poor. Monitoring changes in clinical signs and laboratory values will help indicate the possible prognosis.

What is your Feed Tag telling You?

The feed tag is on feed to give the purchaser information that allows for an educated decision to be made about which feed is best suited for your animal. A feed tag, by law, must state the percent of protein, fat, and fiber, and a list of ingredients in the feed (i.e. corn, oats, soybeans, or in cheaper feeds the grain byproducts, plant byproducts, roughage products, etc.)

What is protein? Protein is used by an equine to supply energy, build muscle and maintain body tissue.

What percent protein is recommended for maintenance of a healthy equine? Nine and one-half percent to twelve percent is considered to be the best range for maintaining a healthy equine and the average of 10-1/2% as the best.

The total ration balance is the average between the protein of all forage, hay and pasture and the grain portion of an equine's diet. Hay's percentage of protein is from 5% to 12% with the average being about 8-1/2%. A mature horse [*not donkey*] will eat about 15 pounds of hay a day. To figure the total ration balance:

15 lb. hay X 8-1/2% protein from hay = 127.5 units
6 lb. grain X 12% protein from feed = + 72 units
21 total pounds and 199.5 total units of protein

Now, take the total number of pounds (21) and divide it into the total units of protein you are feeding your horse (9.5 in this example). When using this equation, it becomes apparent that hay or pasture should not be fed with less than a 12 percent sweet feed.

Donkeys would figure out as follows:

8 lb. hay X 8-1/2% protein from hay = 68 units
2 lb. grain X 12% protein from feed = + 24 units
10 total pounds and 92 total units of protein

Total number of pounds (10) divided into the total units of protein equals 9.2. Two pounds of grain is generally fed to a donkey you are trying to put weight on or to a nursing jennet to maintain her current weight. The weight of the hay will also depend on the type of hay (i.e. pure alfalfa weighs more per pound than does grass hay.

The next ingredient on the feed tag is the fat content. Pound for pound, fat has the highest concentration of calories available to the equine. The minimum acceptable level is 3 percent with some feeds exceeding 60 percent. Fat contains twice as much energy as an equal volume of carbohydrates. Also, it is very good for hair coat condition.

The third ingredient is fiber. Fiber has essentially no nutritional value. A 7 percent level is acquired when mixing equal amounts of corn and oats. Fiber is passed through the digestive track in the same volume as it is fed. Therefore, if your feed is 10% fiber, 10 pounds in your 100 pounds of feed is wasted. If your feed costs $200, $20 is wasted money.

These are just a few items to look for when purchasing feed. Remember, cheap by the bag doesn't mean it's cheaper to feed. Read your feed tag and get as much information as possible about the product you're using to make the right choice for you and your equine. A good grain protein count for donkeys is 12 percent.

Bonnie Wilson of Washington

Salt: Don't Sell Them Short

Salt is the only mineral for which equine have a nutritional "sense." Since most equine feeds are deficient in salt, rations are usually supplemented by adding a small amount to the grain or by providing free access to a salt block or loose salt. If a donkey or horse cannot meet his salt needs through his food, he will make use of the salt block, and this is the most effective way to prevent salt deficiency.

Salt shortfall can have serious consequences including loss of appetite, depression and weight loss. A seriously salt-deprived donkey may develop a depraved appetite and look for things to eat that contain salt or have a salty flavor. Such cravings can be dangerous; donkeys may eat objects such as stones or wood and lick or eat toxic materials such as lead paint.

Salt starvation can also cause a donkey to consume a great excess once given the opportunity and this can have toxic effects if he doesn't also have an adequate water supply.

In hot summer months, donkeys can lose several ounces of salt per day just by standing around and sweating. This can lead to fatigue and exhaustion. Jennets who are lactating also have a great need for salt and lack of it will eventually lead to decreased milk production. Young foals will begin licking on a salt block around the age of four days.

Some donkeys and horses regularly consume as much as two or three ounces of salt per day and there is little evidence that such intake is harmful if water is available, although long-term studies of the effects of salt on the blood pressure and calcium excretion are needed. On the basis of our current knowledge, it is far safer to trust the donkey's "salt sense" by giving him free access than to restrict consumption.

**A salt block in your donkey's
paddock is essential**

Fences for Horses/Donkeys

Introduction
Sooner or later every equine owner must face the problem of providing fencing for the pasture, turnout lots, arena, or aisles. The most important aspects are safe fencing that is strong enough to contain the equine and has an acceptable price and appearance for the owner. This is intended to assist equine owners with the decisions involved in selecting and constructing appropriate fencing for their situation.

Reasons to Fence in Equine
Equinemen and ranchers in states with open-range livestock grazing laws can let their equine wander on open range; however, equine owners in most states are required by law to fence in equine. Equine are much healthier outside in the sun, rain, and even mud, than they are when kept inside. In order to have equine outside without being in danger of automobiles, poisonous weeds, and other predators, safe fences are essential. Fences keep animals from encroaching upon the property of others; and at the same time, fences discourage people from entering the equine's environment.

Selecting the Right Fence
The type of fence needed depends on a number of factors: the type of equine being managed, the intended use of the area, the density of animals on the fenced area, availability of shelter, neighbors, desired esthetics, and the projected budget.

Criteria
What type of equine will be managed? Obviously, draft horses require taller and stouter fences than required for miniature donkeys. Mare and foal pastures need to be made safe and more solid to protect curious foals from danger. Usually old, pleasure horses that are used to fences require less sturdy and visible fences than young horses, or equine that have never been in pastures with groups before. Stallions should have taller and stronger fences to keep them in and also to keep children and curious visitors out.

What is the intended use of the fenced area? If the pasture provides a significant share of the nutrients for the equine, at least two acres per equine should be allowed. If the area is primarily an exercise lot, then the space should be more than 500 square feet per equine. If activity is expected on the inside of the enclosure, then the boards (or other material) should be on the inside. This is primarily because of safety reasons in riding arenas where the fence surface protects the cart or the rider's leg from hitting the post.

What is the equine density in the fenced area? Dividing the total number of equine by the acreage available determines the animal density. Basically, the higher the animal density per acre, the stronger the fence needed.

Is there shelter and water for the equine in the area? Either allow the equine into the woods, build a three-sided shed, or fence the area in a manner that provides a stall or lean-to shed to provide shelter from the sun and weather. The arrangement of fences and gates selected should depend on whether it is necessary to allow the equine to get into a building or shelter to access water. Equine tend to congregate near shelter, feed, or water so the fences in these areas need to be more solid and safe than the periphery.

What is on the other side of the fences? ``The grass is always greener on the other side of the fence." If things attractive to equine such as grain crops, other equine, or even the barn are present on the other side of the fence, then the fence should be stronger and possibly taller.

What does the fence need to look like? The importance of appearance depends on your personal likes and also the priorities in your neighborhood. Fences should be safe, require as little maintenance as possible, and be affordable for the equinemen.

How much am I willing to spend? Prices for most fences range from less than $1.00 per linear foot to more than $4.00 per linear foot. The criteria involved in matching your equine's needs to the attributes of the specific fence become the most important factors in controlling your costs. Building fences yourself takes a lot of time. Your ability to build the fence and the availability of time are factors to consider. Paying someone to install the fence often results in quicker installation and higher quality fences. However, fences such as high-tensile wire and polyvinylchloride fences should be installed by professionals.

Types of Fences

Select a specific type of fence appropriate for your situation. The types of fence available for equine facilities change and improve every year. Those discussed here include board fences, woven wire, high-tensile wire, polyvinylchloride (PVC), pipe, diamond wire, electric wire, and numerous combinations of the above. Description, advantages, and disadvantages, and other considerations follow.

Post and board

This type of fence includes three or four six inch boards hung on wooden posts. Board fences are suitable for line fences, paddocks, and arenas. The ``standard'' design usually includes 16-foot, rough-cut, 1 x 6-inch hardwood boards fastened on the inside of 4-inch minimum diameter wooden posts with each staggered board spanning two posts.

4-board fencing
3-board & batten fencing

There are several variations: 1) setting the posts on 10-foot centers and using 20-foot boards, 2) utilizing square 5-inch posts instead of the round 4-inch posts, 3) using 2 x 6-inch milled planks rather than the full 1-inch thick rough-cut boards, 4) deleting the fourth board and increasing the space between boards to 10 inches (between the bottom board and the ground to 16 inches). A good practical distance between the ground and the bottom board is just greater that the height of your lawn mower deck! This makes trimming fence rows much easier.

Advantages of this type of fence include safety, sturdiness, high visibility for the equine, and popular esthetic appearance. Disadvantages include high maintenance, costs, and board replacement.

Post and board fence

Woven wire. Field livestock woven-wire fence can be purchased in rolls 39-, 45-, 47-, 49-, and 55-inch widths. The top and bottom wires should be at least 9-gauge with the intermediate wires 11-12 gauge. Woven wire with the vertical strands a maximum of 6 inches apart should be used (1047-6-11). The standard design is to hang a 47-inch woven wire 5-6 inches off the ground on the inside of 4-5 inch diameter round wooden posts. A 1 x 6-inch hardwood board is then nailed above the wire, making the total fence 60 inches tall

Tightly woven wire (this wire is a concern as a small donkey hoof could get hung up in it)

Depending on the topography, the wire may need to be higher off the ground, and the board could be replaced by an electric wire no more than 4 inches above the woven wire. Posts on 8-foot or 10-foot centers work well with 16- or 20-foot boards. As with any wire fence, strong brace-post sections must be in the corners to stretch the wire tight. Brace sections also must be in the lowest points of valleys and the top of hills to allow straight stretching without the wire pulling the posts out of the ground.

Advantages include high visibility and low maintenance; disadvantages include stretching and costs.

Diamond wire

Much like the livestock woven wire fence, the diamond wire fence is normally made with 48-inch wire hung 6" off the ground with a 6-inch board along the top, making the whole fence about 60" tall. Brace post sections are needed to adequately stretch the wire. Wire of 9 -11 gauge diameter is available in this design and the wire should be all galvanized steel.

Advantages of the diamond wire fence are the safety and the low maintenance. Disadvantages are primarily cost and the need of brace sections and ways to stretch the wire tightly.

Pipe fence

Fences made of pipe are constructed from 2" to 4" horizontal pipes welded to 4" posts. As with wooden posts, the pipe posts should be driven or set 30" to 36" into the ground. The horizontal pieces should be welded to the inside of the fence or holes cut in the posts so the rails can be slid through the posts. Usually four or five horizontal ``rails" are set 6" to 8" apart. Be sure the top of the posts are rounded or capped so sharp edges are not exposed.

Pipe fencing

Depending on the availability of used well-casing pipe, this type of fence can be economical, sturdy, and have relatively low maintenance costs. The construction requires metal cutting and welding expertise. This fence is more popular in the south where fewer temperature changes cause the need for repainting.

High-tensile wire fence

High-tensile wire. High-tensile wire fences are made with five to seven strands of smooth 12.5 gauge wire spaced 8 to 12 inches apart. Rigid brace sections are required at corners, gates, and fence ends. Eight foot wooden or fiberglass line posts set 30" to 36" into the ground are placed at 50- to 75-feet intervals with fiberglass spacers of the same height every 20 to 30 feet. Alternating wires should be electrified so plastic insulators must be put on the posts on the top and bottom strands and alternating wires in between.

Considering the curiosity of equine, the electrification of this type of fence is essential. Bracing, in-line strainers or tighteners adequate to allow 200 to 250 pounds of tension are needed. The advantage of this fence is that it is sturdy and takes relatively little maintenance, although it does require frequent checks for damage, electrical shortages and tension loss. Disadvantages are that it has low visibility to the equine, it takes specific expertise and equipment to install, foals can get through the fence, and if a section is damaged, the whole line must be repaired or retightened. Generally, this type of fence should only be used with electricity and in areas of at least five acres.

PVC

Polyvinylchloride (PVC). This fence is made of a weather resistant polyvinylchloride material that can be made in flat or round shapes resembling boards OR pipe. The fence appears to be a pipe fence. Round rail fences consist of 5" diameter round posts and 3" diameter rails 16' long and span through three posts. Posts with three or four rails are most common. The plank shaped rails, 1 1/2" by 5 1/2", usually interlock into slots in the 5" round or square posts.

These single- or co-extrusion polymer products can be made in white, brown, or black and have a UV light protection mixed in to keep the product from fading. The advantages of this type of fence is that it looks great, does not need painting, and requires very little maintenance. The disadvantages are that it is expensive to install and is less sturdy in small areas with high animal density.

PVC plank fence

Covered boards. There are products on the market that consist of a 2' by 6" plank, usually 16-feet long and covered with the polyvinylchloride or plastic. This has the sturdy advantages of the wood fences, but the PVC protects the wood and eliminates the need for painting. The board inside can still break and need to be replaced.

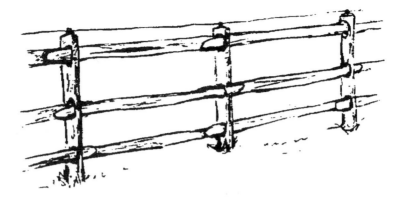

Split rail – can be attractive but you always seem to find rails laying on the ground.

Cable

Usually these fences are made with pipe posts 4" to 5" in diameter with twisted wire cables either run through holes in the posts or fastened to the inside of the posts. At least six cables should be used with the bottom about 6" off the ground and the top strand 54" high. Cables with a minimum of 1/2" diameter should be used. This fence is not recommended in small areas or with foals. It is difficult to keep the equine from entangling themselves in the strands.

Electric and fiberglass webbing

There are a wide variety of electric wire fences having two to four strands of either smooth wire or wire woven into colored fiberglass webbing. This webbing can be 1" to 4" wide and comes in a variety of colors. The key to any electric fence is to make sure that the electrical current is not shorted out by poor insulators, tall weeds, or broken wire. (Electric fence is probably not acceptable for miniature foals.) The electric material must be kept tight but not with the tension of a high-tensile wire fence. The posts can be 20 to 30 feet apart and should be set deeper than 30" in the ground for permanent fences. The advantages of these fences are the economical features, and they can be made temporary by using metal posts. The disadvantages include the low visibility to the equine (with smooth wire) and the constant need to check for shortages so the equine do not become entangled or injured. The fiberglass webbing is safer and higher in visibility.

Nylon or rubber fencing

There are fences made of 2" to 4" strips of belting or inner tube rubber from the tire industry. These strips should be stretched, so the same considerations of tension and bracing are important as they are with wire fences. Rubber and nylon are very durable and safe, but tend to stretch in colder climates and becomes brittle with time. Caution should be used in selecting a product that does not have exposed nylon threads, because equine will playfully ingest these and experience colic. This fence can be very safe, but curious foals may weave their way through it. It will need to be replaced regularly in the colder climates.

Barbed wire

Barbed wire is inexpensive and is very dangerous for equine. Whether electrified or not, this type of wire is not recommended for equine.

Other Considerations

Fencing on the inside of posts. Regardless of the material used for the fence, be sure to fasten the horizontal fencing onto the inside of the posts. When the equine lean against the fence, this pushes the boards, pipe, or wire against the posts rather than off the posts. If boards are put on the outside of the posts, they can easily be pushed off the post, allowing the equine to escape. When boards are put on the inside, there is no need for vertical face boards.

Choosing posts. Round posts generally come from tree stock similar in diameter to the finished post. Square posts, on the other hand, must be milled and wood removed from the original blank; but, this removes strength as well. Thus a 4- inch round post is stronger than a 4-inch square post of the same type of lumber.

Posts should be of western red cedar, osage orange, western juniper heartwood, and black locust, and hard enough to be useful untreated. Treated softwood posts appear more expensive; however, posts treated with salt or other pressure-treated processes last 25 percent longer than untreated posts. They are often guaranteed for 20 years. Your best plan is to buy either treated posts or hardwoods, and then coat the posts with a paint, or other coating before setting them in the ground.

Wooden posts must be used for board fences and woven (or diamond wire) fences with a board along the top. Metal T-posts and other temporary metal posts can be used for electric wire and woven wire fences when no board is nailed onto the posts. The advantage is certainly price and the disadvantage is safety. Equine can hook themselves on the metal posts and even impale themselves of the top of the metal post if not protected with a cap.

Construction and Management Hints

• When setting posts, consider that they are tighter if driven rather than augered and set. The loose dirt must be returned to the hole and tamped. After about a month, most posts need to be re-tamped to be tightened.
• Any stretched fence needs good bracing and regular tightening. Stretching often pulls the woven wire product staples against the posts, so one needs to walk the fence line to loosen staples.
• Newly cut wooden boards are the easiest to fasten to the posts, but they should be allowed to season before being painted or treated. The part of the posts to be set below the ground should be dipped or treated before being set. The lifespan of posts made of hemlock, Douglas fir, red oak, popular, and cottonwood can be increased three to five times if pressure treated.
• Treating with a tar or oil based product will discourage equine from chewing the fence boards. A metal flashing cap is easy to install along the top edge and is inexpensive.
• If using steel posts, drive them at least 6" beyond the bracing triangle. All ``U" channel posts are significantly stronger than ``T" posts of the same weight. They should be driven at least 30" into the ground.
• When using electric fences, test regularly for grounding. During the growing season, regularly walk the fence to knock down any weeds or tall grasses. The danger of equine getting out is greatest after a wind storm and when the fence is either shorted out or knocked down.
• Don't skimp on the quality of gates and gate posts. The gate posts should be set in concrete and set at least 36 to 42" in the ground. Usually a 12' pipe or tube gate is recommended so tractors and other equipment can get through.
• If a ``people entry" is needed, either install a three foot gate, put in an overlapping section, or make a solid wood board section. Do anything you can to discourage climbing over wire fences.

- Avoid putting strange equine in neighboring paddocks and it is often handy to have one paddock that is not directly bordering the pasture. This is especially handy if a stallion is being managed.
- Provide at least one small (less than 1/4 of an acre) paddock to contain the equine when you want them turned out, but not put them on the pasture.
- Plan your gates and access to water so that equine can be turned out into the paddock; and then by opening or closing the gate you may have them in the pasture.
- Cattle guards are satisfactory for most equine, but be sure that they are 10 to 12 feet wide so that equine cannot jump over them.
- Fence around desirable trees if you are concerned about bark stripping. Wild cherry trees, black walnut, and large apples trees should be removed or fenced.

Conclusions

The important consideration in selecting and building fences for equine is that the equine must be safely contained. After determining what type of equine and criteria important to you, build the strongest fence you can afford. Building the fences on your property will likely be the largest cost second to the property itself and the barn. ``Strong fences make good neighbors" is not just an old saying. Nothing will be more comforting than to know that your equine are outside where they are the most healthy, in a fence that you know will keep them there until you come back.

Purdue University Cooperative Extension Service

Stall Bedding

What's best for your Donkey?

Donkeys have adapted well to 'domesticated' life and it is our responsibility as owners to make them as comfortable as possible. Most donkeys prefer to be kept well-fed, dry and warm in winter, and away from insects and hot sun in summer.

If donkey keepers could design the perfect bedding, it would keep them dry and comfortable and would keep our maintenance chores to a minimum. It would also be affordable, ecologically sound, readily available, dust-free, unpalatable to donkeys and easy to transport, store and dispose. Unfortunately, no single material will meet all of these requirements.

Reasons for Bedding

In winter, donkeys need protection against very cold wet weather and muddy ground. A warm donkey keeps in better condition and needs less food. In summer, donkeys need a place to get out of the hot sun and irritating flies.

When treating a sick animal, you need a clean place to work and the donkey needs a clean place to recuperate. Many people keep pregnant jennets stalled at night so they can easily monitor them.

How about underneath the Bedding?

Plain dirt floors in stalls are hard to maintain. There isn't a lot of drainage and every time you clean, you find yourself taking more and more dirt out of that 'favorite urine corner' until before long, you've dug yourself a hole.

Many large horse establishments have concrete flooring in their stalls. Concrete allows you to thoroughly clean a stall and hose it down however, concrete does not allow moisture to flow through it. Concrete is also hard, cold in winter and can be slippery when wet. Concrete floors must be heavily bedded.

Wood flooring can be a good alternative to concrete. Treated wood would be installed with at least 1/2" gap between planks to allow drainage and allow for natural expanding and shrinkage. Wood floors can be extremely slippery and must also be deeply bedded.

The most economical flooring is stone and gravel, sand and clay. Stone and gravel are installed one to three feet below the level of the barn floor. If the percolation value of the soil is good, you may need as little as one foot of gravel and no stone. If natural drainage it poor, you will need up to 18" of crushed rock or stone, topped by a similar depth of gravel. A one-foot deep mixture of sand and clay at a 30:70 ratio is placed on top of this foundation. This mixture is superior to plain dirt because it offers good footing, resiliency and drainage, but does not easily become rutted. If you already have permanent stalls built, dig out an 18" deep "well" in the donkeys favorite urine spot, fill with about one foot of creek gravel and top off with sand/clay or sand/soil mixture.

Rubber matting can be purchased although it can be expensive if you have several stalls. It can cost $250 to $400 to install mats in a 12 x 12 stall and you must use a very absorbent material such as sawdust.

Principles of Good Bedding

Whatever type of bedding is used, it must be dry, soft, clean and fresh. It should either absorb liquids and gases, or allow them to reach an outlet for escape. The choice of bedding material depends a lot on the amount required and its cost, and how easy it is to obtain and dispose of.

Bedding Material

There's a wide assortment of bedding materials from which to choose: straw, sawdust, wood shavings, sand, ground peanut shells, paper, and paper pulp materials.

Straw

Straw used to be the bedding of choice for many years. It is a good insulator, doesn't compact when walked on, absorbs fairly well and has a nice look to it. Wheat straw is by far the best and is less edible. It should be free of weeds and grass and not dusty. Oat straw is less durable and donkeys will eat it. Barley straw is also unsuitable, as it is prickly. Straw does not work well on dirt flooring as the two together can cause strong urine odors. We do use straw in our foaling stalls over top a thick layer of wood shavings to absorb the urine. Foals should not be born on sawdust or wood shavings as they will stick to a wet foal. Many donkeys eat any type of straw bedding. This is not good as there is little nutritional value to straw and it reintroduces parasites. Eating large amounts could also cause a donkey to colic. Straw can be expensive depending on where you live. We have purchased straw for as little as 75 cents a bale and have seen it sell for $6.00 a bale. Some gardeners do not like to use straw mulch in their gardens because it's too bulky.

Sawdust

If you live near a saw mill or a lumbering area, you can sometimes get sawdust for free or at least have them fill up the back of a pickup, for around $7.00. Over the past several years, researchers have discovered just how sensitive the respiratory tract of donkeys and horses are and that sawdust can be damaging. Sawdust soaked with urine can be a heavy load to those of us with weak backs.

Wood Shavings

Shavings are my bedding of choice. I purchase them from a large horse farm which brings in a tractor-trailer load from Canada on a monthly basis. They come baled in heavy paper so are easy to store in the barn. We purchase 100 bales at a time and get them for $3.75 per bale, however we continue to see the price rise so sooner or later economics may come into play. They are currently economical to use because they are easy to pick through. We find the type we get to be very absorbent and easy to clean up. They are clean and give your barn a nice fresh smell. Again, we put a layer of straw on top of the shavings in all the foaling stalls.

Sand

Sand may be used as bedding as it is very absorbent. The downside of using sand is that donkeys may ingest it along with their hay and cause severe colic or impaction. Wet sand is also very heavy to pick up.

Peanut hulls

I have read rave reviews over finely chopped peanut hulls. First of all, I suppose you have to live next to a peanut farm! I do not know of anyone who uses them but I am told that they are lightweight, easy to work with, and are fairly inexpensive. I have read that they can also be dusty, depending upon the manufacturer.

<u>Paper</u>

A few years ago, paper became the 'in' bedding to use. Haven't heard much about it lately. No matter how deeply you bed a stall with paper, its super-absorbency and pulpy texture when wet cause it to mash and compact with urine. This makes it very difficult to clean. It's very heavy when wet and people were finding themselves just cleaning off the top layer and spreading more paper on top until the day came that you were willing to hire someone just to come in and clean the barn out!

You may have to check the availability of bedding products in your area. Sometimes one, sometimes a combination of several beddings, will work best for you. If you aren't sure where to get whatever bedding you choose to use, stop in a few large horse farms in your area and ask where they buy their bedding.

Then......what do you do with it?

For those faced with the job of cleaning out stalls every day, the manure pile is a subject there is literally no getting around. It can get to be a big headache - particularly when you live in a suburban area. Unless your neighbors are livestock owners also, you'll discover that they are less entranced with the sight and smell of that mushrooming mound of steaming what-ever behind your barn.

Consequently, the site of your manure pile should be given careful consideration. Ideally you should have a covered pit, not a pile, built over concrete for easy cleaning. But because this kind of arrangement is prohibitively costly for most, I'll go on with the pile. It has to be close enough to the barn to be easily reached by a wheelbarrow, accessible by truck, far enough away so it doesn't attract flies to the stalls or your house, and located out of sight and downwind of neighbors.

If you own only one or two acres, this will be difficult. However, you are most likely in an area where people have backyard gardens. Come spring, (when the wind shifts) get on the phone and invite them over to get some of the best manure money can buy - for free. If you have a pickup truck, offer to deliver it. We have a local paper with a "Free-Bees" section. Doesn't cost anything as long as what you are selling is free. Last year we put the ad in and probably took us six weeks to get rid of the pile of manure that 65 donkeys made in a year. Then we bought a tractor with a front-end loader and advertised "Free Manure - We load for you". You would have thought our farm road was a major highway. We had trucks lined up and it was gone within a week. They parked their trucks along side our fence and Mike loaded them up over top the board fencing. A few really big trucks showed up and Mike decided to take down a section of fence so they could drive through the pasture to the manure pile as it was about 400 feet from the fence. Thinking he'd only be a few minutes, he'd leave the fence open. Mike did this several times and each time we were roundin' up donkeys in the neighborhood. But we won't talk about that.........and when the horse mare got out and realized she was *free*......well, no, we won't talk about that......

freedom??!!

Caring For Your Miniature Donkey

Manure Management

Proper manure handling and disposal are important whether you have one horse/donkey or one hundred. Owners of one or two horses/donkeys on only a few acres of land in close proximity to neighbors often have difficulties related to manure handling and disposal. If the horses/donkeys usually are confined in barns or small exercise lots, manure handling can be a serious problem.

Suburban horse/donkey owners should plan housing and manure management carefully to avoid difficulties with neighbors and health officials. Flies and odors are the most common complaints. Anyone considering keeping a horse/donkey, especially in a suburban area, should review local zoning and health regulations.

Regular clean-out and removal of manure and wet or soiled bedding to a fly-tight container, storage facility, or field for spreading are requirements of any successful management plan. Regular cleanup reduces the opportunity for insect breeding and odor production. Storage should be designed to exclude rodents and to keep rain and surface water away from the manure.

A complete manure management system involves collection, storage (temporary or long-term), and disposal or utilization. Manure should be collected from stalls and paddocks daily. This is usually done with a fork or shovel and a wheelbarrow, tractor-loader, or trailer. Following removal of manure and soiled bedding, fresh bedding is added to ensure clean, dry conditions. Simply adding fresh bedding and allowing manure and soiled bedding to accumulate in the horse/donkey stall results in dirty animals, provides excellent fly-breeding conditions, and may be unhealthy for the donkeys.

Stored manure must be kept in a fly-tight area during the warm months and should be protected from rainfall and surface runoff. The type and size of the storage facility depends on how much manure is to be stored and the method of disposal or utilization. A horse produces about 0.7 cubic feet of manure per day per 1000 pounds of body weight plus bedding. Storage may be covered boxes, fly-tight concrete or pressure-treated lumber sheds, piles covered with black plastic, or covered garbage cans. Large quantities of manure require a storage designed to allow clean-out with power equipment, that is, a substantially built, strong storage with a wide door and a high roof.

Disposal of manure may also be a problem for the horse/donkey owner with no cropland. Horse/donkey manure should not be applied to horse/donkey pastures because of the risk of spreading internal parasites. Horse/donkey manure with or without bedding can be used in greenhouses, gardens, nurseries and by mushroom growers.

Manure bedding mixtures can be composted to reduce bulk, eliminate odor, and improve handling qualities. Proper mixtures of manure, urine, and bedding or other bulking material (e.g., dry leaves, straw, sawdust, or shavings at approximately 50 percent moisture) composts well in piles that are at least 3 feet square and 3 feet deep. Smaller piles will not retain enough heat to maintain a temperature above 160 degrees, which is needed for composting.

The following recommendations should be considered when planning a manure storage and handling system:

- Dispose of manure daily if possible.
- Provide temporary storage for manure, if daily disposal is not possible. Plan about 12 square feet of enclosed area per horse.
- Locate the storage in an area convenient for loading and unloading.
- If power equipment is to be used, be sure the size of the storage and construction area are adequate for equipment.
- Grade the area surrounding the storage to prevent all surface water from running into the storage and to keep any leaking from the storage from reaching streams, ditches, or groundwater.
- If the storage cannot be emptied weekly during warm weather, provide a fly-tight cover or enclosure.

Prepared by Robert E. Graves, Extension Agricultural Engineer, Penn State; under the direction of the Manure Management Work Group of the Agricultural Advisory Committee to The Pennsylvania Department of Environmental Resources

Cold Weather Care

Donkeys are made to be Donkeys

Here we go again: we're about to be zapped by nasty weather, and with it comes the perennial crop of well-intentioned concerns when it comes to looking after our donkeys. Although these are spawned by a sincere desire to do right by our donkeys, nevertheless, we so often fail to recognize the resilience and hardiness of most donkeys.

All too often, the solutions that we think are correct are misguided; whereas the ones that treat donkeys like donkeys are most sound.

"My donkey is getting thin, I'd better increase the grain ration."

Most adult donkeys do fine without any grain at all. Instead, you should take an honest look at your hay ration and your deworming program. Are you really feeding enough quality hay? Many parts of the U.S. have more than normal amounts of rain, and others have draught, but now the grass is not growing or is of much lower quality. If your donkey is scrounging around picking up every last piece of hay, you need to reevaluate how much you are feeding. Roughage is the foundation of your donkey's diet. If your donkeys are not properly dewormed, the worms will definitely rob your animal of needed nutrients.

"Looks like rain or snow is on the way. I'd better keep the donkeys locked in the barn."

Your donkeys should be turned out every day. We have a large barn and our donkeys and horses come and go at will. The barn is always open for them. We have a board nailed across the donkey entrance so the large horses cannot get into the donkey's part of the barn. Since we have a slight hill in front of the barn, the only time we lock up the donkeys and horses is during an ice storm as the ground is treacherous. Donkeys are outdoor animals and need to be able to get out and interact with each other. It is proven that donkeys and horses who have barns and run-in sheds, that they can leave and enter at will, have much lower incidence of respiratory disease. We once had a jennet experience very painful gas colic from staying in the barn and not moving around enough.

"It's going to get cold tonight, I think I'll put a blanket on my donkey."

Unclipped, healthy donkeys do much better without a blanket as their coats have natural insulation abilities. Blankets mash down the coat and can actually chill a donkey. The only exception may be freezing rain and/or a very cold wind storm. If you are new to donkeys, you may not realize how thick their winter coats are. When they start to shed out in the spring, you'll understand what I mean...

"It's going to be so cold tonight I'd better make sure all the windows and doors are closed on the barn."

Nothing is worse for a donkey than a barn with no ventilation. Stale air and ammonia fumes can invade a donkey's defenses to fight off bacteria and viruses. In an airtight barn, one donkey harboring a slight respiratory virus can quickly spread it to everyone else. If you have a wind slamming against one side of the barn, leave the opposite side of the barn open.

"I'd better check up on my donkey's flu vaccination and make sure he's up to date."

Flu shots are fine but how about that rhino vaccination? Equine herpes virus (EHV) also known as rhinopneumonitis, also known as rhino can be just as deadly if not more so as it pertains to donkeys. Most people just simply call an upper respiratory outbreak the flu when clinical findings may very well indicate that it is rhino. A lot of vaccinations come in 4-way and 5-way and don't include rhino because it has to be given separately, many people think they are fully vaccinating their donkey. We find donkeys to be just as susceptible to rhino as they are flu so do not forget that very important rhino vaccination. And don't forget deworming. A donkey stressed out due to worms has a much greater chance of dying from a severe respiratory illness.

"It's a cold one today, think I'll give my donks a big scoop of grain to keep them warm."

Wrong! Grain provides very little heat to the donkey if any, and this includes corn. Hay keeps the donkey warm because fermenting digestion of the hay generates caloric heat. Donkeys are designed to eat a little, all day long. Feeding good quality hay will keep your donkey warm, over a longer period of time, plus provides plenty of fiber which is important to keep the intestinal tract functioning properly.

"I've chipped off the top layer of ice so the donkeys have water to drink."

Chipping away ice may not be enough. Warming the water to a drinkable temperature has shown to significantly increase consumption. A dehydrated donkey is not digesting its food properly and is very prone to colic and other digestive problems. We have automatic waterers that have a heating element in them that keeps the water in winter at about 45 degrees. If you do not have this luxury (that's what I consider it if you aren't forced to haul heavy buckets of water!) then you need to haul hot water to pour over the ice. There are all kinds of electrical ice melting gadgets out there. Check the wiring often and be careful not to get the water too hot and burn the donkey.

Use your good judgment in caring for your donkeys in winter weather. A happy donkey is usually a healthy donkey.

Cold Weather Care of Weanlings

Most weanlings are between the age of six and nine months during the coldest part of winter. Their care is critical at this time as they are not only facing their first winter but are coming in contact with severe weather and potential health risks.

Winter care should be aimed at minimizing stress to help them remain healthy. Hopefully you have not waited until the dead of winter before weaning your foal from its mother. If you had a late summer or early fall foal, and the mother is in good weight, you may have to keep the weanling with its mother until early spring if you are having a rough winter. You will have to pay extremely close attention to the mother to make very certain that she is not losing weight. With a winter coat, this means feeling her body along the back, rib cage and hips, not just looking, as long coats hide too much.

On most topics, you can ask 10 veterinarians one question and receive 10 different answers. When it concerns winter housing, you will probably only hear one answer. The more they are outside, the better and healthier that weanling will remain. You must also use common sense as we *are* talking about *miniatures.* Miniatures do not and cannot produce the amount of body heat that a full-grown horse can. If you live in Minnesota, the temperature is -10 with 30 mile an hour winds, that weanling needs to be inside a barn.

We have fairly mild winters here in Maryland but do on occasion get snow and extreme temperatures. We have never had a problem with sickness during winter months as we follow several rules of thumb. Seldom are our donkeys locked inside a barn. Our barn doors remain open all year so the donkeys can come and go as they please. There are a few circumstances when we *will* lock the donkeys inside.

1. Expecting a snow storm at night. During the day, the barn remains open as we can keep an eye on things.

2. Freezing rain. The ground in front of our barn slopes down and can become very slippery.

3. Winds in excess of 20 miles per hour along with cold temperatures. Whether it be a barn or a run-in shed, donkeys cannot protect themselves from wind and winter coats alone are not enough protection.
Talk to any professional equine breeder or any veterinarian and they will tell you that airtight barns are a no-no even during severe winter temperatures. When raising donkeys or horses, you always have to keep the respiratory health of your animals in mind. Good respiratory health always means access to clean fresh air void of dust.

If weather dictates that we need to stall weanlings due to inclement weather, we stall them together. Donkeys are very sociable animals so stalling separately would cause undue stress.

Weanlings are playful and need room to run and exercise. One half to one acre is plenty of room for five or six weanlings. If the paddock area is too small, they easily become muddy during bad weather and this increases the probability of injury as well as stress.

Fencing for weanlings is critical. It should be at least five feet high. Never pasture weanlings in barb wire fencing. There are any number of fencing materials available and you can choose whatever suits your needs as long as it is safe for weanlings. Weanlings love to run and play and many times will run into a fence and this is the reason why it needs to be not only secure, but safe. (The same reasoning applies to sucklings as to why they should never be around electric fencing.)

If the donkeys' shelter is a run-in shed, it needs to be well bedded to encourage the weanlings to sleep inside, especially in inclement weather. Add bedding periodically to ensure dryness. Wood shavings are a preferred bedding material.

Weanlings should have been vaccinated at around 4 months of age. One vaccination called a 5 in 1 consists of A1 and A2 Influenza, Tetanus and E/W Encephalomyelitis. Respiratory diseases are a problem with weanlings and it is extremely important to vaccinate for Rhinopneumonitis, commonly called Rhino. This vaccination alone can and will save you many veterinarian bills. Weanlings and yearlings routinely have what is commonly known as "the snots" and vaccinating for Rhino will help prevent these problems from getting serious.

Weanlings should also be on a regular deworming program every 30 to 60 days. A paste wormer is easy to administer to weanlings and results in little stress.

The Equine Comfort Zone

"Should we put the donkeys in tonight?" Usually *you* ask this question when you feel cold. I see my donkeys most comfortable and playful when it's 35 to 40 degrees. So when you are grabbing your coat, your donkey may just be getting comfortable.
In the wild, donkeys would seek out natural shelter such as trees and hillsides. Leaving your barn open at all times, leaves your donkeys the option of going inside when they feel the need.

Nutrition is also significant during the winter. The growth rate of weanlings is slower than sucklings, but it is still high. This growth rate requires considerable energy, protein, minerals and vitamins. A mixture of one half alfalfa and one half grass hay for weanlings is recommended. (This hay may be too rich and too fattening for adult donkeys, however, is a good hay to feed to donkeys who need weight gain.) Always keep a salt block in front of donkeys.

Keep an eye on hooves. Long hooves on weanlings not only cause crooked legs, but are prone to seedy toe and abscesses. Long hooves can also be like sleds on icy ground and are dangerous to young animals who love to run and play. Many breeders also spread sand around automatic outside waterers and other walkways to keep ice to a minimum and provide good footing.

The Battle Against Flies

They lurk, fiend-like, waiting to attack your defenseless donkey. They buzz your face and ears, causing you to flail your arms like a mime gone mad. Yep, it's fly season again. Are you ready to defend your donkeydom?

It appears that a fly's only mission in life is to harass, pester, torment and madden its victims and most people would agree that the only good fly is a dead fly. It is not uncommon for donkeys to injure their eyes as they look for a place to rub their heads against stalls, trees and their own legs. They can also cause harm to themselves by biting at parts of their bodies and rubbing off manes, tails and patches of skin.

The discomfort donkeys go through can cause classic signs of stress - anxiety, depression and overall restlessness. If continually tortured, your donkey could stop eating, lose weight and develop a low resistance to disease.

People in northern states do not have the lengthy fly season that the southern states have, but no matter where you live you can count on some species of flies to live there also. Once the fly's' prime season is over, your donkeys may well continue to suffer from fly induced ailments.

Fly dermatitis results from the bite of a fly which can cause inflammation and if scratched, scabbing and scars. Allergic dermatitis can cause unsightly skin allergies and can drive your donkey mad. Donkeys with particularly sensitive skin can have yearly recurrences for the rest of their life. Spotted donkeys, with pink skin, are more prone to allergic dermatitis and skin sensitivities such as sunburn. Flies are often the cause of eye infections, which causes additional mucous in the eye, which causes severe eye drainage, which attracts the attention of yet more flies, thereby creating a vicious circle. A donkey whose eyes constantly water should have a fly mask to wear.

Flies can also cause internal parasites. Fly transmitted internal parasites include protozoa that live in the equine bloodstream. They are no less harmful for being less visible. Botflies lay their yellow eggs on the hair of a donkey's forelegs, shoulders and chins. When the donkey bites or licks these areas, the eggs enter the mouth. The larvae attach to the stomach walls where months later they are passed in feces where they begin a life cycle again. Heavy infestation of botflies can cause colic, ulcers and general discomfort.

Fungal diseases can also be caused by flies. Implanted into the tissue, fungi can grow beneath the skin causing swelling and local infection. These tiny infections look similar to rain rot or rain scald. Extended periods of wet, warm weather encourage fungal diseases and the flies who serve as carriers.

Bacterial and viral diseases are spread by flies. The fly bites the infected animal and carries that infectious blood or mucous to another animal. In general, blood-borne diseases are the most dangerous to horses and donkeys with biting flies transmitting the disease.

Fighting Back

Fighting off flies, the problems they cause and the ailments they transmit is the key to protecting your donkey's health. You may not be able to fight your neighbor's flies, but you can help prevent encouraging "homegrown pests" in your backyard.

Protected from flies or bank robber? You be the judge.

Daily cleaning of stalls and removing soiled bedding can put a stop to these excellent fly breeding grounds. Stockpiles of manure that you have stored in your pasture can be treated with topical larvicide sprayed on it.

Check on low wet spots in your pasture that collects rain water that sits for several days and fill them in with top soil.

Dark barns are an excellent escape for your donkeys as flies really avoid dark areas. So many people build beautiful little barns then line the roof with skylights thus giving their donkeys no place to get relief from flies during daylight hours. If you have skylights in your barn, do your donkeys a favor and cover them up during fly season.

Automatic fly spray systems installed in barns can be a Godsend. We at *Pheasant Meadow Farm* had one installed years ago and we love it. The systems come with timers that you can set to go off as many times per day as needed.

If you have problem mainly with face flies, you can buy a face mask (sold through *MDT Magazine*) and they work terrific. They also work great for keep dust out of donkey's eyes and for trailering to keep flying bedding out of donkey's eyes.

There are dozens of fly sprays on the market. They all claim to protect equine for days and weeks! Personally I'd like to find one that lasts a full 24 hours. There are pour-on insecticides also. Under perfect conditions - no rain, dust or sweat to dilute its potency, they would probably work better. They are oily to attach to the hair but they also attract dust and dirt. There are roll-on fly repellents that work good on donkeys who don't like spray around their ears.

Bot Fly Season

Fall is the season of the mature bot flies. I am sure you will notice when they get very active and are quite a nuisance to your donkey. The bot fly is that "bee" that has been flying around your donkeys' legs.

Life Cycle of the Bot Fly

The adult bot fly lives only long enough to mate and lay eggs on the hairs of the donkey/horse. Larvae hatch from these eggs in five days when the donkey rubs his lips in contact with the eggs when scratching the legs. The larvae crawl into the donkey's month and then burrow into the tongue. After several weeks they emerge from the tongue and are swallowed. While in the mouth, the larvae can cause irritations and lesions that will be open to infection.

The bot larvae attach to the wall of the stomach for almost a year. Then the bot are passed out in the feces. These bots are the red, short, fat, grub like worms found in the manure. Adult hot flies emerge from their pupal capsules in the manure in 3-9 weeks when the temperature is warm. Bot fly activity starts in the summer, peaks in the fall, and ceases in the winter when the cold weather sets in. There are signs that may indicate a heavy infestation of bot flies in your donkey's stomach. One sign is a thin, rough coat on your donkey. Also your donkey may not have any energy and have a pot belly with ribs showing.

The adult bot fly doesn't bite or sting but each time it touches a donkey, the bot fly lays an egg. The common botfly will lay 1000 eggs per female fly. The constant buzzing and flying around the donkey is very irritating to them.

Treatment

Treatment for stomach bots is delayed until one month after the first frost. This allows the larvae in the tongue and mouth tissues to molt and reach the stomach where the deworming medication is effective against the bots.

It is important to note that the eggs on the hairs of the donkeys legs will continue to be a source of infection long after the frost has put an end to the adult bot flies. Removal of the bot eggs weekly and especially after the first frost will definitely decrease the amount of infestation by bots in the mouth and stomach of your donkey, which is much better for your donkey's health.

Removal of the bot eggs from the hair on the donkeys/horse's legs and body can be done with a dull knife or a lava rock. Many feed stores sell a "bot eraser" which is lava rock. (Lava rock is also used to clean grills.) Washing with hot water of 104-118 on a day when the air temperature is below 60 will make the larvae hatch on the legs and die of exposure to the cold temperature.

Worming in December and again in February with a botacide will kill 99% of the bots provided that you have removed the eggs in November. Worming compounds that kill bots are Eqvalan Liquid, Eqvalan paste, Zimecterin paste, or any other dewormer that specifically states that it kills bots.

Chapter 4

Hoof Care

Handling the Legs and Hooves

You first need to tie your donkey up and once your donkey has accepted being tied up, the next step is to handle his feet. A donkey can never be too young to have his feet handled.

There are different ways in handling the legs and feet. Remember that you are not trying to pick up the donkey's hooves - you are asking him to pick them up for you. There is a big difference.

Tie the donkey up short and start with the left front leg. Stand close to the shoulder facing the rear, scratch his should area to relax him, run your hand firmly down the leg and gently squeeze just above the fetlock joint between the tendon and the bone. This is a "pressure point" and the donkey reflex is to lift this foot. (Don't try it on the hind leg - you will get kicked.) *Lean against the donkey*, your hip against his shoulder, or your shoulder against his shoulder, to push his weight onto the other leg and use your word command "up" or "lift." Until the donkey has learned what your cues mean, you may have to help him to lift up his foot. Put your hand under it to support it, do not grip it, and then put it down again - don't just drop it.

Picking up the front hoof

Picking up the front hoof

When you are both happy with this, try a back hoof. Rub the donkey around the base of the tail and take your hand and go all the way down his leg with it, to help him relax and know what you are doing. Again stand facing the rear and close to the donkey, leaning against him to push the weight onto the other back leg. Keep your hand in front and inside his leg and push the foot up and away from you.

Don't squeeze the fetlock of the back leg, it will make the donkey kick. Always keep your thumb close to the rest of your hand - this way it is safe should the donkey kick. Don't grip the leg. Make sure that it is you who decides when the hoof is placed on the ground again - not the donkey.

Handling the back hoof

Handling the back hoof

What if my donkey has never had his feet handled or I have an older donkey who shows fear of having his feet handled?

Some donkeys need to be taught how to have their legs and hooves handled, or need to be retrained and shown that they need not fear having these parts of their body handled.

Throwing a donkey on the ground to trim hooves is never an option!

First you have to get the donkey used to having the feet handled. Grooming is a good way to do this. Gradually brush further and further down his legs, always retreating just before he starts to object. Only when he is completely confident about your touching his legs, can you attempt to pick up his hooves.

Pick up the hoof as described above, and put it down again immediately. Repeat this, gradually, increasing the time that it is up off the ground; introduce a hoof pick and clean out the hoof while you are holding it up. Talk to your donkey while all this is going on, tell him exactly what you are doing, and why; make sure that he understands. Be calm and relaxed; firm but not rough; confident, never hesitant or tentative.

Back legs can get more agitated than front ones - they wave around backwards and forwards in an attempt to shake off the restriction. To save a lot of exercise, try to put the foot down just before it goes mad. If you miss your moment, let go and try again. Note: Many people feel that when a donkey starts kicking back with a back leg that they should hang on to it with all their might and never let go until the donkey stops. One breeder in the Midwest always did this and ended up with quite a few donkeys with patella damage and locking up. What you want to teach the donkey is that **you** are to decide when the foot goes down, not **him**. Weanlings should have their legs and hooves handled on a daily basis so that they grow into adults who are easily handled.

Why is it that my donkey hates my farrier?

There's a very easy explanation for this - it's called **pain.** When blacksmiths are schooled in how to trim horse hooves, they are taught to lift the leg and position it just above their knees where it can be secured and they can go to work. This is fine for 14 and 15 hand large horses with long legs.

It takes a little more work and effort to trim a donkey's hoof. Why? Because they are half the size of a horse and YOU have to teach your farrier how to hold the donkey's hoof. The drawing below is the proper way to position a donkey's leg. The farrier needs to bend down with his legs. *The lower he can position the donkey's leg between his legs, the better. (See photos in next chapter.)*

The proper way to hold a donkey's leg

The proper way to hold a donkey's leg

It can be placed over top of the person's leg and held in place at the knee with the person's arm and side. The hoof can then be positioned just below the farrier's knees and doesn't have to be twisted and bent upwards which causes severe pain.

Most farriers work fast and just don't take the time to realize that if they hold the donkey's leg the same way as they do a horse, they are causing intense pain to the donkey and a donkey will surely begin to object to having his legs and feet handled by anyone. Give your farrier a copy of this article so that he can learn how to properly handle your donkeys when trimming their hooves. They'll probably thank you for it because it will ultimately make their job easier if the donkey is not fighting the entire time the farrier is trying to do his job.

Rasping and Trimming Donkey Hooves

A newly purchased donkey should have had his feet trimmed just prior to your taking delivery of him. Rasping on a monthly basis will keep the hoof in very good condition. Rasps can be purchased from tack shops and some hardware stores that carry equine and/or farm equipment.

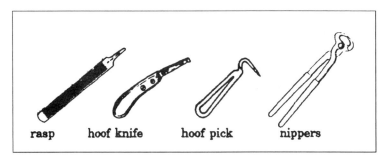

rasp   hoof knife   hoof pick   nippers

It is advisable for you to learn to rasp or trim your own donkey's hooves as farriers can be difficult to find. Some are so busy that if you only have one or two donkeys, they don't even want to come. Also, most farriers charge $12 to $20 to trim a donkey. If you have no idea how to go about trimming a donkey, you may want to get a farrier out first and watch him very closely. Donkey's hooves are not shaped or trimmed like horses' hooves so a farrier unfamiliar with donkeys will probably trim them wrong. It may be advisable for you to remind him that a donkey sits up higher in the heel than a horse. The frog of a donkey's foot is almost never cut. Trimming off straggly pieces hanging down is all that may be required. Miniature Donkeys hooves never need shoes for normal wear because their hooves are more resilient than horses' hooves.

(left) Long hoof that needs trimming
(right) Dirt needs to be cleaned out before you begin

The first thing to do is to use a hoof pick or hoof knife and clean out the bottom of the hoof of all manure and dirt. A farrier will probably remove some of the sole with his knife before cutting back the wall with his nippers. This is not something you should attempt to do without considerable knowledge.

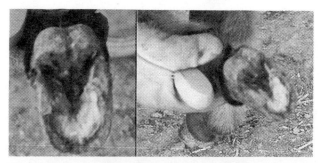

Hoof is cleaned out using a hoof pick and excess flaky sole is removed using a hoof knife. Take note to the toe portion of the hoof. After the hoof is cleaned you can see the outside wall actually sticks out about 1/4" further than the sole of the hoof.

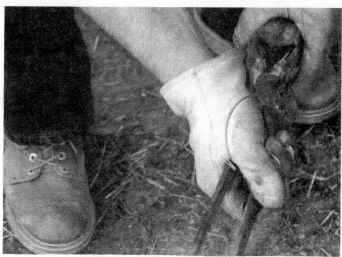

(left) The 1/4" excess wall is cut off with the nippers.

If you want to try trimming your donkey's hooves yourself, we recommend you start by using a rasp instead of tackling the nippers. Wear gloves at first as it is easy to rasp your hands, knuckles and legs. Hoof nippers or cutters, are a bit more difficult to use than the rasp, especially if the donkey won't stand still.

On long hooves, a farrier will cut around the hoof removing the overgrown hoof wall. The cutters should be held in a position which allows the blades to cut the hoof on the same angle as the bottom of the donkey's hoof. Be cautious with your cutters as it is much easier to take off too much hoof than it is when using the rasp.

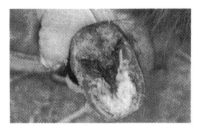

Shows hoof wall cut evenly with sole

Watch carefully how the hooves are held by the farrier while he is trimming. If the donkey seems distressed and begins fussing, ask him to hold the hooves lower to the ground.

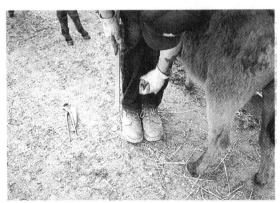

Note how the hoof is held by the legs and below the trimmer's knees. Making a donkey twist his leg high off the ground causes pain.

Filing the hoofs will take some elbow grease. Position the donkey's hoof between your legs just below your knees and commence rasping. Always file from heel towards the toe. Be careful to only file the heel if needed.

Always rasp from the heel to the toe.

The portion to be rasped is the overgrown wall protruding from the bottom of the hoof. Never rasp the outside wall of the hoof as this is a protective hard shell. You can go too far with trimming or rasping, and this is indicated by specks of blood-like dots appearing in the white line. These blood specks will not cause damage, but any further rasping or trimming might. You may also end up with a donkey that is sore-footed.

Hold the hoof then point the toe toward the ground. You want to make sure that the heels are of the same length and even. Uneven heels will cause the hoof to grow crooked and is certainly uncomfortable for the donkey to walk on.

To finish off, turn the rasp over to the finer side and smooth the edges of the hoof. If the growth of the wall at the heel is level or just slightly higher with the heel bulbs, then rasp the toe area only. Both sides of the hoof should be level with each other so the donkey stands evenly.

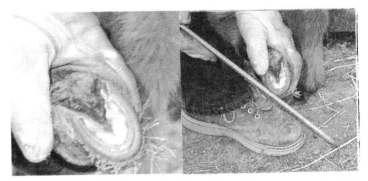

To finish the hoof off, use the fine side of the rasp and slightly round off the sharp edges. This also helps to prevent cracks and splits in the hoof.

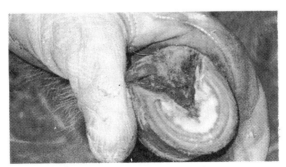

Photo shows a nicely trimmed hoof. Notice that the frog has been trimmed slightly The angle of the hoof should follow the angle of the pastern axis.

Caring For Your Miniature Donkey

Stand back and take a look at your work from all angles. Make sure that one side isn't higher than the other or that one side of the hoof is not flared out further than the other side. Stand directly in front of the donkey and draw a line down the front of the leg and hoof and make sure you can draw a straight line.

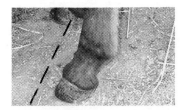

When a donkey is standing, an imaginary line from the point of the toe to the fetlock joint should be straight

Hoof Abscesses

Every spring, most of the U.S. and Canada goes through a thaw from the past winter. That means very wet ground that predisposes equine hooves to a variety of problems.

"But I watched her running and playing last night and now she's only on three legs!" That's just about how it happens. Over night your donkey will become very lame or hopping on three legs. Few conditions are as swiftly and completely disabling as a hoof abscess.

So exactly what happens to cause an abscess? As already stated, wet conditions soften hooves which is step one. Your donkey is walking along and steps on a sharp stone. He may limp for one or two steps but unless you just happened to see this, it will go unnoticed. The stone caused a tiny puncture in the sole of the hoof and as the donkey walks, his sole expands and contracts and acts as a sucking motion to draw the bacteria up into the hoof. A horse's sole is much softer than a donkey's sole. A horse may become lame in several hours but it could take days to weeks for the bacteria to work up into the sole of a donkey to the point where it will cause pain.

Long hooves, without doubt, lay the groundwork for a hoof abscess to develop in the toe area. Why is this? As a donkey walks forward, pressure is put on the wall of the front of the hoof as it pushes off the ground. The longer the toe of the hoof, the more pressure is applied and with each step the wall stretches the white line tissues, separating them, giving bacteria a chance to invade at this point.

Some, mostly inexperienced owners, do what they would do if their own foot hurt. Grab a bucket, grab the Epsom salts and stick the donkey's foot in the bucket of warm water. Unfortunately, this does no good at all. The tiny hole that the bacteria entered has since sealed itself and the Epsom salts cannot penetrate. In the mean time, white blood cells have flooded the sight where the bacteria is, the bacteria fights back, more white blood cells arrive and before you know it, pus has formed in the tiny pocket.

All during the night, pus is forming putting pressure on the sensitive tissue inside the hoof. If left untreated, it could take weeks before the abscess works its way up through the hoof and hopefully exits at the heel. In the mean time, your donkey could be in a tremendous amount of pain.

Telltale Signs

The pain your donkey suffers from a hoof abscess is similar to what a person would feel with a tooth abscess. Some donkeys tolerate pain more than others, but even though, a donkey will be somewhere between limping very badly or lifting the abscess foot up, jumping from one spot to another.

Pick up the hoof and clean it out thoroughly. You may need a bucket of water to get out all the manure and dirt. Look very closely for a puncture hole. It's rare that you'll see one, but sometimes luck is with you. Push on different parts of the sole and look for tenderness in one particular area. If that doesn't work, try pushing on different parts of the sole with your paring knife.

Hoof Testers   Hoof Paring Knife

Your veterinarian has what are called hoof testers. You can also buy these from vaccine catalogs or tack shops. This tool looks like a large pair of pliers, and is used to apply pressure to various parts of the foot.

When the abscess is located from the pressure you apply, the donkey will flinch and try to pull his hoof away from you. When that happens, you've found the abscess.

Treatment

The abscess needs to be located and drained. This is the hard part. Why? Because abscesses don't go in straight lines. They may follow a blood vessel so although you locate the tender spot with the hoof testers, the actual drainage point may be a half inch in either direction. Always start paring at the point where the donkey is most tender. Look extremely close to see if you can see any drainage or any type of a hole. The word "hole" is probably the wrong term to use. You are more aptly looking for an opening half the size of the head of a straight pin. You must keep paring at the hoof until you get drainage. You will not see a glob of drainage start pouring out. In fact, if you aren't looking closely, you may miss it. Usually the drainage that comes out looks like a clear liquid.

What you are trying to accomplish is to find the drainage point with the least amount of paring possible try to keep your paring hole as small as possible. At the same time, too small a drainage hole often reseals and re-abscesses.

Treatment at this point depends on what you found while paring the hoof. If you do not find a hole that clearly drained, but did find some drainage but no hole, the healing process and treatment will take longer. **Important Note:** If you do not get some type of drainage, then you have accomplished very little. We have pared until we've hit blood and still found nothing and at that point called in our veterinarian.

If you find no definite hole, you need to apply something to the hoof that has a drawing affect to it such as ichthammol. Put a good sized glob of ichthammol to several layers of large cotton gauze pads, apply the pads to the bottom of the hoof, wrap the hoof with vet wrap or Elastikon. Leave on for 24-48 hours. If the donkey is not walking better after 48 hours, take off the bandage and again see if you can locate the abscess. Many times the ichthammol pulls it more toward the sole so that it is easier to find.

If you do have a good drainage hole, you still need to apply medication and wrap the hoof. We take a small piece of cotton, apply 7% tincture of iodine to it and put it on top of the hole and then wrap the hoof. If you have a very tiny hole, you may only need to do this twice and leave the bandage on for 2 days and repeat.

Though you may be tempted to reach for an antibiotic when your donkey has a hoof abscess, keep in mind that the location of the pus pocket - between the tissue and the hoof - is beyond the reach of any such medication given by mouth or injection. Only if the wound is deeper will antibiotics reach the actual contaminants. For any uncomplicated abscess, it's better to promote drainage with a sufficient opening, intensive nursing and nature's own ability to heal. If you veterinarian feels that the abscess is very deep, he may want to give the donkey a tetanus shot along with some bute to ease his pain.

Once treatment is initiated, recovery varies. If you found a hole and there was good drainage, you will see immediate results although your donkey will still be very lame, he will be clearly walking on all fours within 12 hours. If you did not get good drainage, it may take 3 days to a week of nursing before you see results. Until the donkey can walk more soundly, he should be stalled. Abscesses are not to be taken lightly. If they become severe, they can proceed up to the coffin bone and then you have real problems.

Thrush or Abscess?

Thrush

Thrush is a foul, black infection of the frog. Whenever you clean your donkey's hooves, if there is a rotten smell once you've removed the dirt and manure, chances are you've discovered thrush. The smell, which is associated with the disease, is from the dead tissue of the frog. In severe cases, it may penetrate the sole and involve vital structures within the hoof. It is characterized by a distinct offensive odor and in more severe cases, a black discharge.

Thrush is caused by the bacterial ground organism or yeast organism. The bacteria and yeast are present in the environment, and when the conditions are right, they will invade the crevices of the frog. Thrush is more commonly seen in dirty stables where the bedding is continuously moist or the donkey is standing in manure most of the time. It can also be caused by standing outside in continuously wet soil or mud. Donkeys are more prone to thrush than are horses, as donkeys hooves are more concave and tend to hold dirt and manure more readily than a horses large flat hoof. Very pregnant jennets are also more prone to thrush as they do not run and play and throw the manure and dirt out of their hooves like jacks or younger donkeys.

The frog of the hoof itself may start to degenerate and chunks of it peel off. In more severe cases, your donkey will show signs of lameness and may flinch when the area is cleaned. This indicates involvement of the sensitive tissues. If this is the case, you should give the animal both a tetanus and possibly penicillin.

Treatment should begin with eliminating the source of the problem. Provide a dry place to stand during wet weather and keep your barn bedding dry and clean. The hoof should be thoroughly cleaned and any parts of the infected frog should be trimmed away. A dressing should then be applied. There are various thrush treatments. For mild cases, a drying solution such as Kopertox (available in most feed stores) can be applied. Strong 7% tincture of iodine can be used also and household bleach can be used on a limited basis until you could get some Kopertox. Iodine and bleach can be very drying so should not be used excessively. You should treat the hoof at least once but preferably twice daily. Treating for two to five days should kill the bacteria and promote healing.

Donkeys especially prone to thrush will benefit if treated weekly with one of the commercial preparations.

Abscess

Donkeys seem to be highly susceptible to abscesses during wet spring months. We have even narrowed it down to a week of wet weather and you can count on abscesses occurring four to six weeks later. A donkeys hoof during wet weather will become much softer which makes it easy for tiny pebbles to pierce the hoof and begin to work its way up through the hoof, causing an abscess.

Ask seven veterinarians how to treat an abscess and you will get seven different answers. We have tried them all! (See *Hoof Abscesses* in this book.)

Norma Haskins of Massachusetts with Peanut Butter at Farm Day Celebration

Seedy Toe: *Causes, Complications, Cures*

What is seedy toe?

This is a disease of the hoof wall normally in the toe region in which the hoof wall is separated from the white line. There is a change in the consistency of the horn that results in "crumbling" of the inner wall. Depending on which veterinarian and farrier you ask, many consider Seedy Toe and "White Line Disease" to be the same thing.

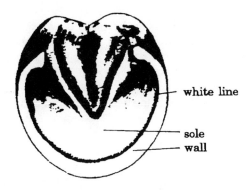

What causes seedy toe?

Letting the hoof grow too long is the major cause of seedy toe. When the wall of the hoof is too long, the weight of the donkey pushes the hoof wall away from the sensitive structures. Debris such as dirt and manure, packs into the hollow space and enlarges the separation. Seedy toe most commonly occurs in the front hooves as that is where the donkey bears most of its weight. Seedy toe is common is damp areas or in areas where in certain months, such as spring, you have a lot of rain. This causes the hoof to soften and predisposes the hoof to seedy toe.

What are the signs of seedy toe?

If you catch the disease before lameness occurs, you will see a cavity filled with soft dark cheesy type material which is really the debris of degenerated or broken-down horn. Seedy toe may be seen in only a small spot or it may appear in the entire width of the wall at the toe. If you catch it early, the donkey will not be lame. In more advanced stages, the donkey will, over a period of a few days, go from a slight limp to extremely lame. A veterinarian will diagnose the condition as primary, secondary, or chronic laminitis, all of which are important to know to determine how it will be treated.

How is seedy toe treated?

Again, there are a variety of treatments depending on the severity of the condition. The severity can often be determined by how lame the donkey is.

Mild Seedy Toe:

The diseased portion of the foot is hollowed out making a cavity between the horny wall and sensitive laminae. The hoof should be thoroughly scrubbed with a diluted iodine solution. The wall of the hoof just in front of the diseased portion, should be filed slightly down so when the hoof is level on the ground, that portion of the wall will not touch the ground. This will keep the pressure off the wall in that area and stop any progress of the disease.

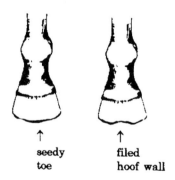

	seedy	filed
	toe	hoof wall

Apply a large piece of cotton soaked in iodine in to the cavity and wrap the hoof. Keep hoof wrapped for two days then repeat and keep doing this until the donkey's lameness eases. In mild cases of seedy toe, most of the diseased portion of the hoof will be trimmed away. Do not wrap the *entire* hoof then turn the donkey loose and forget about it. You are going to have to check the hoof on a daily basis to make sure the tape covering the diseased portion only, is still in place.

Secondary and Chronic

If you have a severely lame donkey, you can be pretty well assured that you have a severe case of seedy toe. *Warning:* If you are not aggressive in your treatment of severe seedy toe, it is entirely possible that your donkey will have to be put down due to non-treatable laminitis. Again, the tip of the hoof wall, or where ever the disease portion is, should be trimmed to keep further separation from occurring.

Severe seedy toe can respond to several different treatments. The problem is, you never know which treatment is going to be successful so you may end up trying several methods of treatment.

1) Soak a large piece of cotton in 7% iodine and put in the cavity that has been dug out. Repeat every two days.

2) Apply a large glob of Ichthammol (you can find this in feed and tack stores) into the cavity and wrap.

3) Tetracycline (or another trade name Oxytet 100) is generally an injectable broad spectrum antibiotic used to treat a variety of diseases. However, veterinarians have found that it attacks the same organisms that causes foot rot in cattle. Apply a generous amount on a piece of cotton, put in the hoof cavity and wrap. Repeat daily, in severe seedy toe, and every two days in secondary seedy toe.

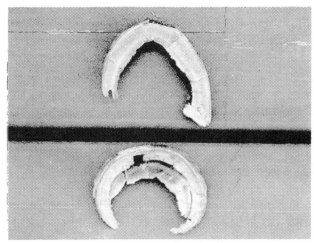

Hoof trimmings from a donkey with seedy toe. Top: healthy back hoof trimming. Bottom: Secondary seedy toe condition. Note dark coloring and separation of wall and sole by diseased laminae

The above are all tried and true methods of treatment. If you start out using one treatment, say the iodine, and you see no improvement in two days, try switching to the tetracycline. You don't know exactly which organism is causing the disease, therefore you might have to try several treatments until you get a response.

Once the donkey is again sound (this may take two or three weeks) the cavity can be packed with a variety of materials to keep dirt and manure out, until the hoof grows out. Years ago, we had a donkey with a very bad case of seedy toe and about 1/3 of her hoof wall had to be removed. We used auto fiberglass which he applied to the remaining hoof wall and actually made a new part of the hoof. It worked great. If I remember correctly, it only had to be redone one time until the hoof grew out. Other packing materials are melted resin, silicone caulking and tub and tile silicone caulking.

In extremely severe seedy toe that has destroyed much of the laminae and caused coffin bone rotation, your veterinarian should already be involved and can steer you in the right direction.

The best prevention for seedy toe is proper hoof care. Have your donkey's hooves trimmed before the wet spring weather hits and always make sure your donkeys have dry areas to stand in.

Added Note: I have looked and looked for equine poultice boots small enough for miniatures to no avail. Instead of wrapping a hoof, sometimes in the case of abscesses, seedy toe, or stone bruises, a boot would be nice to put on after applying medication. I happened to be in a very large pet store and came across hunting dog foot boots. Bought a pair and they work great. They are made of tire rubber and slit on the sides so that you can get them on and all you need to do is tape the boot around the leg one time. For stone bruises, you can apply several layers of cotton pads to the inside sole of the boot for protection. *Warning:* These boots do a great job of keeping moisture in and we found that you should take them off and stall the donkey on dry clean bedding at night as too much moisture softens the hoof and can cause added problems. I purchased size Extra Large which seems to be a good size for the average donkey. If you have a donkey with a little larger foot, go to a size XX Large.

Extra Large measures 3-1/2" from heel to toe
XX Large measures 3-3/4" from heel to toe

Keratoma

What is keratoma? This term applies to an abnormal growth of horn, which begins at the coronary band, on the inner surface of the hoof wall. The actual cause of a keratoma is not known, however it is associated with inflammation of the laminar structures. It is brought on by a puncture wound or an injury to the coronary band, although some odd cases have been diagnosed as being due to an abnormal secretion of hoof material..

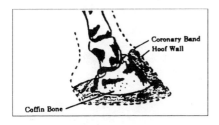

The donkey may or may not be lame. Most of the time, the condition is not noticeable until it is quite advanced. The abnormal growth is cylindrical (moving parallel up and down the hoof) in shape. The bulge begins at the coronet and gradually advances down the hoof wall as the hoof wall grows. This growth pushes the white line in toward the center of the sole, pressing on the sensitive laminae which occasionally causes the donkey to be lame.

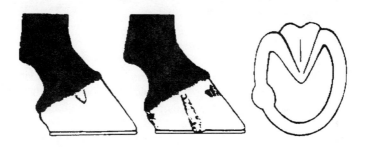

Advancing keratoma. Begins at the coronet and advances down the hoof as the wall grows

How is a keratoma treated? Most of the time, no treatment is necessary. In severe cases, surgical removal of the abnormal growth by a veterinarian seems to be the only treatment for advanced cases. After surgical removal, the hole in the hoof wall is ordinarily filled with plastic to protect the sensitive structures until new horn growth covers the site of removal. This treatment is not always successful because the abnormal growth can recur. In mild cases where the donkey may be slightly lame, a corrective shoe could be applied, but this would be rare.

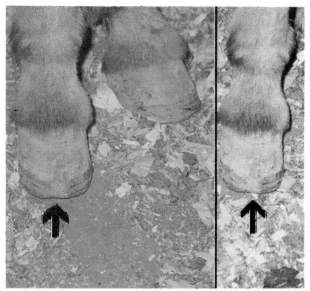

Keratoma on 12 year old jennet

Does a donkey fully recover from keratoma? I have had two jennets with this condition. One jennet was purchased as a 6 year old and had it on her arrival here. No lameness was apparent and ten years later, she still has it and it has never caused lameness. The other jennet was raised here and developed a keratoma when she was a five year old. Again, she was never lame and approximately 14 months later, it had completely disappeared due to growing a new hoof in that time period. If a donkey develops keratoma, and is never lame, it will in all likelihood never cause lameness and no treatment is necessary.

Scratches

Scratches, also known as grease heels, grease, cracked heels or mud fever, is a condition of dermatitis (inflammation of the skin) of the heel and rear side of the pastern area. While it is most common on the hindfeet, it may affect the front ones, or be any combination thereof. It was very common in draft horses, helped by the long hair on their legs. This long hair held dirt and moisture and often covered up beginning signs of the scratches, so it was not noticed until quite advanced. The disease is not contagious, but several donkeys in the same stable may be affected because they are exposed to the same conditions.

Scratches is frequently associated with dirty stables. It can also occur when donkeys stand in muddy corrals or muddy, wet pastures for long periods of time without relief.

Soaps, salt solutions, or irritating liniments may cause enough dermatitis to start a case of scratches. Lime dust from roads or lime left uncovered on stall floors, along with other chemical irritants may cause scratches. Contact dermatitis from clover (dew poisoning) or poison ivy can also start scratches. Infection by bacteria and/or fungi usually occurs as the disease progresses. In some cases, it is impossible to determine the original cause of the problem.

Early in scratches, the pastern area hair falls out and the skin may be sensitive and swollen; it may itch severely. As it progresses, the skin may show heat and be reddened. Serum begins to ooze from cracks and sores on the skin. The exudate may be yellowish or grayish and will have a foul odor. Edema (swelling with fluid) may extend up the leg. By the time it has reached this point, the animal is usually lame and shows severe pain in the area. Dead patches of skin may begin to slough, leaving raw, red sores.

If not treated, the problem becomes chronic. Granulation begins; growths commonly called "grapes" may appear. The skin becomes thickened and hard. The foot may be so swollen as to look like an elephant foot. In severe cases, the infection may extend into the frog. It can even undermine the frog and sole.

Begin by removing the cause, if it can be determined. Cases of scratches which are diagnosed early have a good chance of recovery. Clip all hair from the affected area. Wash the skin gently with a mild soap. Then pat it dry with paper towels or a soft cloth towel. Remove any loose, dead skin and hair. Apply a mild antiseptic product such as calamine lotion or another drying type lotion. In a day or two, change to ointments such as zinc oxide to prevent over-drying it.

If the infection extends deep into the heel or into the frog or if severe granulomatous growths are present, call your veterinarian for treatment of the problem. Small granulations may be removed with a pressure bandage, placed over a soothing ointment or a product containing a corticosteroid, such as Panalog. Corticosteroid ointments are also useful for cases of scratches where the skin is not broken. A mixture of sulfanilamide powder and mineral oil is said to work well when the animal cannot be removed from wet conditions. The oil would act to keep moisture off the skin and the antibiotic would help to heal the lesions. Larger growths will require surgical removal by your vet.

The basic theory in treating a problem with scratches is to dry it up if it is wet, and to moisturize and soften if it is dry. Now that I've told you all the fancy cures for the problem, let me tell you about an old-time remedy that many people swear by. It apparently has cured many minor cases of scratches and also seems to work well on rope burns in the heel area.

Get a large can of sauerkraut, a plastic bag (a bread wrapper is okay) and some bandaging material - adhesive tape, Vetrap or Elastikon. Pull the bag up over the affected foot. Pour the entire can of sauerkraut into the bag, putting most of it on the back side of the foot. Wrap the whole thing well with the tape, putting on gentle pressure and wrapping plenty of tape around the bottom of the hoof to help protect the plastic bag there. Leave it unchanged for three days. When you remove it, the skin is usually clean and fresh-looking and the problem is much improved. Treat it with either softening or drying products as needed. In a few cases, sauerkraut treatment for anther two or three days may be necessary. The treatment works especially well with those cases that are exuding pus and are generally messy.

Andrea Olson of Montana with her donkey Ozzie

Chapter 5

Disease, Illness, Skin

Choosing a Veterinarian

I have found veterinarians who do not prefer to deal with miniature livestock. They were schooled in large equine and would rather stay in that field and have no desire to learn how to care for miniatures.

Where and How To Look

If you have neighbors with horses or other Miniature Donkey breeders in your area, ask them who they use and why they like them. Ask them about other veterinarians they have used and why they dislike them. All veterinarians have clients who love them and others who hate them. What you are looking for is the veterinarian whose name pops up more often, in either case.

I have personally found that I prefer veterinarians who specialize in equine, verses one that works on all types of farm animals. In my mind, if they only work on equine then their expertise is in *this* area instead of having a *general* knowledge of all farm animals. Some veterinarians cater to particular types of equine owners. If a veterinarian generally specializes in Thoroughbred race horses then it's possible that he may not be appropriate for your Miniature Donkeys.

Evaluating Potential Veterinarians

Once you have a few names, stop by their office and see how their practice is run. We have veterinarians in our area who work from 9 to 5, five days a week and if you call any other time, you won't get an answer. I don't know about you, but if I have an emergency, it almost never happens between 9 and 5. Is there more than one veterinarian working out of the clinic? If there is only one, you may not be able to get hold of him/her during an emergency if they are on another emergency. I currently use one equine clinic for all my needs. They have an in-house operating room and one vet is a specialist in equine surgery. The clinic is owned by two veterinarians and they generally have a third resident veterinarian employed. I recently took a donkey to the clinic for x-rays. All three veterinarians happen to be in the office and all three analyzed the x-rays together. I had the expertise of three vets for the price of one! Many veterinarians, just out of school, do not have their own clinic and work out of their homes. If this is the case, you do not have the option of hauling an animal to them for evaluation, and must always pay a farm call fee. Also, they may not have all the equipment you may need such as ultra sound machines.

Personality

A veterinarian's personality is very important to me. We have all known vets who think everything should be a big secret and you have to literally beat information out of them. I like talkative veterinarians. If I ask a question, I expect a thorough, complete answer. I am paying them to not only treat my animal but to avail myself to their expertise. If I have a problem that doesn't require a visit or want to discuss something - free of charge - my vets welcome my phone call any time day or night.

My veterinarians *like* my donkeys. They enjoy their personalities and like the donkeys rubbing on them. *My vets enjoy learning about Miniature Donkeys.* Sometimes they ask me as many questions as I ask them. I like that. They don't come to my farm with an "I know everything" attitude. They get a kick out of the babies wanting all of their attention. I had a new vet out several years ago who acted like my donkeys had the plaque. The further away he could stay from them, the better. Had another vet one time ask me why I didn't raise "decent sized animals." Obviously, I haven't called on either one again.

Should You Switch Veterinarians?

Have you ever had doubts about your vet? Personality conflicts, overwork and simple mistakes do occur. When is one more mistake too many? When do you decide that, no matter how hard you try, you just can't see eye to eye with your veterinarian?

Try to narrow down the problem. Are you uncomfortable with the way your vet handles your donkeys? Is he/she always late or difficult to get hold of? Keep the lines of communication open and discuss the problem with them. Is it just this one particular case that you are unhappy with? More than once I have called several veterinarians to get their opinions on a problem. Most veterinarians will discuss a problem with you on the phone even if they do not know you. Of the different veterinarians I have used over the years, I have never had one get upset with me when I told them that I got a second opinion on a problem. They know how much I love my donkeys and they realize I care enough about them to make certain they are getting the proper treatment.

Tips on getting along with your veterinarian:

1. When calling a new vet, find out when he likes to be paid. Does he prefer payment at the time the animal is treated or will he bill you.

2. Will he bring an assistant with him or will he need your help.

3. Have your donkey ready. Don't expect your vet to walk a half mile to get to your animal or spend an hour trying to catch it.

4. Vets don't like to hear "while you're here doc......". They've scheduled you a certain amount of time according to your initial phone call. If you need other animals treated, let him know a day ahead of time. Remember, there is another client after you who is also waiting on their arrival.

5. Some vets are notorious for talking "veterinarian talk." I always come back with "Oh, yes, it's wonderful you're so well versed in foreign languages, but how about talking to me in English!" I find that most vets honestly don't do this to try to impress you, it's just the way they talk!

6. Don't be embarrassed about talking about certain parts of an animal's anatomy. What ever problem your animal has, vets have dealt with it time and time before. Lots of times we have ladies call *Miniature Donkey Talk* who refuse to talk to Mike about a 'certain problem' with their jennet or jack. We've heard it all before too and I can assure you that you need not be embarrassed - we sure aren't. Things do work both ways - Years ago I had an elderly gentleman vet who could not bring himself to use the word "penis" in front of me. Whenever the topic arose, he always substituted the word "weenie"!

7. Give your vet as much information as you can about the problem. Tell them everything you have seen no matter how minor it may seem to you.

8. Don't be afraid to call the vet and ask him if the donkey should be getting well faster or changing more rapidly. If you don't feel a medication is working, tell him. It may be something that takes longer to work or a change in medication may be necessary.

9. If possible, you should have the donkey's detailed medical history available for the vet.

10. Have the donkey in adequate light. If at night and you have no barn lights, have extra flashlights available and make sure the ground is well lit from the vet's vehicle to wherever the donkey is located.

11. Make sure the donkey is in a clean environment. Don't expect your vet to administer medical attention in a foot of manure.

It takes the cooperation and understanding of both the client and the veterinarian to develop a good working relationship. He needs your business and you need his knowledge. Helping your vet do his job better can only result in better health care for your donkeys.

MGF Sage and Susie Gemmell

Hematology Testing

Test results listed under donkeys is a compilation of NINE Miniature Donkeys and represents the average counts. Veterinarians normally compare test results with the Equine Values listed and as you can see, some counts for donkeys differ greatly. A veterinarian that compares donkey blood chemistry counts to the average range for horses, could very well misdiagnose your donkey's illness. Give your vet a copy of this to keep in your files.

Large Animal Profile: CHEMISTRY
Albumin, Alk, Ptase., BUN, Calcium, Creatinine, Glucose, Magnesium, Phosphorus, SDH, SGOT, Serum Protein, T. Bilirubin, Na, K, Cl

	Donkeys	Equine
1. Albumin	2.9-3.6	2.3-3.9
2. Alk Ptase	117-232	7-177
3. BUN	8-15	16-28
4. Calcium	11.8-12.4	11.6-13.4
5. Creatinine	1.1-1.9	1.2-2.8
6. Glucose	30-73	60-100
7. Magnesium		1.7-2.1
8. Phosphorus	2.9-5.3	2.0-4.8
9. SDH		
10. SGOT	244-378	83-339
11. Serum Protein	5.9-7.4	5.7-7.9
12. T. Bilirubin	0.1-0.1	0.2-5.1
13. Sodium	129-136	138-144
14. Potassium	3.5-5.7	2.8-4.5
15. Chloride	97-107	96-106
16. GGT	48-147	9-35
17. LDH	367-728	200-450
18. CPK	187-538	150-450
21. Fibrinogen	200-400	100-250
Total CO	24-26	20-26
Cholesterol	62-109	75-150
Bilirubin Direct	0.0-0.1	0.0-0.4
Globulin	2.9-4.2	2.6-4.0
Triglycerides	94-195	
HDL	43-65	

HEMATOLOGY

CBC (Hb, PCV, Plasma, Protein, WBC, RBC, MCV, MCHC, Differential)

Donkeys   Equine

	Donkeys	Equine
23. Hemoglobin	9.3-14.3	10-16
26. RBC	4.8-6.9	5.5-10.5
28. MCHC	34-55	35-38
29. MCV	54-64	34-50
30. WBC	7,100-12,200	6,000-11,000
DIFFERENTIAL		
31. HCT	27.2-41	32-52
32. MCH	18.8-22.8	12.3-19.7
33. Seg Neutrophi	2400-4200	3,000-7,000
34. Lymphocytes	55-76	1,000-5,000
35. Monocytes	1-7	0-600
36. Eosinophils	1-7	0-600

Most veterinarians go by #30 WBC (White blood cell) counts to determine if a donkey is sick or not. Healthy donkeys usually have a count between 7,100 and 12,200. A donkey that say has a slight bug, may carry a count around 18,000. At this count, it should be determined whether to treat the donkey with antibiotics – which may shut down the immune system to allow the antibiotics to work – or, to let the donkey's own immune system fight the bug. A WBC of 30,000 indicates a sick donkey that should be treated with antibiotics.

Average pulse (beats per min) 44
Respiration (breaths per min) 20

Average temperature 99 to 101

Household First Aid

There are several household and first aid products right in our own home that can be used on your donkeys. When you need something quickly, instead of wasting time running to your local tack shop or vet clinic, look in your medicine cabinet first.

Epsom Salts or Table Salt are good for soaking a donkey's hoof to treat a mild sprain, puncture wound or treating a hoof abscess.

Tincture of Iodine is good for treating a newborn's navel to prevent navel ill and infection. Thoroughly immerse the navel stump and repeat at least once a day for two days. Iodine is also useful in treating the soles of the hoof if your donkey happens to be extremely tender footed - after a hoof trimming - to prevent stone bruises. Iodine can also be used to prevent thrush (a degenerate disease of the frog). Apply to bottom of hoof being careful not to get any on the outside hoof wall or skin.

Vaseline can be used on your foal's bottom where irritation may occur due to foal heat diarrhea. It may be necessary to clean the foal several times a day and applying Vaseline until the diarrhea clears up. Vaseline is also good to use on a rubbed spot where the hair is gone. It will keep the area soft and encourage hair growth more quickly. It is also good in battling bot flies which lay their eggs on your donkeys. While the eggs should be scraped off the donkey, you will find some eggs hard to reach. Smearing Vaseline on those spots prevents the eggs from breathing by sealing out air thereby killing them.

Pepto-Bismol works well for foal heat diarrhea. Pepto does contain some bacteria fighting agents and is good at coating and protecting the stomach wall. *Remember*, any signs of depression accompanied with diarrhea is an emergency demands **immediate** veterinarian attention.

Kaopectate can be used on persistent foal heat diarrhea, however Pepto Bismol should be tried first. Read the directions and use the same amount you would use on a human baby. Kaopectate is much harsher than Pepto but is good at clearing up diarrhea. Give one dose of 3 cc's.

Hydrogen Peroxide is much better than just plain water for washing out minor wounds. The bubbling action will penetrate portions of the wound that water may not be able to. Hydrogen peroxide mixed with other equine fungicides makes a good flushing solution, as it will carry the fungicide to deeper depths of the wound killing bacteria.

Aspirin is still one of the safest and most effective ways to reduce pain, fever and inflammation. If your donkey is suffering from an injury and you cannot get immediate veterinarian help, you can administer aspirin in the mean time. Dissolve two aspirins for every 100 lbs. of body weight in water, and put into a syringe (without the needle). Mixing in some Karo syrup to make a paste helps prevent the donkey from spitting it out.

The Secret

The Killing Fields
An Innocent Weed May Be Deadly To Your Donkey

When a donkey dies suddenly and the cause cannot be determined, it is often lumped into the category of "poisoning" and a plant or chemical agent is suspected. Hundreds of poisonous plants have been indicted as causing illness or death in livestock.

Most diagnoses of poisoning are not based on laboratory experiments, but rather on field observation and experience. It is difficult to run clinical tests on poisonous plants, because not all plants are toxic at the same time. Nor are they equally poisonous when growing under different conditions, or when compared as fresh versus dried.

As with other toxicity's, there are very few signs that are absolutely diagnostic for plant poisoning. And, few plants cause distinctive changes in a dead animal. In fact, many plants can kill animals without producing noticeable changes before the death occurs.

Weather conditions can influence toxicity's. A storm prevented a group of horses from eating normally for several days. When the weather finally cleared, they were hungry and ate huge numbers of **acorns**. Several of the animals died. This may occur with other plants. When the animals finally eat again, they are so hungry that they may eat whatever is handy rather than what they would normally eat.

As a general rule, poisonous plants are not palatable. An equine will usually avoid them if he has a choice of other, palatable feed - whether growing forage or adequate supplemental hay and grain. Donkeys may be forced to eat poisonous plants when pasture is overgrazed and no other feed is offered. Overgrazing not only reduces the supply of desirable feed species, but by its destruction of valuable range plants, may stimulate the spread of undesirable species.

Donkeys may consume poisonous plants in hay, where the animal cannot separate them out. The problem is less easily controlled. Donkeys may also be affected when poisonous plants are cut and left where the animals are accustomed to eating. *The wilting of some plants can drastically increase their toxicity.*

Equine owners should check hay as it is fed to make sure that it is not too weedy. Animals may be poisoned by plants, such as **oleander**, which have been baled with the hay. Buy hay from the same source all the time if possible and know your supplier. Fortunately, most poisonous plants must be eaten in approximately 1 to 3% of the animal's body weight before toxicity occurs. Continued ingestion of small amounts of some poisonous plants in hay may cause toxicity.

If poisonous plants are noticed in the pasture, they can be removed by digging or using chemical weed killers. Be sure that the weed killer used is compatible with a grazing animal, or remove the equine from the pasture for the recommended length of time after treating the plants. With annual plants, mowing them before they go to seed can result in control of the offending plant within a couple of years. They should be raked up and removed from the pasture after mowing so the animals don't have access to them.

Ditches, fence rows, and spring or seep areas should be closely checked as poisonous plants are often found there. Some plants are only poisonous at certain times of the year and it may be necessary to take animals out of the pasture at this time. In California, for example, yellow star thistle grows mostly in the late summer and fall, when native pastures are dry. Care should be taken to provide the animals with supplemental feed, or they may eat the thistle. If the animals acquire a taste for the thistle, which they sometimes do, it may be necessary to completely remove them from the pasture.

Mineral deficiencies sometimes stimulate equine to eat certain plants. For example, plants high in nitrates may have a salty taste, and are thus palatable. If the pasture is short, it is desirable to provide mineral supplements.

Do not turn hungry donkeys out into strange pastures. At this point, they will eat anything, especially since they don't know what is there. If the first plants an equine finds are poisonous, he may eat them anyway. Fill the animals with hay and then turn them out. Young animals are more curious than older ones, and will often eat dangerous plants.

Well-meaning neighbors can pose another threat to your animals by tossing lawn clippings and shrub clippings into your pasture. There are numerous shrubs which are toxic to equine and clippings from lawns that have been fertilized may contain poisonous substances.

By following these guidelines, you can greatly reduce the chances of your donkey consuming poisonous plants.

1. Learn about poisonous plants. Local county extension agents and universities usually have information and descriptions of poisonous plants in your area.
2. Inspect pastures regularly, especially in the spring.
3. Always check your hay for an over abundance of weeds each time you feed.
4. Be sure not to overgraze pastures. During times when pastures are scarce, feed hay to reduce the chances of your donkeys eating toxic plants.
5. Advise neighbors not to throw branch or lawn clippings inside your pasture. Explain to them the dangers of doing so, as most non-livestock owners simply do not realize the potential harm.

References: Ruth B. James, DVM, Bonnie Gross, Miniature Donkey Talk Magazine

If you suspect your donkey has ingested a poisonous plant call:

National Animal Poison Control Centers:

1-900-680-0000 (U.S. and Canada) The charge is $20 for 5 minutes and $2,95 thereafter
1-800-548-2423 (U.S. and Canada) The charge is $30 per case Have credit card (Visa, MC, Discover, Am Express) ready

POISONOUS GRASSES AND WEEDS

PLANT NAME	SYMPTOMS	COMMENTS
Arrowgrass	Nervousness; muscle tremors; difficulty breathing; convulsions and death	Thick-leaved grass native to the United States west of New Mexico and Montana; commonly found around a water source; not poisonous as long as it has a sufficient water supply; but after drought or a hard frost becomes extremely toxic; causes a notable loss of range livestock each year
Chickweed	Central nervous system disturbance; weakness; staggering	Poisonous whether dried or fresh; often grows among gardens, root crops, cereals and fodder crops
Cocklebur	Dullness and nausea; weakness; inability to stand; difficulty breathing; rapid but weak pulse; animal may lie on its side and paddle its legs as though running until exhausted; death is possible	Germinating seeds and the seedlings are most poisonous; toxicity decreases with plant maturity; mature plant has sharp, prickly burrs which can injure mouth and muzzle area; commonly found along streams and pond beds, fields, roadsides and waste places
Crotalaria	Loss of weight; dullness; periods of excitement characterized by compulsive walking (usually in a straight line, bumping into obstacles); jerking of head and neck muscles; frequent yawning; incoordination; jaundice; dark red or coffee-colored urine; impaired liver function; delirium; death	Has yellow flowers and small pods; first introduced to the Southeast as a soil binder; now grows uncontrolled; grows in wet areas such as river beds; afflicted animals sometimes referred to as having "walkabout" disease because of compulsive walking; causes erosion of esophagus; animal cannot swallow and usually dies of starvation; when harvested with hay or grain, causes them to be toxic also
Groundsel and Ragwort	Staggering; aimless walking; pressing of head against hard objects; sudden attacks of frenzy with violent, uncontrolled galloping; cirrhosis of the liver; pale mucous membranes; hanging head; dragging legs	Herb with yellow flowers in early spring that grows in meadows and pastures; poisonous year-round; must be removed from pastures; though bitter when fresh, palatable when dried; toxic in hay and bedding
Horsetail	Unthriftiness with increasing weakness until muscle control is affected causing frequent falls; difficulty breathing; pale mucous membranes; rapid but weak pulse; convulsions; coma and death	Thrives in sandy, moist soil in meadows, embankments and ditches; especially toxic when dried
Jimson Weed	Increased thirst; nausea; vertigo; dilated pupils; retention of urine; irregular respiration; death	Coarse plant with hard, spiny pods and wavy leaves; commonly grows in fields, barnyards and abandoned pastures; poisonous both green and dried; death is usually quite rapid
Johnson Grass, Milo, Sorghum, Sudan Grass	Slobbering; weak, rapid pulse; increased respiration; incoordination; cystitis; urinary incontinence; urine scalding of hocks and perineum; bladder paralysis; convulsions and death possible; almond odor to breath	Tall coarse grasses often cultivated for fodder; must be properly dried and cured for six weeks before it is safe for consumption; in pastures it must reach a height of one foot before it is safe to graze; second growth after cutting, drought or hard freeze is extremely poisonous

Locoweed	Staggering gait; holding head high; stiffness; loss of directional sense; easy excitability; wild-eyed appearance; incoordination; pressing head against hard objects	Low-growing weed with wide range of colored flowers; most common in the West; once a horse has tasted the plant, he seeks it out and eats it readily until the toxic levels in the body build up enough to cause death; survivors are seldom healthy, trustworthy mounts after the poisoning
Milkweed	Bloated, distended stomach caused by congestion of internal organs; loss of muscle control; staggering; paralysis of rear limbs; labored breathing; death due to respiratory failure	Has milky white sap that seeps from pods; found in uncultivated fields, roadsides and pastures; poisonous year-round, because of its bitter taste, horses usually eat it only when extremely hungry; death is usually rapid; there is no known cure
Timber Milkvetch, Vetch	Hair loss; dullness; cracked hoofs and lameness; stiff joints; staggering; emaciation	Causes selenium poisoning; first sign is loss of the long hairs of the mane and tail; then cracking of hoofs at the coronary band leading to stumbling; there is no known cure, survivors usually suffer from liver damage and extreme sensitivity to sunlight.

POISONOUS ORNAMENTALS

PLANT NAME	SYMPTOMS	COMMENTS
Lantana	Watery lesions and sloughing off of skin; abdominal pain; bloody, watery manure; sensitivity to light; jaundice	Planted for beauty in yards and gardens; also grows wild in South; most poisonous during spring and summer
Oleander	Coldness of extremities; extremely irregular heartbeat; depression; nausea and bloody diarrhea	Evergreen shrub common in yards and gardens in warm areas such as the South and California; extremely toxic despite its beauty and fire-resistant qualities; especially toxic during winter and spring; as little as 30 crushed leaves can kill a 600 pound horse within 12 hours; to remove plant dig up and dispose of it; never burn the plant, the smoke can be poisonous to man; handle the plant with gloved hands, the toxins may be absorbed through open wounds
Privet Hedge	Colic and unsteady gait when large amounts are ingested	No known treatment; death usually occurs within 36 to 48 hours; common landscape planting
Yew	Muscle tremors; weakness; collapse; rapid death	An evergreen shrub often planted for decoration; all parts are poisonous and drying does not lessen the toxicity; contains "taxine" which acts as a strong heart depressant; when large amounts are eaten, death may come so rapidly that the animal is found with parts of the plant still in its mouth

Buckeye - Found in woods. Young shoots and seeds are the most poisonous.

Nightshade - Somewhat resemble tomato plant w/yellow, red or black fruit when ripe. Found in fence rows, hay & grain fields. Leaves, shoots, berries all contain toxic agents.

Lantana - Ornamental shrub used for landscaping. Leaves are extremely poisonous.

Arrowgrass - Found in MT to N.M. and states west, grows in marshy pastures or near water source. As long as plant receives adequate water it doesn't cause poison. Growth stunted by drought or sudden frost and it assumes poisonous trait.

Johnson Grass - Coarse weed grass w/white line splitting the blades in center. Found primarily in south but can dot other countrysides. When stunted by dry weather or when in its second growth, the plant is at its danger peak.

Yellow Jessamine - Favors open woods of PA, MI, Iowa and points south.Grows like vine with leaves.

Castor Bean - Throughout the South. Equine enjoy eating the toxic bean.

Chokeberry - Also called wild cherry, large shrubs, white flowers, cherries. Leaves are toxic.

POISONOUS TREES

Plant Name	SYMPTOMS	COMMENTS
Black Cherry, Chokecherry, Chokeberries	Uneasiness; staggering; breathing difficulty; mucous membranes turn blue; convulsions and rapid death	Shrubs with white flowers and red or black cherry fruit; commonly found along fence rows, thickets and woodland areas; toxic agent is hydrocyanic acid is produced in wilted or bruised leaves; most common danger is from branches blown down during storms or that have been pruned: death is usually so rapid that the animal is found with portions of the plant still in its mouth
Buckeye	Weakness; staggering; severe trembling and twitching of muscles; inflamed mucous membranes; dilated pupils; coma; death	Tree or shrub found in woods and along river banks in the East; seed is glossy brown with a pale scar; most danger occurs in spring and summer
Oak Tree, Acorns	Dullness; weakness, black pelleted manure followed by total constipation which is then followed by bloody diarrhea; frequent urination; dry muzzle; thin, rapid pulse	Common tree of varied heights found all over the United States; leaves and acorns contain tannic acid; especially toxic during spring and summer; heavy rainfall may soften fallen acorns and cause them to sprout which makes them more tempting and palatable

UNUSUAL POISONOUS PLANTS

PLANT NAME	SYMPTOMS	COMMENTS
Avocado	Severe, noninfectious mastitis; milk production is reduced; as inflammation subsides, no more milk is produced	Leaves, bark and fruit are toxic
Blue-Green Algae	Abdominal pain; difficulty breathing; convulsions; death; survivors suffer liver damage and are sensitive to the sun	Some forms highly toxic to all animals; smaller animals at greater risk since they are more prone to drink from shallow water where algae blooms; animals must be removed from the water supply and water treated with algicides
Wild Tobacco	Paralysis and rapid death	No known treatment; animals are often found dead or paralyzed and near death

POISONOUS PLANTS AND SHRUBS

PLANT NAME	SYMPTOMS	COMMENTS
Bladder Pod	Inflammation of the intestines with yellowish diarrhea; frequent urination; short, rapid breathing; death	Tall plant common in the South; produces pods containing two poisonous seeds; especially poisonous in summer; necessary to prevent exposure and remove all plants and fallen pods
Bracken Fern, Brake Fern	Progressive loss of condition: unsteady gait while walking, progresses to swaying, incoordination and staggers; drowsiness; pressing head against solid objects; crouching stance with neck arched and feet wide apart; difficulty swallowing; between seven to 20 days after first symptoms appear, horse lies down and is unable to rise again; death usually follows within a few days	Common to pastures and woodlands; has triangular shaped-fronds and may reach a height of two to four feet; contains a toxin which destroys vitamin B-1; if caught in time, injections of thiamine may prove helpful; poisonings usually occur in early spring and late fall when the fern is the only greenery left in the pasture; also dangerous when dried; may be baled with hay; since symptoms take a while to show up, many horsemen fail to believe that this plant is toxic; horse may be removed from the pasture before the symptoms become noticeable.
Castor Bean	Dullness; severe thirst; nausea; vision difficulty; incoordination; profuse sweating; watery diarrhea; heartbeat that shakes the entire body; colic pain; convulsions and death	Grown as an ornamental planting or weed along roadsides; palm-like leaves and pods containing "beans" are equally poisonous during all seasons; about 150 beans will kill a 1,000 pound horse; symptoms often appear to go away only torecur before the onset of death
Corn Cockle	Inflammation of mucous membranes; diarrhea; vertigo; weak pulse	Has purple flowers, black seeds and fine, white hairs on underside of leaves; seeds are the :most poisonous part; sometimes harvested into grain
Death Camas	Excessive drooling; staggering and incoordination; weakness; inability to stand; coma followed by death caused by heart failure	Resembles the onion with its bulbous root, except that it has flat leaves and no odor; most dangerous in early spring since it is one of the first plants to produce greenery when forage is scarce; also poisonous when cut and dried in hay
Fly-Poison	Excessive drooling; respiratory difficulty; weakness; death due to respiratory failure	Herb with a bulbous root which blossoms; poisonous year-round; an alkaloid which is found in woodlands and marshy pastures; also poisonous when cut and dried; there is no known cure
Indian Hemp (Dogbane)	Increased body temperature; sweating; ears and legs become cold; pupils dilate; linings of nose and mouth turn blue; soreness inside mouth; increased bowel action; weakness; labored respiration; coma: death	May grow as tall as five feet; stems contains milky, latex-like substance; leaves turn bright yellow during the fall; often found in sandy or gravelly soil along roadsides or in fields; extremely poisonous; as little as one half to one ounce can kill a horse: normally has a bitter taste, but some horses try it
Larkspur, Dwarf Larkspur, Staggerweed	Small amounts cause loss of appetite; excitability: falling and staggering; constipation; large amounts cause slobbering; colic; bloating; straddled stance; convulsions and respiratory paralysis leading to death	Grows one to three feet high with blue or white flowers; often grown in gardens, but also in woodlands and along streams

Plant	Symptoms	Description
Lupine	Nervousness; large accumulations of iron in the body; digestive disruption; weak heart; depression, liver damage; convulsions	Shiny green leaves and wide variation of blossom colors; often found in moist areas and foothills in the West; most dangerous from spring until first killing frost in fall; summer is the seed stage
Nightshade (also called Jerusalem Nettles, Jerusalem Cherries, Poison Berry)	Weakness; stupor; staggering; constipation or diarrhea; dilated pupils; muscle tremors; loss of muscular coordination and sense of feeling; cramps; convulsion; death from respiratory paralysis	Grows from one to two feet with white flowers resembling tomato plant flowers; has small, berry-like fruit which turns purplish-black at maturity; all parts are toxic; can be found in woods, fields, along fence rows, farm buildings and in hay and grain fields
Poison Hemlock	Excessive drooling; loss of appetite; muscular weakness; muscular tremors; incoordination; dilated pupils; rapid pulse; pain; bloating; coma; death from respiratory paralysis	Common herbal plant with a purple-spotted stem; leaves resemble parsley; root resembles a parsnip or pale carrot; people are often poisoned by mistakenly identifying the root as a parsnip; all of the plant is poisonous; common around farm buildings, roadsides, streams, fields and ditches
Rattlebush	Rapid pulse; labored respiration; diarrhea; death	Common in the South; has orange blossoms and angled pods; most dangerous in the fall and winter
Rayless Goldenrod	Tremors; dullness and depression; respiratory difficulty; death	Bush-like plant with many yellow flowers; grows readily in various types of soil; can be found around irrigation canals, pastures, woods and fields; no known cure
Silverling	Paralysis and death shortly after ingestion; survivors suffer from weakness and depression	Woody plant from the sunflower family; bears whitish flowers; commonly found in open areas across the United States
St. Johnswort (also called Klamath Weed, Rosin-Rose)	Skin blisters; falling hair and scabs; dry skin with cracked open lesions; all caused by extreme sensitivity to sunlight on white skinned areas or unpigmented skin areas	Has small leaves and many yellow flowers; commonly found growing freely in meadows, pastures and along roadsides; although not deadly, can cause severe skin disruptions in white-skinned animals
White Snakeroot (also known as White Sanicle, Boneset)	Sluggishness; depression; incoordination; trembling; paralysis of throat muscles causing inability to swallow; nasal discharge and respiratory difficulty; death	Herb with tapering leaves and clusters of white flowers; commonly found in woods and shady pastures; poisoning usually occurs in late summer; if plants cannot be eradicated, horses should be removed from the pasture by late July
Yellow Jessamine	Rigidity of limbs; lowered pulse rates; drop in body temperature; weakness; convulsions and death	Vine with yellow tubular flowers; toxin acts quickly
Yellow-Star Thistle	Frequent yawning; stand in abnormal positions; wooden expression; flicking of tongue; paralysis of swallowing muscles causing inability to chew or drink; horse may lower head into water but be unable to drink; death follows from starvation and dehydration	Has bright yellow flowers over dandelion-like leaves with cotton wool film over them; common in California, but found throughout the United States; most poisonings occur in late summer or fall; after onset of symptoms, the mortality rate is very high, since there is no know treatment; in areas infested with this plant, it is wise to remove horses from pasture altogether during the most dangerous season

Note: All horsemen should contact their local county extension agents for a detailed list of poisonous plants in their regions.

Hyperlipaemia and Obese Donkeys

Hyperlipaemia is clinically described as follows: An abnormally high concentration of lipids (fats), mainly triglycerides, in the blood. It is of greatest clinical significance in small fat ponies and donkeys, especially those in late gestation or early lactation. In these equine, there may be a massive release of fats into the plasma causing clinical signs such as dullness, lethargy, poor appetite, rapid loss of body condition, trembling, staggering, fever, diarrhea and resulting in high mortality rates after about 10 days of illness. In certain cases, the administration of insulin and glucose may be beneficial.)

A breeder lost several obese donkeys due to this condition, after they were moved to a different part of the country with a different feed source.

A donkey is not a small horse, says Dr. Gill Whitehead and colleagues at the Donkey Sanctuary. One difference is that the donkey, basically a domesticated wild ass, evolved under desert conditions. Donkeys were once used to wandering for many hours each day looking for sparse vegetation. Domesticated, the donkey on good pasture and slightly pampered with tidbits will quickly gain weight. Bad enough in itself, but also possibly a contributing factor to a common and potentially fatal problem in donkeys - the all-too-familiar hyperlipidemia. This news might start you wondering if you will have to get a triglyceride count on this animal. As a guide to treatment, the answer is yes, if the donkey is sick or is not eating. As a triglyceride count climbs, fat is deposited within the cells of various organs, and the donkey begins to deteriorate.

In the early stages of the disease, the donkey appears listless and loses appetite, may have an elevated temperature, and may pass hard or no feces at all. Abdominal discomfort develops, signaled by the animal paddling its feet or lying down and rolling. Animals may stand drooling over the water trough, later, they will have difficulty in breathing and then collapse suddenly. Some donkeys with elevated triglyceride levels also develop inflammation of the pancreas (as happens in dogs and humans).

The best defense against this disease, say these experts, *is in avoiding obesity through weight control - and avoiding stress.* However, because lack of appetite is a warning sign, it is advisable to check the donkey's appetite every week. Never starve a donkey in order to reduce its weight and avoid sudden changes of feed that may be unacceptable.

The breeder previously mentioned, was feeding a very high fat diet to his donkeys and their metabolism became accustomed to that feed. Upon moving the donkeys to a different area of the country and a lower fat diet, the donkeys bodies attempted to make up for the change by releasing great amounts of fat into the blood.

Most of us are guilty of over feeding our donkeys. This is truly "hard love," so lets see if we can break ourselves of this habit.

Factors predisposing donkeys to hyperlipaemia

Several factors were found to be positively associated with the development of clinical hyperlipaemia. In common with previous reports, female animals were found to be more likely to get the disease than males. However, there were very few pregnant animals among the donkeys and no breeding occurs within the population thus providing evidence that aspects of female physiology, other than pregnancy and lactation are involved in predisposing jennies to the disease. *(Ed Note: I agree with the statement that female physiology predisposes jennets to the disease, however, my experience - and your phone calls - gives evidence to the fact the pregnancy and lactation (foaling) ways heavily in the onslaught of hyperlipaemia. Of all the phone calls I've received all but one jennet had foaled within 30 days of the diagnosis of hyperlipaemia and the one jennet was due to foal in one week.)*

Body condition was also a significant factor in the development of hyperlipaemia. The prevalence of the disease in **fat and obese** animals was higher than in animals in normal or thin condition. This finding supports the observation of Watson et al. Concerning the raised levels of VLDL and triglyceride in overweight donkeys. It was not possible to quantify the effect of concurrent disease in comparison to the non-hyperlipaemic population, 56% of cases were considered to be secondary to another disease process.

Donkeys also seemed to be more susceptible to developing hyperlipaemia at times of social and environmental stress. Changes of housing or mixing with a new group of animals leads to the establishment of new dominance hierarchies, an observation supported by the cases occurring after entry to the population.

Furthermore, animals that were younger (less than 10 years) at times of such stress were less likely to get the disease than older animals, perhaps due to the fact that younger animals are less prone to secondary disease or may be stronger and more successful in establishing dominance.

Factors affecting survival of the hyperlipaemic crisis
Data collected at Dept of Veterinary Medicine, University of Glasgow Veterinary School, UK

Animals that developed hyperlipaemia were divided into survivors and non-survivors and the epidemiological factors associated with each outcome group compared. In contrast to developing the disease, gender was not significantly associated with survival. Whether this would be true of a population where females were allowed to breed is open to debate because the severity of the disease may be exacerbated by the physiological stresses of gestation and abortion. (Note: Again, we have determined that pregnancy is a significant factor.)

Overweight and obese animals were more likely to die than underweight donkeys, which in turn, were less likely to survive than donkeys of ideal weight. However, the most important factor influencing survival of hyperlipaemia was the presence or absence of concurrent disease. In the multivariate analysis, the body condition of the animal was entered as either normal or abnormal, i.e., both over and underweight animals. Considered together, animals of normal body condition were approximately 7 times more likely to survive than fat and thin animals; donkeys with a concurrent disease were 8 times more likely to die than donkeys with primary hyperlipaemia.

Although stress during mixing and entry to the population may have been implicated in the precipitation of hyperlipaemia, survival of animals during this period was good. Close veterinary supervision identified cases early and instituted the appropriate therapeutic measures. The incidence of cases occurring at other times was low but these cases had poorer survival rates. On the whole, this seemed to be due to the fact that secondary hyperlipaemia was more common among these animals.

Conclusions

Despite the fact that the donkey with hyperlipaemia treated by Mair made a full recovery, there can be no doubt that the disease is frequently fatal. Even with the use of heparin and insulin therapy, 60% mortality rates may still be expected. Until such time as human lipid lowering drugs like nicotine acid, which inhibits lipolysis become available to the veterinarian practitioner, the emphasis must be on prevention rather than hope of a cure. To this end, the study reported briefly above provides preliminary points of action.

- Donkeys must be regarded as potential hyperlipaemia cases whenever they experience stress. This includes not only the time of socialization when mixing with new animals but also during transport and introduction to a new environment.
- Physiological stress due to obesity or malnutrition should be minimized by maintaining donkeys at a healthy body-weight. Care should be taken when attempting to control a donkey's weight so that food intake is not reduced to such a level that hyperlipaemia ensues.
- Female donkeys should be considered as high risk animals for hyperlipaemia even if they are not pregnant.
- Diseased donkeys should always be considered as potential cases of hyperlipaemia and attention paid to both primary disease and energy balance. Cases of hyperlipaemia secondary to other illnesses as illustrated by Mair are perhaps the most difficult to avoid. Certainly, inappetance precipitates the hyperlipaemic state and oral drenches of glucose in oral drenches or by i.v. infusion may be the only realistic methods of maintaining a positive energy balance.

The donkey, like man, is susceptible to stress. Attention to lifestyle and removal or prevention of identifiable stressors is important for the well being of both species. Whether it is artherosclerosis or hyperlipaemia, the consequences are all too frequently the same.

The feed requirements of a donkey are 75% of those published for horses, because of a donkeys greater efficiency of food utilization. The dry feed intake should be between 1.75% and 2.25% of body weight total per day. So a 370 pound donkey should receive 6-1/2 - 8-1/2 pounds of dry feed a day. If you are trying to reduce a donkey's weight, the maximum weight loss must not exceed 2 pounds per month.

Plugged Tear Ducts

We get many calls in the spring and summer from concerned owners who feel their donkeys' eyes are infected or have plugged up tear ducts. Many times, the over-flowing tears are due to dust or flies and not infection or tear duct blockage. Some donkeys are overly sensitive to irritating flies or dust but this problem can be solved by purchasing a fly mask (appropriate donkey size is sold by *Miniature Donkey Talk*)

Anatomically, the nasal ostium is usually found on the dorsal surface of the false nostril about 1.5cm from the nasal mucocutaneous junction, easily located if your vet is aware of this difference from the horse. Donkey's eyes do tend to tear more readily than horses, so excessive tearing is not necessarily an indication of disease.

Technically called the nasolacrimal duct, the tear duct extends from the inside corner of the eye to the inside of the nose. The lower opening is a small hole which may be seen inside the nostril, on the inner wall. Normally, it drains excess tears from the eyes into the nose (ever notice how your nose runs when you cry?). They may fill with pus because of infection. Obstruction of the duct can be congenital (present at birth), in which case it is due to malformation or absence of part of the duct, or it can be acquired. Acquired causes include a plug of cellular debris, inflammation, infection, trauma, dental problems, sinus disease and neoplasia.

The first sign is that the donkey's tears spill out of his eyelids. He will have a damp or pus-like streak down the side of his face. Flies and other insects are attracted to this moist spot and may severely annoy the animal. The problem can occur in one eye or in both. The membranes of the eye may be reddened because of the insect irritation, but usually will not be as red as they would with an eye infection.

Call your veterinarian for this one. He will use a small tube and sterile saline solution to flush out the dirt through its opening into the nostril. Often the pus will exude in a long chain or string and float across the surface of the eyeball. This procedure may need to be repeated daily for several days until pus is no longer flushed from the upper opening. Antibiotic/anti-inflammatory medications may also be required if inflammation and infection are involved. In cases where repeated flushing does not resolve the problem or where initial catheterization is very difficult, it is helpful to stitch a catheter in place for at least 2 weeks to prevent the duct re-blocking or scarring closed. Ducts may become permanently blocked due to scarring otherwise.

Ref: Ruth B. James, DVM ; Mark Boddy BVM&S MRCVS ; Bonnie Gross, Editor MDT

Treating Eye Problems

Before you begin treating a donkey's eye, it must be examined to see what the problem is. Your vet needs to be summoned the minute you see the problem.

If there is a film or cloudiness associated with the eye, the next task is to determine whether it is on the surface or deep within the globe. Injuries to the cornea and some other problems will cause a whitish or bluish film on the surface of the cornea.

The tissues surrounding the eye must be examined to determine whether or not they are involved in the problem. Are there any cuts or lacerations in the eyelids? Are the eyelids rolling inward or otherwise causing problems? Is the white membrane which lines the eyelid inflamed, oddly colored or injured?

Corneal Injuries

Donkeys injure their eyes running into objects, such as tree limbs and fences. They can also injure themselves by scratching their heads up against fences, trees and buildings. Owners can mistakenly injure an eye when attempting to discipline the animal by hitting the side of the head.

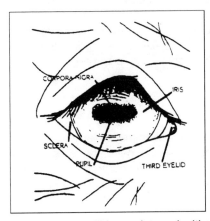

Injuries to the cornea (the clear part of the eye) may be superficial scrapes or may be deep cuts. If the injury has just occurred, the obvious sign is severe pain, with the eye being clamped tightly shut.

One of the first things your vet may do is to use a fluorescent strip. These are small pieces of paper saturated with a fluorescent dye. The orange end of the strip will be moistened with a slight drop of water and inserted in the inner corner of the eye to allow the dye to float into the eye. If there is a spot on the cornea where the green dye sticks, you are seeing either a corneal laceration or an ulcer. If the dye doesn't stick anywhere you next have to determine whether the animal's problem is an infection or a foreign body in the eye.

When the eye is opened, a scrape or scratch may be seen when you look across the cornea. Use a penlight to first look directly into the eye, and then across the cornea from the side. The scrape can be often be seen from the side angle. The wound may only be a small depression, but the pain can be intense. If it is just a small scrape, treat it immediately with an eye ointment containing ONLY antibiotics. Neomycin ointment can be used and/or Atrophate and/or Gentocin ointments. Do NOT use corticosteroid (such as prednisolone), as it can cause enlargement of the lesion and subsequent loss of the eye.

Put the ointment(s) in the donkey's eye a MINIMUM of four times a day. This should only be done with smaller scrapes, say, less than 1/4 inch in diameter. During the course of the treatment (which should only last three or four days) make sure that the lesion is growing smaller instead of larger.

Treatment several times a day is very important and should not be neglected. It helps the eye to heal and prevent infections. Make sure you thoroughly understand your veterinarian's instructions. The donkey may be reluctant to allow you to put ointment in the eye. Talk to him continuously and touch him a lot. Make firm contact with the side of his face before you touch the eye area and work slowly up to the eye.

If the animal has suffered a laceration (cut or tear) in the cornea, it is imperative that your vet be called immediately. Waiting five or six hours before suturing a cut may leave the donkey with a blind eye or no eye at all.

Conjunctivitis

Conjunctivitis is the name given to an inflammation or infection of the conjunctivae. These are the membranes around the eye and down inside the eyelid. They occasionally become reddened and inflamed. This can be cause by various bacteria, by physical conditions such as dust and dry weather, or by irritation from insects. Some cases are probably caused by various viruses.

The membranes around the eye with conjunctivitis are swollen and reddened. They may exude pus which will drain from the corner of the eye and down the face. No signs of corneal damage are seen with fluorescent staining and no foreign bodies are seen within the eye.

The UNDAMAGED eye with conjunctivitis is the place to use an ophthalmic ointment containing both antibiotics AND a corticosteroid. Put the ointment in the donkey's eye four to five times a day for three days. If the problem has not cleared in two to three days, or if it should become worse, have your vet examine him.

Again, eye injuries must be dealt with and treated immediately to avoid the onset of more serious problems or the loss of the eye.

This 3 month old jack was discovered one morning with severe eye swelling and discharge coming from the eye. Upon examination by a veterinarian, a one inch piece of straw was discovered under the bottom eye lid which caused the irritation.

Allergies and their Treatment

Are you one of those people who when the pollen count goes up, your eyes start to itch and your nose runs? Did you know that your donkey and horse could be suffering the same way? Yes, donkeys and horses can have the same kinds of allergies as humans; dust, grass and tree pollens, food, and even some types of flies.

Symptoms range from coughing and trouble breathing, to welts or bumps on the body. Now not all donkeys sneeze or break out, have allergies, it may be a cold or bug bites. Less than half of the donkeys and horses with skin irritations can be related to allergies.

With the help of your vet, you can analyze your donkeys' history and his surroundings and come up with a program for your donkey.

Antihistamines and Cortisone's can be used to relieve the symptoms, and in most cases that is all that is needed. If the symptoms do come back, this treatment can be repeated. In some cases you may want to find out what it is your donkey is allergic to. This is easy enough, there is a simple test. All that is needed is a little blood that is sent to a lab and analyzed for 60 different allergens including grasses, trees, dust, feathers, foods, and flies. Each allergen is given a score and depending on that score, recommendations are made. This is an example of an allergy test:

In this example there are four different things that this horse is positive to, as you can see she is allergic to grass pollens and one tree pollen. This is not her whole test. She was allergic to a couple of other things.

Once you have figured out what the donkey is allergic to you can take a couple of directions for the treatment. You can avoid the things the donkey is allergic to, but in the case of foods, this is the only way to treat it, or you can vaccinate against the allergens.

Regional Inhalant Screen

Group	Allergen(s)	Test Score	Class Score
1	Bluegrass (Junegrass)	154	BL

2 **	Redtop	273	P
3	Bromegrass	142	N
4 **	Orchardgrass	262	P
5	Timothy	115	N
6 **	Ryegrass	392	P
25	Juniper (Cedar)	111	N
26 **	Boxelder	197	BL
27	Willow	154	BL
28	Oak	161	BL
29	Pine	116	N
30	Birch	106	N

The first way is not always possible, as you can see the horse in the example is allergic to some grasses, and you can't really avoid them. The second option, vaccination. Drawbacks are that it costs a little money.

The animal has to go through about 30 shots to start out with, and may have to stay on the shots for the rest of its life. One problem with equine is that they don't grow out of allergies like humans do. In fact, they can become allergic to other things as time goes on. For that reason, it is a good idea to repeat the test every couple of years to make sure something else hasn't developed.

For my example horse, we opted to go with the vaccinations. On the printout, the lab recommended which ones to include in the vaccines (marked with the stars). There was a total of six and we ordered the kit and went to work. It's been about three months and I'm happy to say this horse is doing much better.

As you can see there is much to consider when you are treating allergies, and it is best to discuss it with your vet before you start into anything.

Reference: by Linda Pozo

Lyme Disease

Over the last few years, Lyme disease has become a serious public health threat in the United States. The disease has received a great deal of media attention and is nationally recognized today as a serious problem for human beings. However, little mention has been made of the incidence of the disease in animals, especially equine.

Lyme disease is caused by a corkscrew-shaped bacterium, which is technically classified as the spirochete Borrelia burgdorferi. The disease is transmitted to animals and humans through the bite of certain types of pinhead-size ticks. The deer tick in the Northeast and the black-legged trick in the West are the primary vectors, although other arthropods are believed to transmit the disease.

Dr. Leon Russell, assistant professor of the Public Health Department at Texas A & M University College of Veterinary Medicine, says, "Some cases of human Lyme disease have been associated with fleas. This theory is currently being studied in animals."

The tick-borne disease was first diagnosed in the United States in 1876 in Old Lyme, Connecticut. The majority of the original cases were seen in people and animals living close to wooded areas and high populations of deer. "We have seen a nationwide increase in the disease over the last few years," Russell says. "This may be a direct result of the white-tailed deer population's extensive growth."

Prevention and detection, as well as clinical signs and treatment, of the tick-borne Lyme disease in the equine species and domestic animals are similar in many ways to those aspects in humans. In the United States, the disease is most frequently reported in the summer months. It is rare to see the disease in horses in areas where it is not present in humans.

The signs of equine Lyme disease vary from vague to acute. Warning signs might include weight loss, gait abnormalities, chronic or migrating lameness, laminitis, and occasionally, foal mortality.

Arthritis is the most common sign of Lyme disease in humans and animals alike. Extensive pain and swelling of joints, causing the animal to move as it he is "walking on eggs," is the most noticeable symptom of the disease. Some authorities believe Lyme disease might be lined to abortion and encephalitis as well as kidney, heart, and eye problems in horses.

In 50 percent of human cases, a rash will develop at the site of the tick bite. Unfortunately, this telltale sign does not exist in equine cases of the disease. However, according to Russell, on occasion a rash can be seen on the belly and legs of a dog afflicted with Lyme disease, primarily because a dog's hair is thin in those areas.

Clinical signs vary according to where the infective organism travels within the animal's body. Dr. Noah Cohen of the Large Animal Medicine and Surgery Department at the Texas A & M University College of Veterinary Medicine says, "The clinical signs are so poor, serology is very important. Frequently the diagnosis is based solely on serological tests." The condition has been called "the great imitator," because it has no specific clinical signs and the available tests for it are not always conclusive. Dr. Foy McCasland, bureau chief of the Texas Veterinary Public Health Department, says, "The symptoms of Lyme disease are compatible with symptoms of a lot of other diseases. The disease symptoms are most characteristic of cardiac and arthritic problems."

Lyme disease basically progresses in three stages. The classical clinical signs such as fever and flu-like symptoms, which are often noted in the first two stages of the disease, disappear only to reappear later with more serious consequences. During the third stage of Lyme disease, arthritis can result in permanent joint damage through erosion of the cartilage and bone. Neurological damage also is likely at this point, resulting in seizures and loss of coordination.

Most veterinarians believe that testing is essential to properly diagnose Lyme disease. Nevertheless, controversy still exists over the reliability of the diagnostic blood test, which reveals the presence or absence of antibodies in horses.

Dr. Kenton H. Arnold of the Equiplex Veterinary Hospital says, "When Lyme disease is suspected, two blood samples should be taken, approximately 6 to 8 weeks apart, to determine any changes in the level of antibodies. If an active Lyme infection is present, antibody levels in the second sample will have increased since the first.

Progress has been made toward developing a vaccine to prevent the disease. Currently, a Lyme vaccine for dogs is offering some encouragement to the eventual prevention of Lyme disease in all species. There is not yet a vaccine for horses.

Treatment is relatively expensive, and involves daily injections of an antibiotic, such as tetracycline or penicillin, for a minimum of 2 weeks. "It is good to rule out other possibilities before beginning final treatment, but it is not always technically or financially possible," Cohen says. "Tetracycline has been known to cause diarrhea in equine, which can create other problems."

Fortunately for equines and their owners, not all ticks are carriers of the Lyme organism. The percentage of infected ticks can vary widely from season to season. Researchers also believe that a tick must be attached to its host for at least 12 hours before the spirochete can be transferred. Therefore, frequent visual examinations of the animal's body can cut down greatly on incidence of the disease.

Pheasant Meadow Farm's Bo Jackson

Equine Sarcoid: Frequently Asked Questions

Copyright 1996 Antony Meyer Jones

What is a Sarcoid?

A Sarcoid is a tumor involving connective tissue, i.e. muscle, sub-cutaneos tissue, etc. A tumor which may appear outwardly similar is the Lymphoma (cutaneous lymphosarcoma), which involves the Lymphatic system (glandular system to you or I). Both these tumors are distinct from epithelial tumors (carcinomas & melanomas). The sarcoid begins as a small wart-like growth, but may progress, through stages of rapid growth, to be the size of a tennis ball. Generally being dry scaly masses that may ulcerate and bleed, the main problems with a true sarcoid are those of secondary infection and physical interference e.g. with tack. The key difference between sarcoids and lymphomas is that sarcoids are benign, lymphomas are malignant. Sarcoids exist in several forms, see below for details.

What causes Sarcoids?

Sarcoids are believed to be caused by a virus, though I have failed to find a detailed explanation from any source. It has also been shown that Sarcoids occur more often in the older horse and on sites of previous trauma. From my own experience I noted that sarcoid growth appeared most in spring and early summer; obviously there are many factors that could precipitate this: dietary change, increased UV light, fly strike, changing routine - stress levels to name but a few. I was unable to conclude which factor(s) was the cause.

Are there different types of Sarcoid?

Yes, Sarcoids can be split into several types.

VERRUCOUS SARCOIDS

Typically these are dry golf ball size lumps, though size may vary considerably. They most often occur on head, chest and shoulder or under-leg. Normally lacking hair, they are not difficult to spot.

FIBROBLASTIC SARCOIDS

If a verrucous sarcoid grows and splits or is otherwise physically damage then it may progress to this type. This is the type that tends to cause more problems as it grows and bleeds; some have been known to reach the size of a small football. Ulceration, fly-strike and secondary infection can all be issues to be tackled. Growth rates do vary with these sarcoids sometimes lying dormant for several years.

OCCULT SARCOIDS

These are a flat form of sarcoid which again may become the fibroblastic type if damaged.

NON SARCOIDS

As previously mentioned, sarcoids can be confused with other growths. Identification is important since many of the other growths are malignant and could therefore spread internally. Biopsy by an expert is the most accurate form of diagnosis, but this has its drawbacks.

How common are Sarcoids?

Sarcoids are relatively common particularly in older equine, though severe cases are considerably less common. Fortunately the more serious cutaneous lymphosarcoma is relatively uncommon.

What treatments are available?

Various different treatments are available.

Traditional Surgery

Physical removal of the tumor has been the normal practice. However there are multiple drawbacks to this technique.
1. A high percentage of cases recur within several years.
2. Growth can be accelerated by the physical trauma of the surgery.
3. Possibility of "seeding"; the tumor elsewhere by cell debris. esp. if diagnosis is incorrect and tumor is malignant.
4. Possibility of significant scarring or physical disability due to site of tumor operation.

Cryosurgery (Freezing)
1. This is a technique whereby the area to undergo surgery is repeatedly fast frozen to destroy all tissue before surgical removal. This decreases the likelihood of recurrence and seeding. However

the technique is not suitable for use near sensitive tissues such as the eyes.

Radiation Therapy

This technique is similar to that used to treat human cancer patients; the affected area is irradiated using a localized source. The drawbacks of this treatment are :

1. Localized side effects of radiation
2. Requirement for specially trained staff to administer treatment.

However the treatment may be particularly suitable around the eyes, where surgery is impossible.

Immunotherapy

A technique to activate the animal's own immune system against the tumor cells. Two different methods can be used:

1. Injection of BCG vaccine - Multiple injections into the tumor over a period of some weeks.
2. Introduction of Sarcoid tissue - Deactivated Sarcoid cells introduced under skin to build immune system over several months.

These treatments are only suitable for small tumors and do take sometime to work, however they do have the advantage of being relatively non invasive.

Chemotherapy

Again a technique originally developed to treat human cancer patients. A variety of chemical agents are being studied, the main characteristics being:

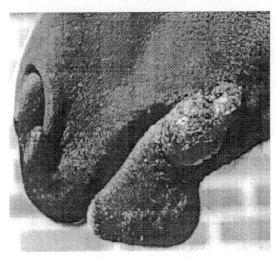

1. Application is topical or injected into tumor - this minimizes the systemic effects of the toxins on the patient.
2. Typically the chemical agents are toxic heavy metal compounds in an inert carrier base.
3. A dosage balance must be struck between tumor eradication and toxic side effects.
4. Beneficial where surgery is impractical or in conjunction with surgical techniques.

**Approximate
Treatment Success Rates**

Success rate defined as % of treated horses with complete removal and no recurrence after 3 years.

Note: This table is merely a rough overview of results that I have read. It is intended as a rule of thumb and as such, is not statistically accurate.

Traditional Surgery	60%
Cryosurgery	80%
Radiation Therapy	70%
Immunotherapy	65%
Chemotherapy	80%
Combined	(Variable but often 85%)
Others	Unavailable

Other Techniques and remedies
A list of misc. other treatments that I am aware of:
1. Laser Vaporization - Use of a hot laser to destroy tumor tissue, typically in conjunction with surgery.
2. Constriction - Application of a band such as a castration ring to remove "hanging" tumors. cf. traditional wart removal.
3. Tea Tree Oil - Applied topically has apparently been of help in some cases.
4. Thuja - Can be given orally as tablets or applied topically as an oil. Thuja is a Chinese herbal remedy that is sometimes available from natural health stores. I have one report of some success with this, on sarcoids that were not responding to traditional treatments.
5. Hyperthermia (Heat Treatment) - localized intense heating of tumor cells using a special instrument.

6. Dermex - A herbal paste made from a plant grown in Wyoming, USA. Applied topically, has been successful on an awkward occult sarcoid. Also useful for reducing fibroblastic size before other treatments.

Are Sarcoids contagious?

Sarcoids are not considered contagious, however they may be spread by contamination with living tumor cells. In other words any mechanism that might scrape cells off the tumor and then place them back in another site, could lead to the formation of a new tumor. As previously mentioned, physical trauma to a sarcoid may accelerate the tumor activity.

What is the prognosis for an equine with Sarcoids?

This depends upon the severity of Sarcoid occurrence. Often small sarcoids will remain relatively unobtrusive and cause few problems for a horse/donkey. On the other hand severe cases that resist treatment may require that the animal be destroyed on humane grounds. Research is continually improving the success rate of treatment; this combined with the fact that Sarcoids are benign tumors, means that in the majority of cases there is little risk to the animal's long term well being.

Hints & Tips

This section includes a list of suggestions that are either not covered elsewhere or that require emphasis:

1. Make regular inspections of any abnormal lumps and bumps on your horse/donkey.
2. If you discover an abnormality, don't panic, keep a record of any changes, this will help your vet.
3. Identification is critical, make every effort to have a positive ID of the tumor type before making any treatment decisions. cf. Risk of aggravation from biopsy.
4. If a Sarcoid is identified consider whether or not it requires treatment. These tumors may not concern your animal if left alone, yet can become problematical after interference.
5. If treatment is necessary discuss the various options and their drawbacks. Not all vets are aware of the full facts, discussing things with your vet can only be helpful to you both.
6. Try to minimize any external aggravation of the tumor. I found that a mixture of Gammexane cream and sunblock lotion helped to reduce summer problems without irritating the Sarcoid tissue.

7. If you don't succeed at first, try again. Keep in touch with research developments, if your horse/donkey doesn't respond to one treatment, consider a different one.

We've had more than the average number of calls recently on sarcoids and donkeys. It is our point of view that Cryosurgery (freezing) is still the treatment of choice for treating sarcoids on Miniature Donkeys when possible.

Several years ago we purchased a donkey with a small marble sized sarcoid on her outer ear. When it tripled in size, it was surgically removed. Follow up treatment involved applying a corticosteroid, Panalog, daily. Three months later it was back and nine months after the first surgery, it again was removed. (Unless absolutely necessary, this surgery should not be done during fly season for the obvious reasons.) One year later, it was again back and was larger than ever. This time we had our equine surgeon treat with cryotherapy with excellent results. The sarcoid never did return. A small hairless area the size of a dime was all that was left of a sarcoid that was the size of a golf ball. Cryotherapy is a relatively quick procedure and quite effective in preventing regrowth. However, most typical equine vets do not have the equipment or the skills to do it. You need to contact an equine surgeon.

Latest research indicates there are several new drugs out for treating sarcoids - Regressin and Cisplatinum are two that I've heard of. We have no experience with these drugs.

RN Oglesby DVM, reports, "An effective treatment is a product called Nomagen® by Fort Dodge. Nomagen has recently been removed from the market by Fort Dodge, hopefully it will return soon. This product works by getting the immune system to reject the tumor and is about 90% effective. If the tumor is large removal may be the best choice and if recurrence occurs, treat those with Nomagen.

Bacillus calmette guerin (BCG) - A similar material to Nomagen is BCG.

Asinine Herpesvirus 3

For the last six years, I have kept my eyes open on anything that may have to do with the 'donkey virus' as I so aptly have named it, and others consequently refer to it. Whenever I come upon something that grabs my attention in the way of a respiratory virus, I always do the appropriate research hoping to some day solve the puzzle of this virus that has struck down so many of our donkeys.

I have been corresponding with Dr. Michael Studdert a research scientist at the School of Veterinary Science, University of Melbourne, Australia. He has identified a new distinct herpesvirus in laboratory testing that although is closely related to the equine herpesvirus 1 and 4, is still different. I'm not going to reprint his research as frankly no lay person could understand it. Don't believe me? In the first paragraph he states, "The predicted amino acid sequence of AHV3 gG has characteristics of a class 1 membrane protein. Two regions within the gG amino acid sequences of EHV1 and EHV4 were previously defined, an N-terminal constant region and an immunodominant highly variable region located toward the C-terminus...." In plain English, although the Asinine (AHV3) Herpesvirus is different than the equine herpesvirus, it is closely related.

Dr. Studdert states that Asinine herpesvirus 3 was originally isolated from a weanling donkey. The horse is host to three distinct alphaherpesviruses, designated equine herpesvirus 1 (equine abortion virus), equine herpesvirus 4 (equine rhinopneumonitis virus) and equine herpesvirus 3 (equine coital exanthema virus). Both herpesvirus 1 and 4 are closely related. It was originally thought that the donkey virus may be EHV1 since donkeys had been shown to have high serum neutralizing antibody titres to EHV1. However, DNA fingerprints were distinct from those of EHV1 as well as EHV4.

Now that I've got that out of the way, we've got good news and bad news. I contacted Dr. Chris Brown whom I originally consulted with when MDT (*Miniature Donkey Talk Magazine*) was the first to report on this virus back in 1989 - and we have tried to keep you updated on a yearly basis. I sent Dr. Brown my research findings and the report by Dr. Studdert. Unfortunately, Dr. Brown cannot confirm that this is the same virus ONLY because thorough research in the U.S. was never completed.

The good news is, I also consulted with one of MDT's Consulting Veterinarians and received the following report from Dr. Craig Landa.

"According to these authors Asinine Herpesvirus 3 (AHV3) is mostly related to Equine Herpesvirus 1 (EHV1). EHV1 causes abortion in horses, but is fairly closely related to EHV4 which causes respiratory disease in horses. There have been reports of vaccine cross-reactivity in EHV1 and 4. For example, if you vaccinate for EHV1 you do get some protection against EHV4. These authors provide no information on cross protection between EHV1 and EHV4 and AHV3. Since this virus AHV3 is most closely related to EHV1, it would follow that it may be suspected in asinine abortion. Because these diseases are viral in origin they cannot be treated with antibiotics. *(Ed Note: If you recall, the many times I have reported on how to treat the donkey virus, I always reported that penicillin produced no results and should not be use.)* I know of no company that manufactures an AHV3 vaccine but we may assume that because of its close necleotide association with EHV1 that you may get some protection against the virus when vaccinating against EHV1."

Bottom line: Every breeder I ever talked to who had the virus on their farm and lost donkeys, stated that they did NOT vaccinate against rhino. The rhino vaccine offers protection against both EHV1 and EHV4 and now apparently may also help protect your donkey against EHV3 if this is in fact what we now have in the U.S.

….For those new to donkeys, several years ago a deadly virus raised its ugly head and killed around 20 donkeys the first year it appeared. All the donkeys caught the virus at sales or their owners brought it home on their clothes to their farms so the donkeys didn't even have to be at the sale to catch it. It was especially hard on weanlings and yearlings who do not yet have built up immune systems. Every one we spoke with you lost donkeys did not have their animals vaccinated against rhino. If you take your donkeys to sales or shows, buy at sales or even attend sales, make certain your donkeys – both at the sale and at home are vaccinated.

Reference: Bonnie Gross, Editor, Miniature Donkey Talk Magazine

New Discoveries on Rhino Virus

If you have been getting *Miniature Donkey Talk* for any length of time, you already know the importance of giving Rhinopneumonitis (Rhino) vaccinations to your bred jennets. We have also advised you the importance of giving the Rhino vaccinations to your younger weanlings to control this respiratory virus that donkeys are so susceptible to.

It has been known for quite a while that the virus consisted of several subtypes. It was thought that the subtypes were merely variants of each other however, research has now shown that they are actually different viruses.

The two main subtypes are EHV-1 (subtype 1) which is blamed for causing abortion and a milder form of respiratory infection. EHV-4 (subtype 2) causes a more severe form of respiratory disease. Understanding the damage caused by the two *different* viruses will result in better vaccines and protocols for better breeding farm management.

EHV-1 can cause respiratory disease but less often than previously thought. This form of the virus is responsible for abortions and various degrees of neurological problems which may follow an abortion or respiratory disease.

EHV-4 has been shown to be responsible for causing respiratory disease and as yet, has not been associated with actually causing abortions.

Both EHV-1 and EHV-4 infections start in the respiratory tract. If the donkey has never been exposed to the virus, he will typically show signs of nasal discharge and a fever. After repeated mild infections, some older animals develop a certain degree of immunity, therefore will show no signs of the disease even though they are carrying it and will later abort. This is especially true of the EHV-1 form of the disease.

Regardless of which subtype is involved, a donkey can carry the virus in their bloodstream where it lays dormant and can usually be triggered by some form of stress.

EHV-4 infections generally begins and ends in the respiratory tract. EHV-1 travels on to the lymph nodes surrounding the lungs, enters the blood and is carried to other areas of the body. From the bloodstream, EHV-1 either settles into the placenta or the blood vessels and tissues surrounding the central nervous system resulting in abortion. Rhino induced abortions in donkeys generally occur between the 7th and 12th month.

A fairly new vaccine on the market is **"Equine Rhinopneumonitis Vaccine" by Prestige with Havlogen**. It greatly reduces reactions in the form of lumps on donkey's necks like they get with other types of Rhino vaccines. Another new vaccine on the market is a combination of Rhino and Flu. We have heard of some reactions with this combination when used in donkeys but it has not been tested enough on donkeys to come to any sound conclusions.

A vaccination program is the key to keeping the Rhino disease in check. Bred Miniature Donkey jennets should be vaccinated in their 5th, 7th, 9th, and 11th month of pregnancy.

Vaccines, which are either killed pathogens or pathogens that are so damaged that they cannot produce disease, induce protection through a simulated infection giving the body a chance to manufacture antibodies. **Check your vaccine label!** Not all Rhino vaccines will protect against abortion. If there is no abortion protection claim on the label, the vaccine probably only protects the jennet against the respiratory form on the infection.

Cutter Equine Vaccines/Mobay Corporation is introducing a new vaccine called **RhinoGuard.** A spokesman for the company claims it gives a combined protection against both EHV-1 and EHV-4 in the same vaccine. RhinoGuard will initially be introduced as effective only against the respiratory syndrome, but field trials of the product's effectiveness in preventing abortion are under way and the new vaccine could eventually be approved by the USDA as an anti-abortogenic.

Dryland Distemper (Pigeon Fever)

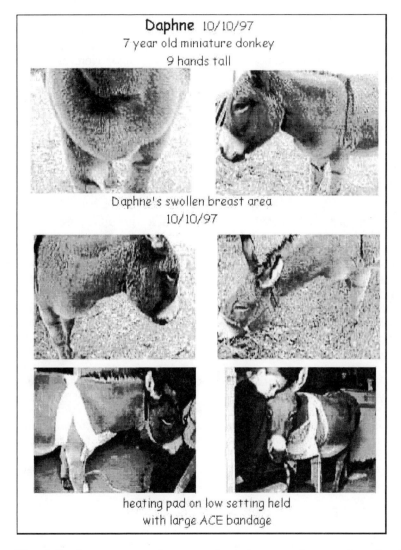

Daphne 10/10/97
7 year old miniature donkey
9 hands tall

Daphne's swollen breast area
10/10/97

heating pad on low setting held
with large ACE bandage

The following correspondence and photos are from a breeder in California whose donkey came down with Dryland Distemper.

10/10/97...Today I took some digital photos of Daphne's chest area. I'm sending them by email and hope you are able to "see" the swelling.

Her "breasts" are swollen the size of half-grapefruits. They are quite firm. The area between her front legs is swollen, but soft. Her temperature is 100 degrees. Her appetite for carrots is great. I have given her 1/2g of Bute today. I very gently rub the swollen areas and have applied a heating pad on the low setting twice so far today for 20-minute sessions. I took her and her companion, Jackson, on a 1/2-mile stroll. I felt it would help her spirits and circulation. She did fine, but we were caught in a sudden rainstorm. Of course, they were not happy about being wet. I did bring her in the house, she seemed happy to be there.

10/14/97...Just a quick update on Daphne. Veterinarian Betty Nunes came out yesterday.

She felt it was Pigeon Fever, but asked if we wanted her to do a culture to be certain. We said yes. She withdrew separate samples from the two hardened areas in Daphne's breast.

She sedated Daphne and asked permission to shave the chest areas to be lanced. We agreed. She shaved the two areas and gave Daphne a local anesthetic. She made two deep 1 1/2" incisions in the swollen areas. She had my daughter hold a bag underneath the incisions while she "expressed" a mixture of pus and blood from each area. My husband estimated that approximately 4 oz of material came from each area. The vet did not want to get this on the ground as it would be a contaminant. We need to flush out the wounds with a saline/mild povidone solution twice a day. She advises 1/2g bute twice a day. We will hear back on the culture by the end of the week.

She advises fly spray for all of our horses & donkeys (we usually do this anyway) and SWAT around the perimeter of any wounds or scabs.

Unfortunately, we had to remove Daphne's companion donkey, Jackson, from the area until she recovers. The vet was worried that he might get it.

Daphne is doing well this morning. She really loves to put her head in your arms and be rubbed.

10/16/97...Daphne is doing well, although the incisions look pretty gruesome. Yes, there has been continuing drainage from the incisions. My husband flushes them out twice daily and I keep SWAT around the perimeter. I am thinking of modifying a large fly mask to protect the chest area. The culture came back, it is definitely Pigeon Fever. The vet felt that the bacteria could continue to live in the soil if we allowed the infected drainage material to drop onto the ground. Also flies could transmit the infected material to other equines.

The vet is coming back on Friday to check her. She felt the prognosis was good although it could take 10-12 days for this to run its course. The wounds need to heal from the inside out.

Daphne is braying again; she tries to kick me when I attempt to take her temperature; she will only take the BUTE if it is hidden in whole wheat bread; her appetite is good. We are encouraged, but it is very difficult to see her go through this.

Dryland Distemper

Horses and donkeys in arid regions of the Western states are most at risk for this disease.

We can blame this disease on a very talented bacteria called "Corynebacterium pseudotuberculosis", which can cause a lot of problems in different animals. **Dryland distemper is also known as pigeon fever due to the development of abscesses in the ventral and pectoral region.** The chest and underbelly become swollen, then abscesses form in these areas within one to four weeks. Other clinical signs include anorexia, lethargy, fever, and lameness. The duration of the disease varies from weeks to months, depending on the severity of the abscesses.

Most abscesses occur under the skin of the chest or along the underbelly, but can also form in the armpits and sheath, near mammary glands and on the legs. The bacteria is also capable of entering the bloodstream and forming internal abscesses inside the chest and abdomen. If these internal abscesses rupture, it is usually fatal. Luckily, this rarely happens. While reoccurrence is possible, most horses/donkeys get the disease only once.

The bacteria that causes dryland distemper also causes "caseous lymphagitis" in sheep and goats and "ulcerative lymphagitis" in cattle and horses. It has also been found in deer and in the ticks that feed on deer. For these reasons, dryland distemper has appeared in areas where infected sheep and goats are present. It is uncertain how contagious it is or how it is transmitted, but biting flies and insects are suspected.

Dryland distemper occurs in arid regions of the western United States, with California having a high percentage of the cases. The disease can occur anytime during the year, but most cases occur during the fall and early winter months. At this time, there are no effective vaccines to prevent this disease, and only moderately effective antibiotics to treat it once the animal contracts the disease.

Strangles – Equine Distemper

Called strangles, this is a bacterial disease caused by a type of bacteria called Streptococcus equi. It has no relationship to dog distemper (which is caused by a virus) or cat distemper (which is caused by a virus totally different from that of dog distemper). Equine distemper is most commonly seen in young animals, but may occur in equine of any age who have not been previously infected. Infection passes from one animal to another in pus from the abscesses which form in lymph nodes around the head, or via the pus which may be discharged from the animal's nose. The bacterium is quite resistant and may survive for months in barns or on objects, such as halters.

The incubation period for equine distemper is usually three to six days. However, equine who are exposed to it may not all come down with it at the same time.

One person had distemper in a herd on pasture, which went on among this group of horses for over three months. One horse would come down with it, and just about be healed, when the next one would get sick, and so on-through six animals. Only two horses did not get it. Both were old mares who could have reasonably been expected to have had the disease earlier in their lives and to be immune to it.

SIGNS

Often the first sign that an owner notices is that the animal does not eat or drink. The temperature may go as high at 106 degrees F (41 degrees C). Swelling of the lymph nodes under and behind the jaw will usually develop within a couple of days. Drainage from the nose often looks like pus-thick and greenish or yellowish. The animal may not wish to swallow and may stand with his neck extended. Abscesses may also occur in lymph nodes inside the back of the mouth. These contribute to the discomfort and to problems in swallowing. Abscesses in the throat which are very large may cause the horse to have trouble breathing, giving the disease one of its common names, "strangles." When the abscesses finally break and drain, relief usually follows rapidly. The animal feels better immediately and will show more interest in life. The appearance of abscesses is almost a foolproof sign of distemper. Once you have one case of the disease in a herd, it is a warning to be on the lookout for more of them.

Complication include: pneumonia, laryngeal hemiplegia, guttural pouch empyema with secondary cranial nerve dysfunction, paranasal sinusitis, suppurative foci in any organ (bastard strangles) and purpura hemorrhagica (particularly if the equine has been recently vaccinated). Early treatment with penicillin can reduce the incidence of complications.

The disease lasts about two weeks in an individual. Like the viral upper respiratory diseases, distemper is rarely fatal. Fatalities usually occur in young or very old animals or in those with another illness which weakens them. When death does occur, it is usually due to central nervous system involvement or internal abscesses. Most equine recover without permanent damage.

Animals with an inadequate immune response may develop a form of distemper commonly called "bastard strangles." This will only affect an individual animal - it is not a herd problem. Also, treatment of the animal with antibiotics, especially when used before the abscesses break, may force the bacteria into the animal's internal organs, creating a case of bastard strangles. This then necessitates very long-term antibiotic therapy-in some cases, procaine penicillin must be given for up to a month.

TREATMENT

Penicillin is often the drug of choice for a chronic case of distemper. In routine cases, most veterinarians do not use any antibiotics at all for fear of causing a case of bastard strangles. Antibiotics may be needed if the abscesses break but the animal is not showing signs of recovery, is still very ill, and not starting to eat. If you do start antibiotic treatment, it must be continued until the temperature returns to normal and has remained there for several days.

The animal should have complete rest and nursing as described under viral respiratory diseases. Hot packs may help the abscesses come to a head. They may then be drained at the soft point. This is usually a job for a veterinarian. You would hate to cut a major blood vessel or nerve while draining an abscess! However, in the absence of a veterinarian, you can make an incision right at the point of the abscess when the skin over it is stretched tightly and the point of it feels soft and ready to burst. Use a very sharp blade (disposable scalpels are best) and make a puncture at the very point of the swelling, about ½ inch long. As soon as you make the puncture, the pus will begin to pour. Let it pour out until it is finished draining.

Now, enlarge the incision to about 1 inch long, depending on the location of the abscess. It is also a good idea to make two cuts at right angles to the original cut, making the opening into an 'X" shape. This helps to keep it open and draining. Making a small hole is not a kindness - it tends to close and causes problems. Do not hesitate to cut a good-sized hole! It will heal over, and a lot more readily if it is larger instead of small. Amazingly enough, there is rarely a scar over the abscess area. It will take some time, but nearly all abscess areas heal back to completely normal and hair over. So, don't worry about a large hole in the jaw of your show animal - it WILL heal, even if it looks as if it never would.

After the abscesses break or are drained, the cavities should be swabbed out with strong (7%) tincture of iodine. Using three or four of the long cotton swabs together helps make the job a little more efficient and less unpleasant. You may also want to cover your hand with a plastic bag or disposable glove to prevent both the pus and the iodine from running down it. The disposable plastic obstetrical sleeves that your veterinarian uses for pregnancy testing are ideal for this use-you may be able to buy some from him or from an artificial inseminator or livestock supply house. Saturate the swabs in the iodine and work them around inside the opening of the abscess to clean out the pus and debris.

Make sure the hole stays open. If it scabs over, do not assume that it is healing O.K. It should heal gradually from the inside out like other open wounds. You should be able to get the swabs in a little less each day. You should not be able to get them in an inch and a half one day and not get them in at all the next. The object is to help the hole heal from the inside out. If you allow it to scab over before the infection inside is all cleaned out, it will only break open and drain again, prolonging the course of the disease. So, pick off the scab and keep swabbing!

Occasionally, the swollen lymph nodes will put enough pressure on the animal's air passages to make breathing difficult or impossible. Your veterinarian should be called immediately. It may be necessary for him to perform a tracheotomy to make it possible for the animal to breathe. In some cases, he may insert a metal tracheotomy tube into the animal's neck to keep the incision open until the swelling goes down enough for the animal to breathe by himself.

PREVENTION

Killed vaccines (called bacterins) are intermittently available for prevention of distemper. Many veterinarians do not use these products any more because of some adverse side effects. In the past, some of the available bacterins have caused a disease called purpura hemorrhagica. Many veterinarians decided that they were losing more horses to the purpura than they ever did to distemper. It also caused   other side effects, such as swelling and hardening of tissues where the injection was given.

If the bacterin is used, most veterinarians feel that it must be started when the foal is about two months old and continued religiously. Using this bacterin in older horses sometimes causes purpura; this may have something to do with the animal's previously having been exposed to the bacteria which cause the disease. Bacterins for immunization against distemper should ONLY be used on the advice of your veterinarian.

Reference: Ruth B. James, DVM

Reference Information received from Robert Oglesby, DVM states:

Your best protection is to be careful where you stall your animal. The disease frequents trading barns, or you may contact if at a show by stalling your animal next to a coughing or snotty nosed donkey. Recently it has been found that clinically healthy carrier horses may be important in the cause of this disease. The guttural pouch was found to be one area the organism persisted in.

The modern Strangles vaccines have been associated with the serious complication of purpura hemorrhagica. Also swellings at the injection site are common. The vaccine is about 67% effective and the duration of protection about 6 months. Because of these factors vaccination should be reserved for the donkey/horse that is likely to come into contact with Strangles.

Recent work on strangles ability to persist in the environment has shown:

- survives on wood for 63 days
- survives on glass for 48 days at 68 degrees
- survival time is effected by temperature
- Phosphoric acid and chlorine bleach were poor disinfectants.
- Povidone iodine, chlorhexidine, and glutaraldehyde were good disinfectants.

It has been stated that the effects of the vaccinations can actually, in some cases be worse than contracting the disease. Also, a horse that gets a bad reaction from the shots can infected an otherwise healthy horse, so we're darned if we do, and darned if we don't!

There is an answer to this dilemma. Everything said about the downside of this vaccine is true and more. The incidence of local reactions (swelling, stiffness, fever) is as high as 44%, with some of these reactions abscessing open. The incidence of the life threatening reaction, purpurea hemmoragica, is as high as 1 in 300 in one study of a 1000 horses on the booster vaccination. This study was conducted by the manufacturer of the best killed vaccine available. Did you know that the vaccine only protects 65% of those it is used on properly, and the majority of that 65% are still going to get the disease, just in a milder form? These mild colds may be hard to recognize as Strangles and may result in the disease being spread more. I have long noticed that year after year there is more Strangles in areas that vaccinate than areas that do not, this may be the reason.

One of the best differing clinical 'signs' between respiratory disease and Strangles is abscessing lymph nodes though it is not a 100% reliable, particularly in older or vaccinated horses. In both types of disease the nodes can enlarge but breaking open and draining is far more common in Strangles. Generally the fever in viral infections is much higher, up to or over 105 degrees, than in Strangles and is not as persistent as Strangles. Viruses have a fever spike that will come back down in 24 to 48 hours then may spike again in the next few days. My personal feeling is that viral fevers are more responsive to anti-fever medication like bute. On the other hand Strangles fevers will generally hover in the 102.5 to 104 range for day after day even with bute treatment. There may also be differences in the complete blood count with Strangles causing an elevation in WBCs and viruses causing a depression. Unfortunately none of these indicators are a 100% so if you can not be sure consider a full course of penicillin.

Strangles always comes from contact with a infected horse or its stall, water bucket, etc... New horses recently recovered or not yet showing clinical signs or your horse visiting a new place are the two ways he will get Strangles. If neither of these two things have happened in the past 14 days, Strangles is very unlikely if your farm has no history of Strangles in the past 12 months. Sometimes viruses seem to crop up from nowhere however. These ideas are the basis for protecting your horse from Strangles:

Is there a place for vaccination? I only recommend it to horses that are known to be coming in contact with the disease and only before they develop any clinical signs.

Diarrhea
Just a mess or is it more meaningful?

The equine digestive tract is generally a marvel of assembly-line performance. It mixes just the right amounts of enzymes and water, translates those raw materials into energy, growth, repair and reproduction.

It's easy to take all of this for granted until something goes wrong. Instead of the semi solid muffins that you usually see, you now have blobs or puddles of possibly foul-smelling fecal material.

It is true in that the majority of cases strike your donkeys the same way it strikes people - it comes without warning, it lasts for about 24 hours and it mysteriously disappears. However, it is also a sign that something serious could be wrong. Serious diarrhea can be debilitating to the point of life-threatening.

Diagnosing

Typical causes other than illness

Just looking at the diarrhea isn't going to tell you a thing. You must take everything into consideration. We all know that donkeys love alfalfa. A donkey used to being on pasture or grass hay, then given a flake of alfalfa will surely have green diarrhea by morning. You already know the reason, so it is of no concern. If not given any more alfalfa, the diarrhea will quickly disappear. The same holds true in spring when the lush green grass is quickly growing after a donkey has spent a long winter on dry hay. In spring the donkey may have loose stools for several weeks. Anxiety is another typical cause of diarrhea. The stress of being loaded and shipped usually always triggers it.

We have also talked about "foal heat diarrhea" before. This usually occurs around the time the mother is going through her first heat cycle after foaling. It used to be thought that it was caused by the jennet cycling and a change in the milk but later studies show that it is caused by the foal starting to ingest grain, hay, grass and eating its mother's manure to introduce necessary bacteria into their systems. It is necessary to keep the foal's hindend clean to prevent scalding of the skin. You can do this by applying either mineral oil or petroleum jelly to the area. No other treatment is generally needed but you should keep an eye on the foal in hot weather to make sure they are nursing and do not become dehydrated. If the foal becomes depressed, I usually treat with 3 to 5 cc's of 1/2 Kaopectate and 1/2 Pepto Bismol and also take the temperature at least every 12 hours. Less experienced owners should also discuss this with their veterinarians. Foals are very small and have limited reserves of fluids and energy.

Foals can also develop diarrhea due to a mother who is a heavy milk producer and a foal who is greedy. I have only had this happen once. In this case you have two options. You can muzzle the foal for part of the day (try to find a muzzle that tiny!) or you can milk out the jennet several times a day to reduce the amount available for the foal.

Is the donkey sick? Diarrhea can precede an illness or can lead to an illness. If it is due to illness, other signs may be lack of appetite, fever and an overall look of weakness.

Causes relating to illness

Diarrhea can be associated with a life threatening situation. Severe diarrhea lasting more than 24 hours is cause to call your vet.

Has the donkey recently been on antibiotics? Has he recently undergone a lot of stress for whatever reason or is acting depressed? Salmonellosis is associated with the above. According to the Marion du Pont Scott Equine Medical Center in Leesburg, Virginia, salmonellosis is the most frequently diagnosed infectious cause of diarrhea.

Heavy doses of antibiotics can cause gastro-intestinal irritants, and mold growth because the normal intestinal bacteria have been killed by the antibiotics. Any time a donkey on antibiotics starts with diarrhea your veterinarian should be notified immediately so that the drug dosage can be changed or a different antibiotic administered. The most commonly used pain medication "bute" (phenylbutazone) can damage mucous membranes when used in excess.

Diarrhea may be seen with some of the upper respiratory virus diseases. Virus diarrhea problems may also occur, unaccompanied by respiratory problems. Viral diarrhea's are usually acute conditions in which the animal generally feels well or is only slightly depressed. They usually clear up by themselves.

Chronic Diarrhea

Diagnosing long term diarrhea can be expensive. Some donkeys will act sick and others will go on like nothing is wrong with them.

**Internal parasites are often the
cause of long term diarrhea.**

Suspicions should be raised if:

- the donkey is in declining body condition and has a dry dull looking coat despite having a healthy appetite.
- the donkey's deworming history is not known or deworming has been very inconsistent
- the donkey has been dewormed repeatedly with the same dewormer and worms have become resistant to the dewormer.

Several fecal checks may be necessary to determine if the donkey needs deworming. A good dewormer such as Strongid or Zimecterin should be used and the donkey should be dewormed a maximum of every 2 months and a minimum of every 3 months.

Water management within the digestive tract determines the consistency of the manure. In cases where a cause cannot be determined, along with supportive therapy, your vet may also advise you to withhold water for a short time frame.

For folks living in the south, sand ingestion can cause diarrhea especially if the donkeys are fed hay on the ground. Consult your vet on which laxative product works successfully in your area and put feed in hay feeders off the ground.

Infectious organisms particularly rotavirus are major causes of diarrhea in foals and weanlings. The actual cause of foal diarrhea can be difficult to determine. Helping to prevent outbreaks means keeping premises as clean as possible of manure, quarantining any new donkeys coming on to the property and hoping the foal received sufficient antibody transfer from the mother's colostrum.

Sometimes the best therapy for diarrhea is a few months of living as close to nature as possible. This includes 24 hour turnout on pasture, with no grain, plenty of plain grass hay and plenty of fresh clean water.

Foal Diarrhea
It can be deadly to a Miniature

Diarrhea in foals (also called scours) is frequently due to bacterial infection, although some diarrhea in foals is probably caused by viruses. The animal is generally weaken by other factors. He may have been weak and chilled by bad weather right after he was born. He may have been born in a dirty environment and picked up infection in a contaminated stall. Foals also may be seen with a jennet who is a good milker and a foal who is greedy and actually getting more than his body can actually digest.

The foal may show scours when the jennet comes into heat. This is called "foal heat diarrhea." It was once thought that this was due to hormonal changes appearing in the jennet and therefore in her milk, however it is also seen in orphan foals being fed milk replacer. This typical diarrhea which first appears at 7-9 days, is now thought to come from bacteria entering the foal's digestive system for the first time. Foal heat diarrhea, although something you should keep an eye on especially in miniatures, generally does not show complications and there should be no temperature rise. Reducing the amount of grain given to jennets who are nursing foals at this time may help reduce the effects of this problem.

If you live in the south, and have many days that hit the mid and upper 90 degree mark with humidity levels also in the 90's, we find that some Miniature Donkey foals do not do well in this kind of heat. They will get bouts of diarrhea, have a slight rise in temperature and may stop nursing. The average body temperature for most Miniature Donkey foals is 100-101. During these hot spells, donkey foals may develop diarrhea and have a temperature of 102. At this time you must be very certain that the foal continues to nurse. You can check this by checking the jennet's udder. If it is filled and hard to the touch, your foal has stopped nursing. (Note: foals can take a stance beside their mothers and "appear" to be nursing. If you are not sure, get down on your knees and make sure the foal has the teat in his mouth and is sucking.) If this happens, you must immediately milk the jennet and force feed the foal. Miniature Donkey foals are so tiny that they can dehydrate in a matter of hours.

You can mix 2-1/2 cc's of Pepto Bismol and 2-1/2 cc's of Kaopectate and put in a 10 cc syringe. If you use a syringe to give this mixture be sure you do not squirt it in the foals mouth as you could choke the foal or it could go into the lungs causing pneumonia.

Bowel movements may vary from thin and sticky to thin and watery and of various color. Fresh bright red blood is a sign that you have a serious problem. If your foal's temperature rises above 102 and the foal looks droopy and weak and shows signs of depression, you should contact your veterinarian immediately. In fact, whenever your foal has diarrhea and looks depressed or stops nursing, this is a true emergency and your vet should be summoned immediately.

Foals - especially miniatures - are small and have limited reserves of fluids and energy. They can dehydrate and become ill very quickly. If your vet suspects infection, he may take a sample of the feces to send to a lab to find out exactly which antibiotics will kill the bacteria causing the diarrhea.

The foal's hind end may become scalded by the feces and you will have to cleanse the area with warm water. After it is clean, you can apply some petroleum jelly to help protect the area.

Foals may have diarrhea **because** they have been treated with antibiotics, especially if these are given orally so if your foal develops diarrhea do not automatically give it a shot of penicillin. Some drugs are more prone than others to kill off the foal's intestinal bacteria - the critters which help him to digest his food.

Does My Donkey Have Arthritis?

The best defense against arthritis and degenerative joint disease (DJD) is early detection. Yet, because the early signs of joint disease are subtle, owners must be trained to look for mild joint swelling and heat, rather than lameness.

Early warning signs may include changes in performance, such as a reluctance to change leads, turn barrels, set a steer or take jumps, pull a cart. Although these problems may be related to behavior or training, the possibility of early joint disease should not be overlooked.

While all donkeys and horses are at risk of developing DID, several predisposing factors put some animals at greater risk. If the animal has crooked legs or toes in or out, its joints will have uneven pressure placed on them. (For example, an animal that toes out will have greater pressure placed on the inside of the coffin, pastern, fetlock and knee joints.) This predisposes these joints to soft tissue inflammation and uneven wear of the cartilage, and may eventually lead to the development of DJD.

Older horses/donkeys are more prone to arthritis. From birth to two years old, an equine's joints manufacture more new cartilage than they wear away. From two to about 15, cartilage replacement roughly equals normal joint cartilage wear. However, from about age 15 and above, cartilage wear begins to outstrip replacement. As a result, the cartilage wears thin, increasing bone-to-bone concussion and injury to the joint. Tendons and ligaments in older animals also become less elastic, making them susceptible to tears, leading to joint instability and inflammation.

All joints are unique and respond to injury in slightly different ways, making early signs of joint disease difficult to see. Early signs may include heat or swelling of the joint; pain on joint flexion; and various degrees of lameness. The vet's examination includes observing the animal trot in a straight line and in circles on a hard surface, as well as using nerve and joint blocks (local anesthesia) and X-rays. Other diagnostic tests such as joint fluid analysis, ultrasound and arthroscopy (insertion of a tiny flexible scope to show the inside of the joint) may also be warranted.

Once the affected joint or joints are isolated, additional X-rays will be used to determine the severity of the condition and to rule out other joint problems such as fractures, bone chips or foreign bodies.

Equine Infectious Anemia

Equine infectious anemia (EIA) is a disease that causes anemia, intermittent fever, and severe weight loss in horses, mules, and asses. EIA is highly contagious and sometimes fatal. There is no vaccine or effective treatment. EIA is often difficult to distinguish from other fever-producing diseases, including anthrax, influenza, and equine encephalitis. EIA is also known as swamp fever, malarial fever, mountain fever, and slow fever.

Monitoring

The U.S. Department of Agriculture's Animal and Plant Health Inspection Service (APHIS) is responsible for monitoring the prevalence of EIA. APHIS works closely with individual States to develop suitable control programs and analyzes diagnostic tests for EIA at its veterinary laboratories.

Signs of EIA

Infected animals may experience a sudden rise in temperatures, from the normal 100F to 105F or higher. Fever attacks may be intermittent or continuous. Infected animals may also sweat profusely, breathe rapidly, and appear depressed. They may lose weight, even if they continue to maintain a normal appetite. Eyes become bloodshot, with a slight watery discharge. Urination is frequent, and an infected animal may develop diarrhea in severe cases. Swelling of the legs (known as stocking up) and the lower parts of the body (dropsy) may occur. The weak animal will develop a wobbly or rolling gait; sometimes its hindquarters may be paralyzed. As the disease progresses, the infected animal develops anemia. Its mucous membranes become pale or yellowish, its pulse weakens, and its heartbeat becomes irregular.

Not all EIA-infected animals exhibit clinical signs. Visibly affected animals may show only a few signs, and some animals with the virus in their blood never show any signs of the disease.

Forms of the Disease

In the acute form, febrile attacks usually last 3 to 5 days. Occasionally, the first attack is fatal; more often, infected animals have several severe attacks before they die.

In the chronic form, animals often appear to recover, except for continued weight loss and deteriorating condition. They may continue to live for many years. Although the disease recurs, intervals between attacks are longer and signs are less severe than in the acute form. Infected animals may eventually die during or following an attack.

In the hidden form, infected animals continue to carry the virus in their blood for as long as they live. These carriers of EIA do not show signs of the disease. However, the hidden form may change to the acute or chronic form after severe stress, hard work, or the presence of other diseases.

Transmission

EIA has been reported in all parts of the United States and in many other parts of the world where equines are present. New outbreaks are usually of the acute form, while the hidden form is more common in areas where the disease is well established.

The disease is transmitted naturally by virus-causing insects, especially horseflies. EIA may be transmitted from mare to foal, or by giving healthy animals blood transfusions from infected animals. In addition, EIA can spread by using unsterilized knives, syringes, and tattooing or bleeding needles previously used on infected animals.

EIA kills from 30 to 70 percent of infected animals. Death rates are usually higher when the disease is introduced into a new area. Bronchopneumonia, which frequently follows infectious anemia, may be a direct cause of death.

Equines normally develop infectious anemia 2 to 4 weeks after exposure. However, signs may appear up to 2 months after exposure.

What Equine Owners Can Do To Help

Owners of equines can take a number of precautions to reduce the risk of infection:

◆ Use disposable syringes and needles. Follow the rule: one equine-- one needle.
◆ Sterilize instruments used in working with animals. Clean all instruments thoroughly after each use; then boil 15 minutes to

sterilize. This will prevent the spread of disease by knives, needles, and dental and surgical equipment.

♦ Control biting flies in stables and pastures. The local Extension Service agent or veterinarian can provide information about approved insecticides and other insect-control measures.

♦ Do not expose infected animals to those without EIA or breed equines that may be infected with EIA.

♦ Keep stables and immediate surroundings clean and sanitary at all times. Remove manure and debris promptly, and make sure the area is well drained.

♦ Isolate all new horses, mules, and asses brought to your premises. Test for EIA before grouping new equines with other animals.

♦ Obtain the required certification of negative EIA test status for horse shows, county fairs, racetracks, and other places where many animals are brought together.

♦ Abide by State laws that govern EIA.

If You Suspect EIA

If you suspect an animal may have EIA, call your veterinarian immediately. He or she will examine the animal, review the recent history of exposure in your area, and submit a blood sample to an approved laboratory. Both the Coggins and the immunosorbent assay (ELISA) blood tests are used to diagnose this disease in the laboratory.

Reference: U.S. Department of Agriculture

So Your Pet Has Cancer

Terminology

Your pet has been diagnosed with cancer. Cancer is a disease that is due to the uncontrolled and purposeless growth of cells in the body. The terms cancer, malignancy, and neoplasia are synonyms. Cancer is not a single disease since it can arise from any tissue in the body. Therefore, there are many types of cancer.

Some forms of cancer have the ability to spread to other sites in the body which are often far from the original site. This occurs when cancer cells enter the blood or lymph vessels and are then carried to other organs. Cancers with this type of behavior are considered malignant.

Oftentimes, it is the spread of a cancer that causes the greatest problems. When a cancer has spread in this fashion, it is said to metastasize. Some cancers lack the ability to metastasize but may cause significant damage due to growth and invasion into local tissues. Tumors that do not metastasize and are not invasive are considered benign. The term, tumor, is a general word for cancer whether it is benign ("good" cancer) or malignant ("bad" cancer).

Oncology is the branch of medicine dedicated to the study of cancer and the veterinarians treating your pet are oncologists.

Tumor Evaluation (work-up): Tumor Staging

The first task of your veterinarian is to determine the extent of the tumor. This information is vital for several reasons including determination of your pet's prognosis (i.e., the expected outcome for your pet as a result of the cancer) and formulation of a plan for treatment.

To gather information that can help to determine the extent of the cancer, your clinician will need to evaluate your pet by several methods. These usually include blood tests (e.g., blood count, chemistry profile), urinalysis, radiographs (X-rays), tissue aspirate, and biopsy.

Tests which your local veterinarian may have performed might be repeated due to the changing nature of your pet's illness. In addition, as indicated for specific patients, other testing procedures may include: ultrasound, specialized radiologic studies (e.g. nuclear scan, CT/MRI scan, dye contrast studies), bone marrow aspirate, lymph node aspirate, endoscopy (direct examination of the stomach, colon, or bronchi with a specialized scope), and immunologic studies. The collective process of obtaining this information to ascertain extent of the cancer is referred to as tumor staging. It is important to realize that medicine is not an exact science and that despite these staging procedures, small sites of tumor or tumor in organs that are difficult to study may not be detected.

Once the tumor staging has been completed, your veterinarian will be better able to discuss treatment options for your pet. The goal of such therapy will also be discussed. Tumors that have metastasized extensively are usually not curable. Therefore, the objective of therapy for these animals is palliation (i.e., afford relief of symptoms and possibly prolong life without providing a cure). Localized tumors that are not deeply invasive have the best chance to be cured.

Cancer Therapy

There are several types of therapy used to treat cancer in small animals at the University of Pennsylvania. These include surgery, chemotherapy, radiation therapy, and immunotherapy. For some tumors, treatment will consist of a single type of therapy, while combination therapy may be recommended for other types of cancer or for animals with more advanced stage of disease. On occasion, due to the rarity or biological behavior of a particular tumor, a precise treatment recommendation may not be known.

In an effort to test newer (and hopefully more effective) forms of therapy, you may be asked to enroll your pet in an investigative clinical trial. The purpose of such a trial is to learn more about the specific type of treatment (that may be of value to humans and other pets with cancer) as well as hopefully providing a benefit to your pet. Only pet owners of animals with tumors for which there is no effective treatment or tumors that have not responded to conventional treatment will be offered investigative therapy for their pets, if appropriate investigative treatment is available.

Should you treat your pet?

Treating animals with cancer is not appropriate for every pet or family. It takes a strong commitment on the part of the owner. Therapy requires frequent trips to the veterinary hospital and can be expensive. For some forms of cancer, treatment, once begun, is never stopped during the animal's life (although the frequency of treatments can be decreased).

Your veterinarian cannot do it alone since treating pets with cancer is truly a team effort and the pet owner is on the team. It is important for you to present your pet for treatment precisely when requested to do so by your veterinarian since the timing of cancer therapy is critical for obtaining an optimal outcome. In addition, medicines to be given to your pet at home should be administered by you exactly as requested by your oncologist.

Any abnormalities or problems you encounter should be reported to your local veterinarian or oncologist promptly. Always feel free to ask questions and communicate with us.

Keep in mind that your veterinarian is as concerned about the quality of your pet's life as you are. The goal of therapy is to keep your pet happy and minimize discomfort.

Although some animals may experience transient discomfort from therapy, treatment of most pets with cancer can be accomplished without major distress or detraction from your pet's enjoyment of life. Just because an animal has been diagnosed with cancer does not mean its life is immediately over. Your commitment to your pet and your veterinarians' dedication to providing state-of-the-art care will work together to keep your pet as happy as possible.

Reference: Authors: Dr. Kim Cronin, Dr. Lili Duda, Dr. Syd Evans, Dr. Karin Sorenmo
Affiliations: Clinical Oncology Service Veterinary Hospital of the University of Pennsylvania (VHUP)

Choke

It is not uncommon for a food bolus to become lodged in the esophagus of the equine. It happens for a number of different reasons and clinical signs develop rapidly.

Symptoms

When an equine becomes choked, he will immediately start showing signs of distress. If it is his first time, he may even appear colicky; throwing himself to the ground repeatedly. He may thrash his head around attempting to dislodge the obstruction. When choked, the salivary glands go into high gear and rapidly fill the esophagus. The excessive salivation then comes out the mouth and nostrils usually mixed with food. The nasal discharge can be copious. This is the hallmark of esophageal obstruction: food tainted saliva issuing from the nose. Equines that have had the problem before become much more stoic and learn to put their head down so the air ways can drain and they can breathe easier.

Causes

Probably the most common cause is gluttony. The equine attempts to swallow large amounts of grain or pellets without first chewing and moistening the food bolus. Anatomical abnormalities in the esophagus can cause food to lodge there also but I think this is rare. Pellets seem to predispose to the problem. Whatever the cause, once an equine has choked it usually means he will do it again if you do not change the way you feed.

Treatment

The equine's response may appear dramatic but, choke is not usually a life threatening situation. In fact, if left alone the bolus will usually pass in a few minutes. It is important to leave the equine alone so that he can accommodate the fluid in the back of his throat. Tying up his head will probably result in aspiration of food and fluid into the lungs and a very difficult to treat pneumonia developing.

When the obstruction passes, the nasal discharge will abruptly stop and the equine will calm down quickly. If the obstruction persists for longer than 10 or 20 minutes call the vet and he should be able to get the bolus to move with a nasogastric tube and water. By repeatedly flushing water over the bolus it will break down and move. He may have to give a mild sedative to work on the equine but heavy sedation should be avoided.

I have had donkeys choke in the past and it can last anywhere from 1 hour to 24 hours. If the donkey does not seem to be in severe distress, some vets will advise holding off any type of treatment to see if the excessive salivation will work - and it always has in my cases here. Withhold all feed until the choke has subsided but always have a bucket of water available to the donkey.

Hypothyroidism
Misdiagnosed and Misunderstood

Insufficient levels of thyroid hormones - is difficult to diagnose. The accuracy of tests for the problem is questionable, and there are questionable effects of treatment when the ailment is misdiagnosed.

Thyroid hormones control protein synthesis. They are responsible for the overall metabolism of the equine and have bearing on the animal's energy level. Hypothyroidism is due either to insufficient levels of thyroid hormones or inappropriate release of hormones from the thyroid gland.

Signs of hypothyroidism include lethargy, muscular weakness, decreased exercise tolerance and goiter. Obesity, cresty neck, frequent bouts of laminitis, poor hair coat, mare/jennet infertility and foal tendon problems have all been reported to be associated with hypothyroidism, but are not scientifically documented.

Although the frequency of hypothyroidism is unknown, many equine are placed on treatment - which consists of thyroid hormones given as a feed additive - for lack of other diagnosis. Symptoms often remain unexplained, and hypothyroidism can't be ruled out.

The test for hypothyroidism adds to the confusion. The easiest laboratory test measures T4, or sometimes T3 thyroid hormone levels in a single blood sample. There are many variables in using this method of testing.

Some commonly used drugs, such as bute, and some diets have been reported to cause low levels of thyroid hormones. Thus <u>the tests do not give an exact quantity of the active form and often are inaccurate</u>.

There are natural daily and monthly fluctuations of the forms of hormones in the body. <u>A single low-serum level of T4 or T3 does not prove that the equine is suffering from hypothyroidism</u>.

THE BEST MEANS of measuring the function of the thyroid balance in the horse/donkey is to take repeated blood samples over a period of time.

Supplementing equine with a synthetic thyroid hormone works, but, in fact, it could lead to more problems than it solves.

Excessive supplementation can lead to decreased production of natural thyroid hormones. Normal mechanisms that detect the supplemental hormones conclude that it's naturally produced and may suppress the activity of the thyroid gland.

Supplementation may actually cause hypothyroidism, with the animal's body adjusting to and becoming dependent on the outside source of thyroid hormones. Excessive supplementation in humans causes heart palpitations and other cardiac effects associated with changes in the cardiac muscle. Whether such effects occur in the equine is unknown.

There simply is not enough known about the function and regulation of thyroid hormones in the horse to consider hypothyroidism as a common condition or one to treat with "best guess" supplements. Until more research is done and better testing developed, diagnoses should only be based on a combination of laboratory values, physical signs and response to therapy, keeping the risks of that therapy in mind.

Reference: Mike Beyer, DVM

Goeffary & Sylvia Rome in the United Kingdom with their champion imported herd sire "Cody" from All Creatures Small Farm in Texas

Heaves *(Emphysema)*

(*Note*: I had a breeder from the mid-Midwest area call to tell me that she has found that some breeders in her area routinely keep young stock locked inside a barn for the entire winter. Following their advice, she did the same for a month. She advised her veterinarian of this who promptly admonished her for this practice and told her of the respiratory illnesses she could be causing her donkeys. This breeder called me to get my advice and I totally agreed with her veterinarian. Apparently these breeders feel that they are protecting their young donkeys from the elements of cold weather, when in fact, they are most likely causing more harm than any simple cold could cause.)

Donkeys are just as susceptible to "heaves" as horses. You can almost always find a few donkeys at sales showing signs of heaves. We at Pheasant Meadow Farm very very seldom lock our donkeys inside the barn. The barn is kept open year round for donkeys to come and go as they please. The only exceptions are a few times each winter when it is extremely cold along with high winds making the wind chill factor very low or an ice or snow storm. We also do not allow foals, under the age of one month, out in the rain. Depending on where you live, newborn foals should be kept inside under heat, if the outside temperature is below 40 degrees or if you are having strong winds.

Heaves is also called *chronic pulmonary emphysema* and is characterized by an expiratory distress, that is, when the equine attempts to breathe out, he is unable to fully empty his lungs. This results in extra effort trying to do so, a heaving motion of the abdomen from which the disease gets its name. Animals who have this disease may have a continuous cough. The cough is a deep, dry, hacking one that seems to come from the bottom of the equine's feet. There is rarely a nasal discharge, and the animal (at least early in the course of the disease) will otherwise look and feel normal. These animals may make a wheezing noise when they breathe, particularly on breathing out.

Causes:

Heaves is usually started by an allergy to something that the equine is inhaling such as mold and dust and leads to a chronic cough. The cough leads to a chronic bronchitis and then to the lung damage. It is commonly caused by dusty or moldy hay. The problem seems especially bad with alfalfa hay perhaps because it is more difficult to put up good alfalfa. Dusty pens or stalls will also initiate coughing. Dusty straw or other poor quality material used for bedding may also start an animal coughing. Virus or bacterial infections of the respiratory tract may start the cough that starts the heaves.

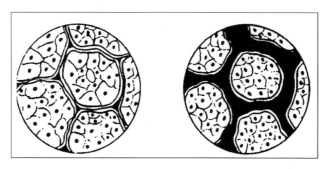

Microscopic views of the alveoli. On the left, normal alveoli. On the right, air is trapped between the alveoli, so they cannot expand and fill with air.

Whatever initiated the cough, in time a chronic bronchitis helps to keep the animal coughing. After he has coughed for a period of time, the small air sacs in the lungs, called **alveoli,** begin to rupture. Their walls break down, leaving less area for absorbing oxygen, leaving the lungs much less efficient. As they break down, relatively large air pockets form in the lungs. These pockets are the cause of the difficulty on expiration and account for the wheezing. Heaves is not a contagious disease, but may be seen in whole groups who are exposed to the same environmental causes.

When the equine takes a breath, he will often hurry as if gasping for air. His nostrils may be flared. The animal has to make an extra effort to try to push the last of the used air out of his lungs in preparation for taking another breath. After he has finished a breath - before he inhales the next one - he will make an extra push upward with his abdominal muscles. The belly muscles are used to help expel the air from the animals' lungs. After a period of time, this continued effort thickens these muscles into a ridge along the lower side of the abdomen. This ridge is called a "heave line".

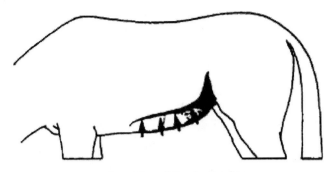

Location of the heave line

Signs

The animal with advanced heaves falls into a breathing rhythm: gulp a breath of air (quickly), breathe out (slowly) and push often wheezing at the same time. A constant amount of nasal discharge is commonly seen in advanced cases.

Heaves is usually a progressive disease. The disease may appear to be worse at some times of the year than others. It is often worse in hot, dry weather and will be more severe when the animal's surroundings are dusty.

Early cases of heaves are difficult to diagnose because they look much like other respiratory diseases.

Treatment

How do you cure heaves? You don't. This is not to say that nothing can be done for the animal. The only thing that can be done is to manage the animal in an attempt to stop the disease from getting any worse.

The best treatment is to get the animal out on a good, clean pasture. Your veterinarian will advise you to never lock the animal in a stall unless absolutely necessary and then you should wet the stall floor down. When feeding hay, you must take a hose and immediately before feeding, wet the hay. If the only hay you have is dusty your vet may advise buying complete pelleted feed which contains both hay and grain. If feeding grain, you should feed a sweet feed with molasses in it to cut down on dust.

In more advanced stages of the disease, your veterinarian will give you an expectorant to feed daily and antibiotics to be given during stages when the animal is going through a bad spell. More and better medications have been developed over the past few years. Discuss these with your veterinarian.

As with most diseases, the best cure is not to develop the problem in the first place. The best prevention is to not lock up your animals in a stall or barn unless absolutely necessary. Feed good quality, mold and dust free hay.

Remember, if you have a donkey locked in a stall and it gets chilled, it has no way of warming itself. Donkeys out on pasture are almost constantly on the move, generating body heat. Weanlings and yearlings love to run and play on a daily basis not only generating body heat but also getting their respiratory rate high enough to help clear dust and debris from their lungs.

Years ago, we purchased a 6 year old Tennessee Walker Mare who developed heaves six months later. The breeder we purchased the horse from stated that he stalled all his horses during winter months around the clock. After numerous tests, the finger was pointed directly at the dust in the barn causing the heaves. The disease progressed quickly and one year after purchasing - and falling in love with - we had to put this mare down. Heaves is a terrible disease that you would not want to see your donkey go through.

by Bonnie Gross, Editor MDT and Ruth B. James, D.V.M.

Hot weather Hauling and Heat stress

If you are new to donkeys, you have probably discovered that most hang on to their winter coats much longer than horses. Some of our donkeys are not completely shed out until mid July. Very hot weather early in the year means a little extra care and attention to your donkeys welfare is needed.

Hauling can, and usually is, stressful to any animal. As part of the research for this article, I rode in the back of our horse trailer for one hour with a jennet. If you have never done this, you should give it a try. Every bump in the road is magnified 100% not to mention the noise and clanging of the metal trailer.

Donkeys attempt to lean against the wall of the trailer for balance and they do a constant and continuous balancing act. All you have to do is look at the donkey and you can see how much stress they are under. Some people who own miniature animals build their own home-made trailers. They are usually made of wood with only two tires and a small opening in the back. These closed in trailers can act like a stove on a hot summer day. Adequate air flow is a must in all trailers.

In human medicine, there are three forms of sunstroke. (1) Heat exhaustion causing failure of the action of the heart, (2) Heat shock in which exposure to great heat appears to paralyze the nerve centers of breathing and blood circulation and (3) Heat fever in which the nerve centers become exhausted from over-stimulation due to prolonged exposure to heat.

A donkey suffering from heat exhaustion will try to cool itself by sweating heavily, taking rapid, shallow breaths and flaring its nostrils. Its body temperature will elevate to a point between 105 and 108 degrees.

If your donkey shows signs of either heat exhaustion or heat stroke you must locate a vet immediately. Donkeys do not have to be pulling a cart or running out in the pasture to suffer from heat exhaustion. Standing in a hot trailer under direct sunlight without shade or in a poorly ventilated trailer is enough to cause a hypothermic condition. If you are out in no-where-land when you realize you have a problem, wet down the donkey's legs, chest and neck area only, then proceed on to find a veterinarian.

Good ventilation in your trailer is a must. Ventilation helps move the heat away from the donkey's body.

We have also found that Miniature Donkey foals, under the age of two months, do not do well in extreme heat of 95 plus degrees. On days like this, we usually wet the chest and legs of young foals during the hottest part of the day. In severe heat, we do the above and also put them in a stall with a fan to keep them out of the sun.

Hauling during hot summer days, should if all possible, be done at night. If this is not possible, a well ventilated trailer is a must. Remember that you not only have the sun beating down on a metal or wood roof but you also have the heat rising from the hot road. Frequent stops must also be made to offer the donkey water.

If you are on a long haul and need to stop to eat at a restaurant, *always* pull the trailer under a tree or some type of shade. Just as you would never leave a dog in a hot car, you should never leave a donkey in a hot trailer.

Upward Fixation of the Patella

"Patella" is the technical name for the kneecap. In the normal equine, it rides in a groove in the lower end of the femur exactly like your kneecap or mine. An affected equine has the kneecap slide upward and "catch", causing his leg to lock straight rather than being able to bend normally. The problem can be hereditary in animals with overly straight, upright hind legs. Fixation can also occur because the animal is injured while the leg was overextended. *Animals who are weakened and thin are more prone to it than are animals in normal condition.* Fixation generally is seen in only one hind leg at a time, but often occurs in either hind leg in susceptible animals. It is common in Shetland ponies and has been seen fairly often in Miniature Donkeys.

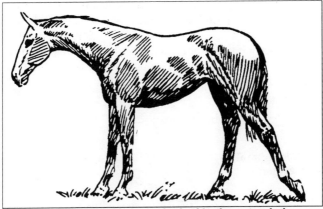

***The animal's leg is locked in the extended
position, stretched out behind him.***

The animal cannot flex the stifle and hock, but can still move the fetlock. The leg may unlock and then catch again in a few steps or it may stay locked for hours or days. Some equine have the kneecap catch as they move, giving a rough, jerky gait, without its ever locking and staying locked. If the animal is forced to move while the patella is locked hard and fast, he may drag the front of the hoof on the ground. A snapping sound can sometimes be heard as the kneecap pops in and out of place without locking.

If fixation happens to your donkey suddenly and does not relieve itself shortly, first-aid to get the kneecap popped back into place may be in order. Pull the leg forward, at the same time, push the kneecap toward the donkey's body. This will often push it back into place. Other animals benefit by being backed while someone pushes inward and downward on the kneecap.

In mild cases of fixation of the patella, where a donkey only occasionally locks up, the donkey appears uncomfortable. In severe cases, where an operation is needed, the donkey shows mild pain and is somewhat reluctant to run and play and has an overall appearance of being somewhat depressed.

I once purchased a weanling jennet (sight unseen) who arrived in poor malnourished condition. Shortly thereafter, both back legs locked up. She was put on a stringent worming program and a high protein/vitamin feed program. We also did daily physical therapy on her back legs. We were advised that with proper exercise and nutrition, there was a possibility for her to outgrow this condition. She improved greatly, however, as a yearling both her back legs continued to lock so we opted for surgery. The surgical correction for upward fixation of the patella is a "medial patellar desmotomy."

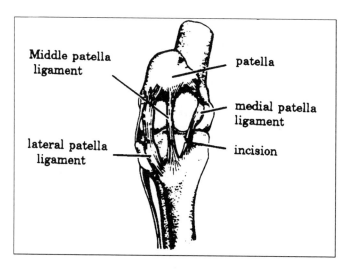

Middle patella ligament

patella

medial patella ligament

lateral patella ligament

incision

Medial Patellar Desmotomy

The surgical site is shaved and scrubbed with an antiseptic, and a local anesthetic is injected into the area.

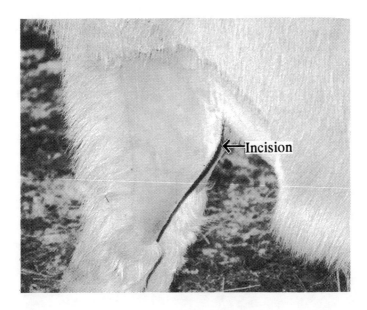

The jennet was tranquilized and in a standing position. A small incision was made over the middle patellar ligament, through which a knife is placed underneath the medial patellar ligament. The knife blade is turned so that its sharp edge is against the ligament which is then severed. One suture was used to close the small incision in each leg.

Important Note: The medial patellar ligament will eventually grow back together over a three month period of time. I spoke with several other breeders who had this procedure done, and in most cases, the operation was **not** a success. All other breeders advised that they were told to stall their donkeys for several weeks and eliminate as much exercise as possible. My equine surgeon, on the other hand, advised me the exact opposite. He wanted me to begin exercise the very next day - Preferably by trotting the jennet up hills. The purpose of this was to build up the hind leg muscles. These muscles would help hold the patellar ligament in place as it grew back together. This jennet was given the proper exercise and the operation 90% successful. I say 90% because this jennet does occasionally lock up to the point where she jerks the hind leg up. She does not totally lock and I see no evidence of pain. I firmly believe the fact that we exercised this animal had a great deal to do with the success of this particular operation.

I also feel this condition had caused this jennet a good amount of stress. She was always very laid back, however since the operation, has been a very playful and much happier animal. I might also mention that I have seen jennets in their last month of pregnancy occasionally lock up and feel there must be a correlation between the extra added weight and stress that is put on the ligaments during this time frame. The fees for this procedure were $175.00.

Misconceptions About Salmonella Infection

Many people think that when a donkey eats something moldy or unsanitary, they immediately come down with salmonella poisoning and become very sick. People usually think of salmonella as it pertains to "food poisoning" in humans. Actually this is only half right. Anyone who has had blood work done on a sick donkey knows that the lab always checks for salmonella.

What is Salmonellosis?

Salmonellosis is an inflammation of the small intestine caused by the bacteria *salmonella typhimurium.* The condition can be mild or severe, from the donkey being a healthy carrier to acute illness in which death is almost a certainty.

What are the signs of Salmonellosis?

Infected donkeys may show little or no interest in food but may drink water freely. Depending on the severity of the infection, fevers can range from a mild 103 to an acute 108. Some form of diarrhea is usually present and may contain blood and mucus. Donkeys will also become dehydrated from the diarrhea. Most donkeys will show signs of severe abdominal pain. Certain strains of salmonellosis can cause abortion between the 4th and 8th months.

What causes salmonellosis?

The disease is most frequent in animals under stress. Long hauls which exhaust donkeys, surgery, weaning, pregnancy, heavy worm infections, exposure to inclement weather and administration of gastro-intestinal irritants such as heavy doses of antibiotics. You may be treating a donkey for a hoof infection or an infected cut and unknowing cause salmonella due to massive antibiotics.

Stress causes debilitation of the donkey allowing the salmonella to greatly multiply, resulting in abscesses and tissue death in the membrane of the intestine. The presence of this massive infection in the body is responsible for the congestion and blockage of the blood system of the intestines, and spread of the infection to the liver, lungs, spleen, joints and the membranes of the brain.

How is Salmonellosis Diagnosed?

A veterinarian can diagnose the disease from the animal's history, clinical signs and bacterial culture samples of the feces, along with a blood test. The white blood cell count will be found to be reduced markedly. Vets often use an animal's gum color to judge the presence and degree of shock that the animal may be experiencing.

How is Salmonellosis Spread?

The bacteria is present in the feces of infected and carrier donkeys and contact with the feces is the usual means of transmission. When feces of rats and birds contaminate feed and water, infection may occur. Man can contract the disease and also spread it throughout the barn.

When donkeys with poor immunity come in contact with these bacteria, the donkey becomes ill. Also, many horses and donkeys carry potentially dangerous salmonella strains in their own intestines which then cause the donkey to become ill *only* when it is stressed. Equine deaths caused by severe salmonella diarrhea, result in a significant loss to the horse industry each year.

What is the Treatment?

Two things make infections by salmonella bacteria much worse than plain diarrhea. First, unlike other intestinal bacteria, salmonella actually invade the body by going right through the walls of the intestine. This results in a deadly condition known medically as "septicemia" which is bacteria in the blood. Secondly, salmonella produce chemicals called "endotoxins" which have profound effects on the blood vessels, kidney, lungs, liver, and other organs. This is why animals with salmonellosis get so sick, so fast and is particularly true in young foals. If the infection has gone on for any length of time, organs such as the large intestine and the kidney become so badly damaged that they cannot heal.

Treatment consists of intravenous and intramuscular administration of broad spectrum antibiotics and sulfonamides. Mass amounts of fluids will be administered intravenously for dehydration. Recently, the availability of an antiserum that protects donkeys/horses from the bacteria and its endotoxins has shown very good results. However, the endorserum is expensive and must be given very soon after the disease starts if treatment is to be successful.

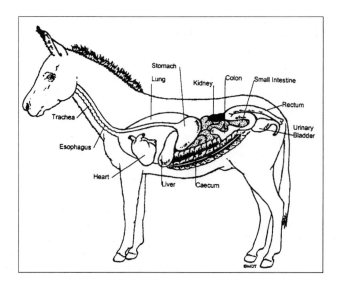

Can Salmonellosis be Prevented?

Control is difficult because of the way it is spread. Proper manure disposal, fly control and feed storage are essential. Sick animals must be isolated from healthy animals. Rest animals frequently while traveling and avoid possibly contaminated public drinking troughs by hauling your own water.

A vaccine is available for equine salmonella. However, it can cause painful local reactions and a transient fever. In addition, while some animals are very well protected by the vaccine, others make little or no immune response. Unfortunately, it is hard to tell which animals are going to be protected and which will not.

Selenium Deficiency
White Muscle Disease
Should YOU be Concerned?
YES! If you live in the U.S. or Canada and raise livestock

Ed Note: Many weeks of research went into this article. My sincere thanks to the following people for their personal contributions: Dr. Cooper Williams, Dr. Michael Harrison, Dr. Dave Galligan -New Bolton Center, University of Pennsylvania; Dr. H.F. Hintz, Professor Animal Nutrition, Cornell University; Dr. Stephen Dill and Dr. William Rebhun both of Cornell University..

The following article contains portions of an article entitled "White Muscle Disease in Foals", Vol. 7, No. 11, Dept of Clinical Sciences of New York State College of Veterinary Medicine, Cornell University. I have changed certain words, contained in brackets [ ], to make the article easier to read and understand. I have also included personal comments in italics based on interviews with the above doctors.

White Muscle Disease occurs when there is an inadequate dietary intake of selenium and vitamin E, and severely affects the muscles of the animal. Vitamin E and selenium function jointly to protect and stabilize cell membranes, including muscle cell membranes. Vitamin E serves as the "first line" oxidant, which decreases peroxide formation by the tissues. Excessive peroxides are destroyed by the selenium-containing tissue enzyme.

Vitamin E and selenium [work together] in effect stabilizing cell membranes and therefore both are generally believed to play a part in the [production and development] of white muscle disease. The independent and joint roles of vitamin E and selenium in this disease have been established in other species. Controversy over these roles in horses still exists. Selenium administered alone (without vitamin E) seems to be effective in both treatment and prevention of white muscle disease. This finding suggests that, in field situations, inadequate dietary intake of selenium may be more important than inadequate vitamin E intake in the development of the disease.

White muscle disease occurs primarily in areas of the United States and Canada that have selenium deficient soil, which in turn results in selenium deficient grains and forage.

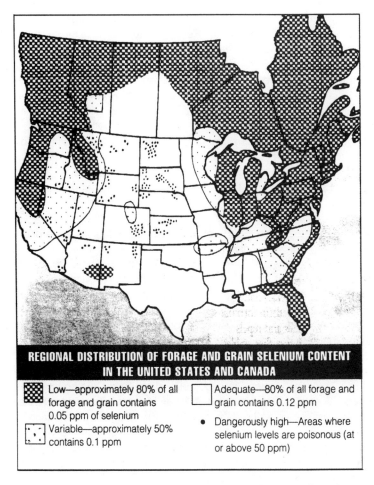

REGIONAL DISTRIBUTION OF FORAGE AND GRAIN SELENIUM CONTENT
IN THE UNITED STATES AND CANADA

Low—approximately 80% of all forage and grain contains 0.05 ppm of selenium

Variable—approximately 50% contains 0.1 ppm

Adequate—80% of all forage and grain contains 0.12 ppm

• Dangerously high—Areas where selenium levels are poisonous (at or above 50 ppm)

This article summarizes the histories and clinical signs of 11 foals with white muscle disease that were presented to the Large Animal Clinic at the New York State College of Veterinary Medicine, Cornell University. Autopsy findings of 6 of the 11 foals that died in the large animal clinic and 4 foals that were sent in after death from the surrounding area are also given.

History and Clinical Signs

The foals affected with white muscle disease were from New York,

Pennsylvania and Maine, which are known to be states with selenium-deficient soil. Mares of affected foals and foals old enough to eat solid food were on diets composed of locally grown crops. The incidence of the diseases was not apparently breed or sex-related in these foals. *(Ed Note: There is documentation of Miniature Donkey foals dying and Miniature Donkey jennets aborting due to white muscle disease.)* Onset of signs in 14 of the foals varied from birth to 11 months of age; five foals were affected at birth, one at 7 hours of age, one at 4 days of age, four between 2 and 8 weeks of age, and three between 4 and 11 months of age. One fetus with histologic [tissue] lesions of white muscle disease was aborted at 10 months gestation. One foal (11 months old) was affected after its first period of exercise following a winter of confinement. The disease had a seasonal incidence corresponding to the foaling season; 13 of the total 15 foals studied became ill between February and June.

The 11 foals presented to the Large Animal Clinic initially were bright and alert. Depression was only apparent in the terminal state of the disease. Rectal temperatures were recorded in 10 foals and ranged from 97 to 104 degrees. Three of the 10 foals had temperatures higher than 101.5 degrees. Of these three foals, one had [existing blood poisoning], one had pneumonia and the third had excessive muscular activity (thrashing attributed to unsuccessful attempts to stand) that was thought to have caused the [fever].

Muscle [malfunction] was apparent on physical examination in all 11 cases. The clinical signs varied, depending on distribution of muscular lesions. Weakness was present in 10 of 11 foals. The one foal that was not weak presented [difficulty in swallowing] as its only abnormality. Eight foals were unable to rise without assistance; the muscles of the chest and/or pelvic limbs were affected in these foals. A few of the eight foals made active attempts to rise but would violently fall and roll, which was occasionally misinterpreted as colic. In 5 of the 11 foals presented, a stiff, painful gait was observed; tense painful muscles were palpable in 4 foals. [Difficulty in swallowing] was evident in 7 of 11 foals as oral or nasal regurgitation of milk after nursing. Two foals were unable to nurse because of pain associated with extending the neck.

All foals had an elevated respiratory rate. Three foals had [difficulty in breathing], two of these had [bluish] mucous membranes.

Clinical Data

Urine was a coffee-brown color grossly in three of the seven patients from which urine was obtained. Protein and blood were reported in all of the urinalyses except one foal.

Treatment

Physical exertion of the foals was minimized to avoid further muscle damage. Vitamin E-selenium (E-SE® - Schering) was administered by intramuscular injection at a dose of 1 ml/45 kg of body weight. This was repeated in the surviving foals at 3 days and again at 8 to 10 days after the initial injection. Foals that exhibited [difficulty in swallowing] were given milk and oral electrolytes by nasal tube. Severely dehydrated foals were treated with intravenous fluids.

Anti-inflammatory drugs were administered to help reduce muscle pain and swelling. Because these drugs can cause ulcers in foals, they were only administered for two days. Foals were put in well-bedded environments with good footing to minimize further muscle trauma associated with efforts to rise.

Postmortem Findings

Six of the 11 foals admitted to the Large Animal Clinic had advanced signs, failed to respond to therapy, and died. [Autopsy] findings confirmed muscle degeneration in all cases.

The location of the affected muscles varied but correlated well with the clinical signs displayed by each foal. Affected muscles included those of the thoracic limbs, pelvic limbs, and heart; cervical muscles; the diaphragm and the tongue. [Lesions of the heart muscle] were evident in 5 of the 10 foals autopsied including a fetus that had been aborted at 10 months gestation. Aspiration pneumonia was apparent in two foals.

Conclusions

The clinical diagnosis of white muscle disease is based on a combination of clinical signs showing muscle disease, elevated enzymes in muscle, decreased blood selenium and response to vitamin E-selenium administration. [Observation] evaluation is more important than laboratory evaluation in arriving at an accurate prognosis. Foals where appropriate therapy is delayed have a very poor prognosis. *(Ed Note:*

Unfortunately, in the case of tiny miniature donkey foals, by the time a diagnosis is made, it is usually too late for treatment to be effective. The best treatment is prevention discussed later in this report.) Foals that are unable to support weight with assistance have a poor prognosis, as do foals with dark brown urine. Unfortunately, definitive diagnosis requires autopsy or biopsy. Relative assurance of a clinical diagnosis of white muscle disease, elevation of muscle enzymes, and decreased blood selenium.

If a diagnosis of white muscle disease is suspected, blood selenium values should be determined in the sick foal as well as in other foals and jennets on the same farm to assess the selenium status of the herd.

(Ed Note: In an interview with Dr. Hintz of Cornell, we were advised that if a foal is diagnosed with white muscle disease, all future foals out of that same mother should be put on an immediate prevention program. She should be fed selenium supplemented feed and blood evaluations should be done on her every 3 months to monitor blood selenium levels.) Evaluation of the herd is important because mild selenium deficiencies may result in decreased immune response to infectious diseases in foals.

White muscle disease can be prevented in foals by injecting selenium and vitamin E at birth and by selenium supplementation of pregnant jennets. Feed should be supplemented with selenium at 0.1 to 0.2 ppm [parts per million]. *(Ed Note: USDA has recently approved a .03 ppm additive to grain. Selenium is extremely toxic so you must first do several things. You must first determine the deficiency of selenium in your area. This can be done by (1) having your soil tested and (2) drawing blood from several donkeys in your herd and having selenium evaluation done. This will tell your feed dealer whether he needs to add 0.1, 0.2 or 0.3 ppm to your feed. Everyone in selenium deficient areas should have selenium added to the grain they feed their donkeys, however the question remains as to how much is to be added.)*

Although the FDA has approved maximal selenium supplementation at 0.3 mb/kg of dry matter in complete feeds for cattle, sheep, and swine, selenium supplementation of EQUINE feeds is restricted only by nutritional recommendations and industry practices. The selenium requirement of the horse was estimated at 0.1 mg/kg of diet. It was concluded that there was no advantage in supplementing the mature idle horse with more than 0.1 mg of selenium to prevent problems associated with selenium deficiency. *(Ed Note: In the above mentioned interview with Dr. Hintz of Cornell, we were advised that a premixed feed with 0.1 mg.kg of selenium (feed 1-1/2 lbs of grain per day per donkey) was adequate in all areas EXCEPT the states of Oregon and Washington which need supplementation of 0.3 mg/kg mixed in feed.)*

Selenium supplementation of pregnant jennets should be started six to eight weeks [before birth] in jennets found to be at risk. Important Note: Only limited amounts of inorganic selenium cross the placenta, but organic selenium appears to cross the placenta more readily.

(What this means is in areas of the country where natural selenium is in the grass and hay, enough passes through the placenta to protect the foal. Inorganic selenium would be selenium that is injected into the jennet before she foals, which this report indicates is NOT sufficient as not enough of it crosses the placenta.)

A foal's blood selenium levels at birth are about one half of the blood selenium levels of its supplemented dam. Foals considered to be at risk should be treated at birth with 1 cc E-SE per 100 pounds of body weight administered intramuscularly. This could be repeated at approximately two and six weeks of age in an at-risk foal.

(Because this is a toxic substance, donkey foals must be weighed and treated with the exact amount. THERE ARE 3 DIFFERENT TYPES OF INJECTABLE SELENIUM!!! The three different names are "BO-SE", "MU-SE", and "ESE". All three have different dosages. The "ESE" is specifically made for equine, however, I am told that in areas heavily populated with cattle, some vets give the "BO-SE" (made for cattle) to equine. I have not yet heard of any bad effects however, I would recommend you have your vet give you the "ESE" for your donkeys. A 25 pound miniature donkey foal would receive 1/4 cc (of the "ESE"). You can get 1 cc syringes, (size 25G X 5/8) from vaccine catalogs in the dog sections).

Jennets on selenium supplementation have a higher milk selenium content than jennets not on supplementation, BUT selenium is not concentrated in the milk in sufficient quantities to protect the foals from developing white muscle disease. Therefore, pre-injecting pregnant jennets before foaling is not a solution.

Some controversy exists as to the usefulness of vitamin E in commercially available injectable vitamin E-selenium preparations. The amount of vitamin E provided at the recommended dose is not generally a sufficient quantity to be of value to a foal. Some question also exists as to how well vitamin E is absorbed when given intramuscularly. As mentioned previously, the precise roles of vitamin E and selenium in contributing to the onset of white muscle disease remain to be determined. Despite these controversies, parenteral treatment includes the provision of both selenium and vitamin E. Vitamin E and selenium interact to protect and stabilize cell membranes, including the muscle cell membrane. Selenium may enhance vitamin E uptake and storage.

(Ed Note: Since selenium deficiency is directly related to muscle inadequacies, SE-E deficiencies could also tie in with fixation of the patella discussed in this book. Strong leg muscles are needed to hold the patella in place. If your donkeys lack adequate muscle tone, you may want to consider selenium deficiency as the culprit.)

Miniature Donkey Talk Magazine Exclusive

New Research on
ESe (Equine vitamin E, Selenium vs. BoSe (Bovine vitamin E, Selenium)

Many years ago, when we at *Miniature Donkey Talk Magazine* did our original research on the importance of Selenium/Vitamin E as it pertains to donkeys, we found that many sections of the U.S. and Canada had selenium deficient soil. Selenium deficiency can cause numerous problems in donkeys including White Muscle Disease in foals (which they do not normally survive), locking patella's in youngsters and adults, muscle weakness in newborns, excessive unexplained cowhocks, prolonged foal-heat diarrhea, low conception rates, and more.

Our studies with Cornell University indicated we should be using ESe (Equine Selenium, Vitamin E) in donkeys and not BoSe (Bovine Selenium, Vit E) or MU-Se (another selenium, Vit E combination generally used in cattle). As previously stated, "The ESe is specifically made for equine, however, I am told that in areas heavily populated with cattle, some vets give MuSe or BoSe to equine.

Over the years it has come to my attention that fewer and fewer veterinarians are carrying the ESe and have been suggesting their clients give BoSe. Most veterinarians regularly carry BoSe as it can be used on calves, lambs and ewes.

I decided last year to again use our donkeys at *Pheasant Meadow Farm* as guinea pigs, so that I could give you accurate data on the use of injecting BoSe in newborn donkeys.

If you compare the ingredients of these two drugs you will find them to be exactly the same except that BoSe contains less selenium than ESe.

Each milliliter of these drugs contain:

ESe (Equine Vitamin E, Selenium) 2.5 milligrams selenium
50 milligrams vitamin E

BoSe (Bovine Vitamin E, Selenium) 1 milligrams selenium
50 milligrams vitamin E

As you can see, they both contain the exact same amount of vitamin E, however, the ESe contains two and one-half times more selenium than does the BoSe.

What we have been doing is injecting our newborns with *2-112* times the dose of BoSe than what we normally would have given using ESe.

What this boils down to is this: Instead of giving an average 20 pound newborn donkey foal 2/10th of one cc of ESe, we are now injecting them with 5/l0th (or 1/2 of one cc) of BoSe.

This dose of course gives the donkey more Vitamin E than they would normally get using the Equine Selenium/Vit E, however, the body quickly sheds off the excess amount of Vit E that it does not use. In fact, currently researchers at Oregon State University and elsewhere are continuing to examine the role of vitamin E in horse health, including disease prevention and therapy. Vitamin E generally is supplied through green forage, with little added to most concentrate feeds. Storage can destroy some of the vitamin E in foods. Currently, Linda Blythe, DVM, PhD, a professor of neurology at Oregon State is working on Equine degenerative myeloencephalopathy (EDM) a disease of the spinal cord and brain stem. Massive vitamin E supplements given to EDM foals can halt disease progression and often can return a horse to usefulness. Blythe points out that, "Vitamin E has been shown in people and horses to augment or make the immune system work better. Vitamin E may help the immune system do the final killing the parasite where antibiotics don't destroy all of it."

The bottom line is, I will continue to give my foals BoSe in place of ESe as in my opinion, I see even less foal-heat diarrhea in our foals than I did giving newborns ESe and the extra vitamin E may be the explanation for this.

Note: I have NOT done any studies on MuSe and cannot recommend giving it to donkeys. Our research has been in BoSe and ESe only. **However. I can tell you that MuSe contains 5 milligrams selenium which is WAY too much and should NOT be given to newborn donkeys.** MuSe is simply too easy to over-dose and should not be used.

As always, check with your veterinarian before making any changes in your own health care program as selenium can be toxic when overdosed. I also do not recommend selenium powder or pellets in donkeys as there is no way of accurately determining how much intake of these substances your donkeys are ingesting. Before giving selenium make certain that your hay and pasture is deficient of the mineral.

On the other hand......

Selenium Intoxication

Selenium intoxication can result from excessive supplementation with selenium compounds. Toxicosis can also occur where the selenium content of the soil is high. Soils that contain more than 0.5 ppm of selenium are considered potentially dangerous. Seleniferous soils are found in the Great Plains south to Texas and Mexico, west to California, and east to Alabama in the United States and the prairie provinces of Canada.

The toxicity of selenium depends on the chemical form of selenium ingested, the duration of intake, and other components of the diet. Organic selenium compounds found in plants are most toxic. Acute selenium intoxication occurs in animals accidentally given excessive amounts of selenium compounds and in animals that rapidly consume large amounts in plants. Acute toxicity results in respiratory distress, diarrhea, prostration and death. A single oral dose of 3.3 mg of selenium per kilogram of body weight can be lethal to horses.

Subacute or chronic selenium poisoning, also called "alkali disease", occurs when livestock consume feeds containing 5 to 40 ppm of selenium. Excess selenium can build up in the equine over a period of time causing various symptoms of hoof degeneration, lameness cirrhosis of the liver and others. Affected equine are often emaciated and lame and as the condition progresses, the hoof separates at the coronary band. Loss of mane and tail hair is often seen.

Lilli Olson of Montana has Ozzie dressed in his finest parade attire

Tetanus
A killer during all seasons

No animal on earth is immune to tetanus, including our beloved donkeys. Tetanus is one of the oldest and most serious diseases. Often associated with a penetrating wound, tetanus has also been linked to compound fractures, obstetric complications such as a retained placenta, infections after castrations, severe skin ulcerations and umbilical infections.

Equine are the most sensitive of all species, with the exception of humans. The most common cause of tetanus is a puncture wound to the hoof wall, resulting from a nail or other penetrating foreign body. If conditions are right, even the smallest wound can provide a point of origin for the life-threatening infection. This would include trimming the hoof too short and hitting the blood line. The infecting bacteria is unable to survive in normal tissue, therefore, dead tissue is a prerequisite for its development.

Signs

The incubation period for tetanus varies from several days to nearly four months. By the time the donkey develops tetanus, the injury through which the bacteria have entered may be completely healed.

Early signs of infection include lock-jaw where attempts to eat and drink result in excessive salivation and food and water often leak from the nostrils. He is usually unable to chew. Another early sign is stiffness involving muscles of the hindlimbs. After 24 hours, additional signs become more noticeable. The animal may become hypersensitive and may go into intermittent spasms. The legs are usually extended stiffly, with his neck straight and head upward or even bent back toward his withers. The ears may be held at a rigid upright position.

The third eyelid may show prominently over the inside corner of the eye. The donkey may have an anxious facial expression. The nostrils are usually flared. The animal may show constipation and other signs of colic. Because of this, an early case of tetanus may be confused with a simple colic until further signs develop. Sweating is frequently seen with tetanus as is a rise in body temperature and heart rates are more rapid than normal. Extremely high temperatures - in excess of 106 usually occurs late in the course of the disease, when terminal brain damage has occurred.

Treatment

If the disease is caught early, large amount of tetanus antitoxin may or may not be of value in helping the animal recover, but it is worth the attempt. Your veterinarian will probably treat the donkey with antibiotics, usually penicillin or tetracyclines. He may also administer tranquilizers or muscle relaxants to help relieve the severe muscle spasms.

As with other diseases, nursing is of the utmost importance to the animal's recovery. Stress must be kept to a minimum for the tetanus patient in order to not elicit convulsions. An animal with tetanus should be confined to a quiet dark barn with plenty of bedding. Feed and water should be placed high enough where the animal can reach it without lowering its head. If the donkey will not eat, your vet may have to feed him via stomach tube.

Approximately 70% of the equine affected with tetanus die and those who recover take 3 to 6 weeks of careful - and expensive - treatment and nursing before they recover.

Prevention

Tetanus is easily prevented with an annual vaccination and booster program. Yes, it is confusing!

We prevent the disease with "toxoid"
and treat the disease with "antitoxin".

If you are giving it to a young donkey or one who has not been immunized previously, he will initially need two injections, two to four weeks apart, depending on the vaccine. Follow the instructions on the label. The first injection is usually given at 2 to 4 months of age with the second dose two weeks later. Give a third dose six to nine months after that. Then, he gets an annual booster after that. Considering a donkey or horse can die from tetanus, it's cheap insurance against this possibility.

A donkey who has never had any tetanus toxoid is usually given a product called tetanus antitoxin as a part of wound treatment. Instead of stimulating the animal to produce his own immune antibodies, this merely puts some into his body, giving him instant protection against the disease.

Jennets should have a booster dose of tetanus toxoid four to eight weeks before they foal. This gives the animal a durable immunity to protect her if she is injured or torn during foaling. It also boosts the antibodies against tetanus which are in the colostrum; these help to give the foal a good immunity for the first few months of his life. This is considered to be much more effective than giving antitoxin to the newborn foal.

Many veterinarians insist that if you are present for the birth of a foal and iodine the navel immediately after it breaks, there is no reason to give a tetanus antitoxin.

Harold and Ursula Kohrs of Alberta Canada have Eddie and Semour dressed for Mexican Day

Bladder Stone Removal in Miniature Donkey

Report from: Allendale Animal Hospital
P. Jeff Shivell Jr., V.M.D.
Kingsport, Tennessee

Hugh and Ann Alley called me about their donkey, Sonny Q, a twelve year old Sicilian jack. They had noticed that for a few days he would occasionally strain to urinate. I had recently had surgery and was not doing farm calls yet so they asked if I would dispense medication to treat Sonny Q. I dispensed some antibiotics to treat a urinary infection.

On October 21, Sonny Q was in a lot of pain and the Alleys called me again. It sounded like he may have colic. Sonny Q is small and very gentle so I went to see him. When I arrived he was dripping urine and was very uncomfortable. I gave him an injection for pain and passed a catheter into his urinary bladder and drained his urine. I felt an obstruction at the end of my catheter and there were small stones in the urine specimen I collected. The stone was too large to pass, so the decision was made to send Sonny Q to the veterinary hospital at the University of Tennessee.

Dr. Sam Meisler was in charge of Sonny Q's care and treatment at U.T. where they surgically removed a one and one-half inch calcium carbonate stone from his urinary bladder. The report from Dr. Meisler is enclosed.

Uroliths (urinary stones) are not very common in equines, and since we do not see very many Sicilian donkeys this was an unusual case with a happy resolution.

Report from: University of Tennessee
Sam D. Meisler, D.V.M.
College of Veterinary Medicine

Sonny Q, a male 12 year old Sicilian donkey, owned by the Alley family, presented to the University of Tennessee's College of Veterinary Medicine; he had been experiencing periodic bouts of abdominal pain and difficulty urinating. We performed a battery of initial diagnostic tests to determine what was causing these symptoms.
These tests included a few basic blood tests and a urine analysis. In his

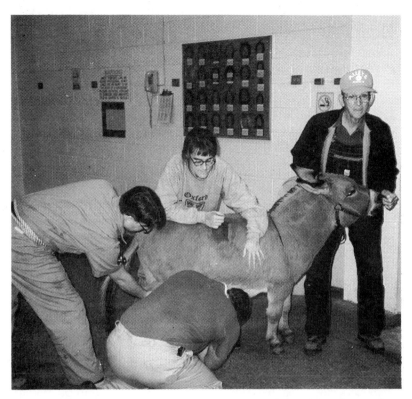

Dr. Steve Adair removing sutures with Hugh Alley holding Sonny Q

urine, we found microscopic crystals which were of calcium carbonate origin; some normal horses and donkeys will have crystals in their urine but usually of calcium oxalate origin. Also, in comparing his urine salts to those in his blood, we determined that he had undergone a small degree of kidney damage.

At this point, we suspected a possible kidney, bladder and urethral stone(s) based on his symptoms and the finding of abnormal crystals in his urine. Sonny Q was sedated lightly and a fiber optic endoscope was passed up his urethra all the way into his bladder - a total distance of about 70 centimeters. This enabled us to visualize the inside of his urethra and bladder. In the bladder, we found our answer: a one and a half inch diameter bladder stone spherical in shape with a rough, spiculated surface. In addition, Sonny Q had a bladder infection secondary to the stone formation and subsequent irritation of the bladder wall by the stone. It was determined by ultrasound that the kidneys were free of any stone formation but that the part of the kidney that fills with urine before it flows down to the bladder via the ureters was very swollen and dilated. It appeared that the bladder stone was partially blocking the urethers so back flow of urine had occurred into the kidneys.

Our only option at this point was to surgically remove the bladder stone under general anesthesia; this was done without significant complications. Sonny Q has since recovered fully and subsequent tests have revealed that his kidneys are also functioning normally. To prevent this from happening again, Sonny Q has been put on a low calcium diet (i.e., no alfalfa hay, etc.), a salt supplement to keep him urinating frequently, and antibiotics until his bladder infection clears up completely. At the Alley's farm, the water source for Sonny Q is not very far away from a limestone quarry. It was recommended that Sonny Q have a new water source just in case the lime content in the water had anything to do with his stone formation.

It is difficult to determine exactly what caused Sonny Q to form a stone in his bladder. Causes that have been implicated in other patients include chronic kidney disease, a deficiency of vitamin A, an excess of vitamin D, bladder or kidney infections, and an inherited tendency. Dietary calcium levels may also be part of the development of this disease.

Report from: Hugh & Ann Alley

Here is the report on Sonny Q and a picture at the University of Tennesse with Dr. Steve Adair removing sutures. Sonny Q sure made a hit with everyone at U.T. They had to move him up close to everyone so he could see what was going on. They put signs on his door: TV Star, Escape Artist and a cup for him to drink his coke from. Everyone loved him to death.

End Stage Liver Disease
In A Miniature Jennet

Jenny #529 was only 12 years old when severe liver degeneration left her owner with no option but to put her to sleep humanely. The exact cause of her shrunken, scarred liver will never be known, but its inability to function properly and keep up with the demands of the jenny and her unborn fetus cost mother and foal their lives.

Jenny #529 has been owned by Mr. Lamb for six years before she had shown any signs of illness. She had always produced strong healthy foals up until the 1991 foaling season, during which she failed to produce a foal but cycled normally. Mr. Lamb breeds his jennies on pasture, and he knew that #529 had been covered in the fall of 1991 after failing to produce but was unsure if she had conceived.

He called his field veterinarian when he noticed that the jenny was standing off by herself and acting lethargic. She was depressed, stood with her head down, and did not display her normally good appetite. Another donkey, a jack, had displayed similar symptoms and responded to treatment with the antibiotic Procaine Penicillin G intramuscularly, so #529 was also given antibiotics and vitamins over the course of five days.

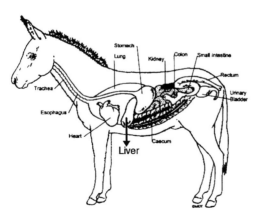

On week later, #529 was still depressed, not eating and inactive. She was referred to the University of Illinois College of Veterinary Medicine for further evaluation. Upon admission, a thorough history was taken and recorded by the veterinary student on duty, and a thorough physical examination was performed by both the student and the equine clinical resident. Jenny #529 was in fair overall condition with a normal temperature, increased heart rate, and normal respiratory rate. Her hair coat was rough, dull and shaggy. Examination of her mouth revealed gums that were pale, slightly purple and red tinged around her teeth. The skin over her neck and shoulder area was gently pinched to test her hydration status. Instead of readily bouncing back to its normal position, the "tented" area of skin stayed pinched for three to five seconds indicating moderate dehydration. A stethoscope was used to listen to her chest cavity and abdomen. There were harsh respiratory sounds and a general absence of the normal gut sounds that indicate a normally active gastrointestinal tract. A rectal examination confirmed that sluggish intestinal motility and a history of poor appetite had led to an empty abdominal cavity with only scant, hard dry feces. A nasogastric tube was passed through her nasal cavity into her abdomen, and water with electrolytes (to replace essential body salts) and mineral oil (to prevent impaction and provide lubrication to the GI tract) were administered. An additional finding during the rectal examination was that the jenny was pregnant with a three to four month old fetus.

A blood sample was drawn and submitted for a complete blood count, serum fibrinogen, total protein, and serum chemistries to be performed. Pending the results of the laboratory tests, an intravenous catheter was placed and systemic antibiotics and fluids were administered in order to rehydrate her and protect her against a bacterial infection. The jenny was monitored in intensive care so that her condition could be watched carefully and intravenous fluids could be given continuously.

The blood test results reflected her dehydrated state, and the serum chemistries revealed extensive inflammation and damage involving her liver. Several values for enzymes that are normally inside liver cells and released when the cells are injured and dead were four to five fold above their normal range. The degree of damage already suffered by the liver and the poor prognosis for recovery even with intensive medical care resulted in humane euthanasia for Jenny #529.

A necropsy was performed to further determine the extent and hopefully the cause of her liver disease. The results indicated an ongoing and active source of the inflammation that was present in the liver up until the time of death. When examined grossly, the liver was small, very firm, and grayish yellow. Sections of her liver showed that nearly all the liver cells were affected and that the cellular response would be consistent with a toxic insult, possibly due to mycotoxins or plant toxins. Unfortunately, no definitive cause could be determined for the severe liver damage from the necropsy results.

Hepatic disease occurs frequently in horses and donkeys as well. In general, however, the liver has a large functional reserve and 60% or more of the liver must be damaged before the animal will show any signs of liver failure. Liver disease has been reported in horses that are fed mycotoxin contaminated corn (moldy corn poisoning), and aflatoxin is the most likely specific mycotoxin to cause liver disease in the horse. In some parts of the world, horses grazing alsike clover or klein grass may also sporadically develop liver disease. Clogging of the vein that drains blood from the intestinal tract into the liver and resultant liver failure has been seen in a foal grazing on fescue pasture. In certain areas, the ingestion of plants that contain pyrrolizidine alkaloids is the most common cause of liver failure. Plants that contain this toxic principle include Amsinckia, also called tarweed, Senecio, also known as groundsel, ragwort, fireweed, and Crotalaria, whose common name is rattlebox or rattlepod. Consumption of these plants most commonly occurs through the ingestion of contaminated hay, especially spring cut alfalfa and alfalfa cubes. The clinical signs are often shown within six months following ingestion of the toxic plant.

In addition to these toxic causes of liver damage, systemic diseases such as cancer, abscesses, and diseases of the pancreas can also be involved. Even gastrointestinal diseases such as colic associated with obstruction of the large colon, or obstruction of the bile duct can have serious consequences on the liver. Other causes of liver disease include foals with a congenital infection of herpesvirus type 1, serum hepatitis from the administration of an equine origin biological, and Tyzzer disease in foals from the systemic infection with the bacteria *Bacillus piliformis.*

The clinical signs from liver disease without liver failure can be undetectable unless associated with other systemic failures. Once a substantial amount of the liver is affected and failure occurs, clinical signs can be shown and usually involve the central nervous system. Affected animals are depressed, and they may walk and circle uncontrollably. Incoordination, excessive yawning, head pressing, seizures, and coma may also be seen. Mild colic, fever, jaundice, and progressive weight loss occur in some cases. The diagnosis is usually made by finding abnormally high serum liver enzymes through blood testing. Additional information can be acquired through the use of ultrasonic imaging and liver biopsy.

The therapy for liver disease and failure is primarily supportive, aimed at maintaining the animal's hydration, acid-base status, and blood glucose (which is usually low). Antibiotic therapy may be instituted if a bacterial cause is suspected. The workload of the liver can be decreased by dietary management. During the recovery of animals from hepatitis and for the life of animals with chronic liver disease and permanent impairment, it is important to provide a diet high in energy. A reasonable diet includes one part beet pulp with one quarter to one-half part cracked corn mixed with molasses and provided in four to six small meals per day, up to a total of 10 to 15 pounds for a 500 pound animal. Vitamin supplementation with vitamins B1 and K should be done weekly. The grazing of mixed grasses can be permitted, but exposure to sunlight should be minimized due to the possibility of photosensitization.

While some individuals may be supported medically and recover from liver damage, all too often the results are like Jenny #529. The insidious nature and silent progress of liver disease can render its victims beyond help before the diagnosis is made. Liver disease takes its toll in the equine and donkey world each year, and through continuing research, we hope to more fully understand the various causes of the disease and develop more sensitive tests for detection and prognosis. It was Jenny #529's owner, Mr. Paul Lamb's hope that by writing this article, her death and the loss of her unborn foal could at least serve to further the knowledge about liver disease in the miniature donkey among the breeders and enthusiasts of this wonderful animal.

Reference: Khristina Kirkland, DVM

Treating the Open Wound

Finding one of your donkeys injured can cause immediate alarm but knowing what to do can eliminate serious problems later on. A fresh open wound needs immediate treatment to give it a better chance of healing without scarring.

Most people can treat superficial or minor wounds by themselves but cuts that involve torn muscles or tendons require a veterinarian. You must remember that **if a wound needs to be sutured, it must be done within the first six hours.** Usually after six hours, the exposed tissue has died and the wound has become contaminated.

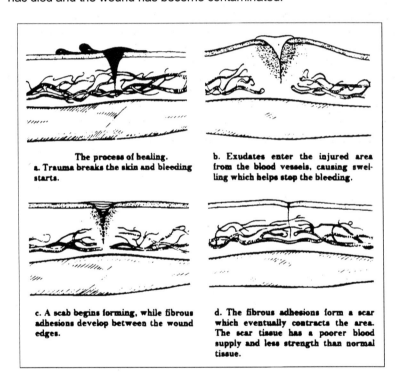

The process of healing.
a. Trauma breaks the skin and bleeding starts.

b. Exudates enter the injured area from the blood vessels, causing swelling which helps stop the bleeding.

c. A scab begins forming, while fibrous adhesions develop between the wound edges.

d. The fibrous adhesions form a scar which eventually contracts the area. The scar tissue has a poorer blood supply and less strength than normal tissue.

With most cuts the owner should give the donkey a tetanus toxoid, especially if it has been more than six months since the donkey has had one. If the donkey has not had any prior vaccination, it should be given a tetanus antitoxin. A simple scrape may not require a vaccination, however, it is better to be safe than sorry.

Cleaning the wound is very important. If you feel the wound will need to be sutured, you should only clean it with water and bandage it while waiting for the vet. Putting antibiotics on may interfere with the vet's examination of the site. If you don't feel sutures will be necessary, you can apply a topical antibacterial spray or cream to combat infection.

Sometimes it is better not to wrap a bandage around a wound especially if it is on a leg. The bandage can rub the wound preventing a protective scab from forming and actually rub dirt and bacteria further into it.

Hydrogen peroxide is a good cleanser for a deep wound. Hydrogen peroxide will oxygenate the wound and keep anaerobic bacteria from entering the site. An antibacterial cream or spray should also be used.

Sutures are usually left in place from 12 to 14 days. Severe wounds can take as long as six months to heal depending on where they are. Wounds on a joint usually take longer because of continuous movement. In this case, the donkey may have to be stalled to deter movement so granulation tissue can form and the wound can begin to heal.

Patience and follow-up care are very important for any type of wound. If you have a bad wound, don't just treat it for a few days then think you can forget about it. Be sure the wound is completely healed before discontinuing treatment.

Identifying the Cause of Weight Loss

CAUSES OF WEIGHT LOSS:

Inadequate Intake or Utilization of Feed:

1. inadequate amount of feed
2. dental problems
3. impaired prehension, chewing or swallowing
4. feed refusal
5. poor feed quality
6. protein losing enteropathies and malabsorption syndromes
7. competition for food with other animals

Increased Metabolism or Need for Calories:

1. increased exercise
2. decrease ambient temperature
3. lactation
4. stress from illness, injury, or cancer
5. equine infectious anemia

Organ Dysfunction: chronic heart, kidney or liver failure

DIAGNOSIS

The diagnosis begins with an examination for the more common causes of weight loss: management problems. This would include reviewing the deworming program, examining the feed and the quantity fed, and the conditions under which the animal is fed. If no cause for the weight loss can be identified then the physical and laboratory work up should be performed.

The animal should be examined to rule out other abnormalities other than weight loss: liver disease, cancer, kidney failure, infection, inflammatory disease and heart problems. Gross fecal examination for diarrhea or sand should be done, and rectal palpation is indicated if the initial exam and history do not point to an obvious reason for the weight loss.

Laboratory tests that may help identify the cause include complete blood count, fibrinogen, blood chemistry panel, Coggins test and fecal flotation.

Additional tests may include fecal sedimentation for sand, fecal occult blood, urinalysis, serum electrophoresis, cytologic exam of peritoneal fluid, and gastrointestinal absorption tests. The results of these tests should indicate whether further tests are needed.

Donkey Weight Condition Chart
Drawings Copyright © 1998 MDT Magazine

Very Poor Condition

Sunken rump with skin tight over bones. Prominent backbone and ewe neck. Dull Coat

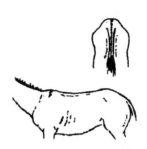

Poor Condition

Sunken rump, ribs visible, backbone shows, prominent hips.

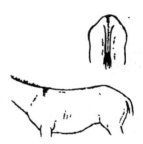

Moderate Condition

Skin flattens out on either side of top of rump, neck narrow, coat only slightly shines

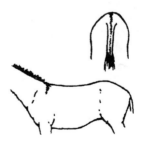

Good Condition

Nice rounded rump, ribs
covered, neck firm but
no fat, shiny coat

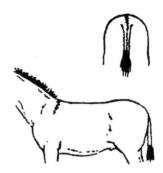

Fat Condition

Well rounded rump with
slight dip along
backbone, slight
fat roll on neck.

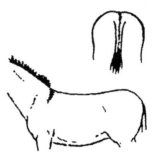

Very Fat Condition

Bulges of fat appear
around rump, deep
gutter along back bone
and over rump,
breast bone covered
in fat, thick fat roll
on neck.

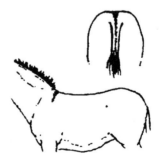

Laminitis (Founder)

What is it?

Laminitis is the inflammation of the sensitive laminae of the hooves. The sensitive laminae are fine, leaf-like filaments which lie between the pedal bone inside the hoof and the insensitive laminae which form the wall of the hoof. The laminae are abundantly supplied with nerves and blood vessels and they form an important role in the rather complicated vascular system of the hooves and lower limbs and in transferring the weight of the animal from the pedal bone onto the wall of the hoof.

What happens when the laminae become inflamed?

The inflamed laminae swell and exude a blood stained fluid which causes congestion so that blood can no longer flow away from the feet. This causes increased pressure in the hoof and, because of its rigid nature, extreme pain.

The laminae separate and break down and often an infection can occur. Healthy laminae hold the pedal bone in its correct position inside the hoof but when they are damaged the pedal bone (coffin bone) can rotate downwards and press on the sole of the foot. In severe cases the pedal bone can actually penetrate and protrude through the sole.

What causes laminitis?

Laminitis is thought to be caused by an allergy and there are several possible triggers.

1. Diet. Over zealous feeding. Overweight and obese donkeys are extremely at risk. Donkeys do very nicely on high fiber, low protein diets and feed which is too rich or too much is very unhealthy. If your donkey is overweight, put him on a (very slow) diet. Lock him in a bare yard for part of the day until he is out of danger.

2. A sudden engorgement of gain or over rich feed. This could be a flush of spring grass, a sudden change of diet, moldy feed and sure disaster, your donkey breaking into a silage shed.

3 A stressful situation such as traveling, ill health, excessive work.

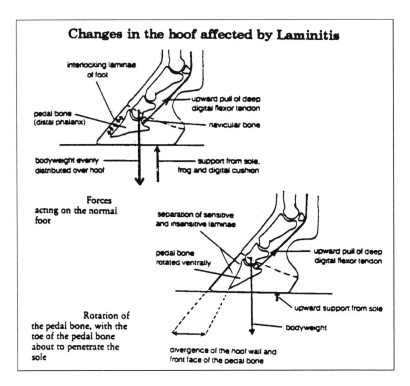

Changes in the hoof affected by Laminitis

interlocking laminae of foot

upward pull of deep digital flexor tendon

pedal bone (distal phalanx)

navicular bone

bodyweight evenly distributed over hoof

support from sole, frog and digital cushion

Forces acting on the normal foot

separation of sensitive and insensitive laminae

pedal bone rotated ventrally

upward pull of deep digital flexor tendon

upward support from sole

Rotation of the pedal bone, with the toe of the pedal bone about to penetrate the sole

bodyweight

divergence of the hoof wall and front face of the pedal bone

Signs of laminitis

The donkey will be very lame and reluctant to move. It is unusual for only one foot to be affected.

The hoof will be hot to touch.

The coronet will be inflamed and swollen.

The donkey will try to take the weight off his hooves by standing on his heels. His stance will appear unnatural with his legs either stretched as far as possible in front or behind, or bunched up under his body.

In chronic cases the donkey will appear normal but have difficulty walking up hills. Some donkeys seek water to cool their feet.

Treatment

X-rays by your veterinarian to determine how much the coffin bone has turned to determine how aggressive treatment will be.

Drugs to relieve the pressure, inflammation, congestion and pain.

Gentle exercise to stimulate the circulation as soon as the pain is sufficiently relieved.

Standing in cold water or hosing the legs and feet.

Acupuncture and laser treatment to stimulate the healing process.

Careful trimming of the feet to restore the normal shape. In severe cases extensive removal of the wall and a corrective shoe might be necessary.

Biotin to promote growth of the hoof.

Corrective trimming usually involves removing the toe and lowering the heel

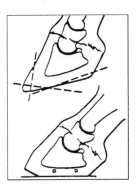

Conclusion

Is there life after laminitis? If chronic or severe, maybe not. Once the laminae have been damaged, the original strength is never restored and the donkey is apt to founder again. It is a very painful condition. Permanent deformation of the hooves is likely to occur and they will be more susceptible to separation and seedy toe. The treatment of acute laminitis is very time consuming and demanding on the owner of the donkey.

Prevention is therefore so much easier than treatment. If your donkey is overweight, put him on a strict – but very slow - diet now.

Skin Problems

Treating the most common skin ailments

Equine are subject to some 50 primary skin diseases and dozens more secondary ones. Fortunately, only a handful are quite common and their signs offer clues to a condition's identity and solution. There is a single rule of thumb to follow: all bumps emanate from *within* the skin, while scurf, flakes, crusts, hairless patches and weeping secretions point to trouble *on* the surface.

Inside The Skin

Of all the skin conditions your donkey is likely to contract, the majority will be of the bump variety and the most common will be from *insect bites*. Some donkeys are very sensitive to fly and mosquito bites. The best treatment is preventive. If you find your donkey very sensitive to insect bites, apply a daily fly repellent each morning - and evening if you are in an area with a high population of mosquitoes.

A second type of bump you may detect is the result of an allergic reaction. Known as *hives* these groups of various sized bumps arise when the donkeys internal defense system produces antibodies against a particular ingredient. Hives are rarely life threatening unless there is a great amount of swelling in the throat area.

Two rough and hairless bumps that appear in horses and donkeys quite frequently are *warts* and *sarcoids*. Slow growing and covered with abnormal skin, both are the result of viral tumors. Warts appear mostly on the muzzles of weanling donkeys and usually disappear within a year but can take up to two years. Sarcoids are difficult to treat and frequently reappear after treatment. Some sarcoids can be removed by surgery although cryosurgery (freezing) is much more effective.

Slightly scaly bumpy areas followed by hair loss can be caused by internal parasites. The areas can trigger furious itching by the donkey and can make them very miserable. They can be treated by deworming your donkey with ivermectin. Your vet may want to prescribe some sort of steroid treatment to ease the itching which could cause open sores on the donkey.

On Top Of The Skin

Itchy, thick patches with hair loss are usually indicative of **sweet itch** seen on the shoulders, withers, rump and tail. The condition appears when insect saliva causes an allergic reaction on the donkey's hide. A donkey will rub himself raw to relieve the itching. Insecticides help along with corticosteroid preparations but the donkey may have to be sheltered in a dark barn during the day until the condition improves.

During winter months, your donkey may become infected with **lice**. Lice can be contacted from donkeys being sheltered near chickens or from birds building their nests in barns and stalls. Lice mainly affect donkeys who still have their heavy thick winter coats in the winter and early spring. **Farnam** puts out an excellent louse powder. Cover the entire donkey with it and again in two weeks to kill lice eggs that are hatching.

A condition called **scratches** is similar to chapped hands in people. It first starts as scabbing in the back of the donkey's pasterns and left untreated can become infected and extremely painful. Treatment usually means washing the area, trimming the long hair around the area and treating with antibacterial ointment. You must also keep the donkey in a clean dry environment to help healing. If a donkey is very prone to this condition, you may well want to apply antibacterial ointment on a weekly basis around the area.

A condition called **rainrot** is very common in Miniature Donkeys. It affects donkeys on the back causing them to lose hair and have raw patches of skin appear. It is caused by donkeys standing out in too much wet weather. All donkeys should have shelter from rain, snow and wind and since they truly dislike all of the above weather elements, it could be considered a form of abuse by making them stand out in it.

Rain that mixes with dirt under heavy coats causes bacteria which causes scabbing and infection. The first step in treatment is to keep the donkey dry at all times. Brush the donkey and remove the crusts where possible. Dab on mild iodine antiseptic, or in summer months you can wash the entire donkey with an iodine shampoo.

Rainrot or Rain Scald

Note: Antifungal preparations are ineffective in the treatment of rain rot since this is a bacterial, <u>not</u> a fungal disease. Intramuscular injections of penicillin may be necessary to clear up more serious cases. Healing usually takes three to four weeks however, the signs of the condition - rough hair coat - can be seen for up to three months.

Another surface ailment that we get loads of phone calls on every spring is **dew poisoning.** On donkeys, it normally appears on the muzzle and is caused by clover and other different types of weeds and grasses that eject a juice when dew falls on them in the early morning hours during the spring. The donkey's entire muzzle will be coated in crusts. Veterinarians will tell you that you can treat it and it will clear up or you cannot treat it and it will clear up. It is so severe on some donkeys that the skin will crack and weep which requires a twice daily treatment of ointment. Most vets recommend that you use a product called **A & D Ointment** applied to the muzzle. The condition usually disappears in two weeks.

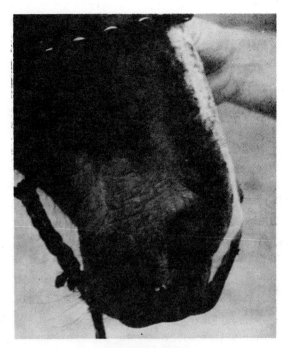

Dew Poisoning

We always get many calls during the spring regarding mysterious skin conditions. If nothing you do for your donkey seems to help, have your veterinarian take a tiny skin graft of the condition and he can have it analyzed to find exactly what is going on.

Ringworm:
It isn't even a worm, but this condition can attack a whole herd of donkeys

Ringworm is caused by a fungus and is probably the most commonly seen of the skin conditions cause by fungal infections.

Ringworm is characterized by the following signs:

1. intense itching (usually but not always)
2. small, rounded lesions which spread in circular patterns
3. inflammation of the skin accompanied by breaking or shedding of the hair in affected areas.

Ringworm appears as hairless patches. The patches may be scaly or they may be covered with crusts. If the scabs are removed, the area underneath may be red and raw and may also contain pus. Spots are often first seen on the head and neck. From there, they may spread until they appear all over the body.

The incubation period for ringworm is usually one to four weeks, but may be as little as four days. Dirty, warm, damp stables encourage ringworm infection. Sun and fresh air help to prevent the spread, but do not necessarily kill the infection once it starts on a donkey's skin. Animals which have been treated excessively with antibiotics may have a lowered resistance to ringworm. Nutritional deficiencies will make the animal more likely to get ringworm. Donkeys may also be infected by other animals, for example, cattle and cats, and by contaminated halters or grooming tools. Young donkeys are particularly at risk and may contract infection during transportation, at shows or in sale rings. It is common for such donkeys to develop the initial signs of ringworm within two weeks of such events.

Treatment of ringworm

Good nutrition helps to get the skin into condition to fight off the fungus. If the diet is lacking in vitamin A, you may need to give a feed supplement to the donkey. This can be common in northern states.

Strong (7%) tincture of iodine should be rubbed into all of the ringworm spots, using a rough piece of cloth to help remove the scabs and assure that the iodine reaches the skin. Be extremely careful not to drip it into the donkey's eyes. Another cure which works well for ringworm is household beach, such as Clorox, diluted half-and-half with water and dabbed onto the lesions. There are also commercial preparations for ringworm sold in feed and equine supply stores, however, they do not necessarily work any better, just cost more.

If the donkey has large parts of his body covered with ringworm, treat the bare spots with iodine and the spaces between that still have some hair with the clorox/water mixture. Don't expect to see results immediately as it may take three or four weeks until the hair grows in.

Ringworm is contagious to humans, so normal sanitary precautions should be taken. Use rubber gloves when working with the donkey. Wash all towels, bandages and other washable materials which have had contact with the donkey in hot water with detergent and bleach. Soak all brushes, combs, halters and lead ropes in 10% bleach solution for several hours, rinse well, then put out in the sun to dry. If you catch the ringworm yourself, contact your doctor (your people doctor, not your veterinarian!).

The following tables will serve as an aid in the diagnosis of skin diseases

Itchy Skin Disorders

Insect Bites	A common cause of itching in fly season. Bumps, blisters, scabs, crusty areas and occasional hair loss occur where insects bites.
Queensland Itch	Common insect bite allergy in equine caused by knats. Crusts and scabs. Intense itching with hair broken and rubbed off.
Ventral Midline Dermatitis	Caused by the migrating phase of hair-like worm transmitted by knats. Produces moist, crusty, shallow ulcerations, typically centered along the midline on the under surface of the abdomen but sometimes on the face. Hair is lost around ulcerations.
Hives	Round raised wheels scattered all over the body with hair sticking out in patches. Swelling of the face or eyelids can occur. Usually caused by inhaled allergens; occasionally by allergens in feed.
Irritant Contact Dermatitis	Red bumps with crusting and hair loss. Found around the muzzle, feet, legs and other areas of irritants. Healed skin may turn white.
Mange	An intensely itchy disorder caused by mites. Red lumps, followed by scabs, crusts and patches of hair loss are found all over body but especially on poll, mane, tail and legs. Mites in ear canal cause head-shaking.
Photosensitivity	Requires exposure to sunlight. Redness, swelling and weeping of serum. Outer skin may peel as in sunburn.
Summer Sores	Caused by the larvae of stomach worms deposition in open wounds and sores. Occurs only in fly season. Mild wound suddenly enlarges and becomes covered with reddish-yellow tissue and bleeds easily.
Pinworms	Intense itching and tail rubbing primarily in weanlings and young donkeys. "Ratty" look to tail.

Disorders In Which Hair Is Lost

Patchy Shedding	Normal type of shedding. Produces bare patches up to 10" in diameter. Skin is healthy, hair grows back in e weeks. Many donkeys begin their shedding process with two bare spots on the rump on either side of the tailbone. This is normal.
Ringworm	Usually occurs in fall and winter. Scaly, crusty or red circular patches with central hair loss are typical. May see matted clumps of hair which fall out easily. Highly contagious.
Seborrhea	A flaky, scaly condition which looks like dandruff. Bare circular patches occur where crusts peel off.
Rain Scald (Rainrot)	Occurs in rainy weather. Tufts of matted hair. Tufts come off leaving bare patches. Skin sometimes becomes secondarily infected.
Lymphosarcoma	A subcutaneous mass or nodule with overlying skin ulceration and loss of hair.

Skin Infections

Abscess	Painful, hot inflamed skin or pockets of pus beneath the skin. Look for an underlying cause (foreign body, puncture wound, etc.) Abscess beneath jaw suggests strangles
Furunculosis	A deep-seated hair-pore infection with draining sinus tracts to the skin.
Tail Pyoderma	Abscesses that occur on the skin of the tail from rubbing or biting self. Look for underlying itchy skin problem such as tail mites or pinworms.
Ulcerative Lymphangitis	Begins as wound infection with swelling of the leg and appearance of abscesses long the lymphatic channels. The abscesses open and drain pus. Infectious.
Malignant Edema	Begins in dirty wounds around legs and face. A soft, hot painful swelling that progresses rapidly. Infectious.
Sporotrichosis	A draining sore or ulcer at the site of a puncture wound, usually the leg. Discharge pus and heals slowly. Caused by a fungus.
Grease Heel	An infection at the back of the fetlocks and/or heels. Characterized by a greasy exudate that mats the hair. Grape-like clusters may appear.

Lumps, Bumps and Growths on or Beneath the Skin

Warts	Smooth raised flesh-colored bumps on the muzzle and lips of young donkeys. Usually disappear in 3 months but can take up to one year.
Sarcoid	The most common tumor in equine. Cauliflower, or red firm growths found anywhere on the body. All ages affected. Cryosurgery (freezing) works better on donkeys than surgery.
Tender Knots	Frequently found at the site of a shot or vaccination. Often painful. No treatment usually necessary
Cattle Grubs	Painful nodules beneath the skin, found at withers, neck and back. May have a breathing hole to the skin.
Squamous Cell Carcinoma	Hard flat or ulcerating growth found on older equine, especially light pigmented breeds. Most common on face and genitalia.
Melanoma	Dark brown nodular growth, usually on underside of tail, sometimes on vulva, anus or mouth.
Phycomycosis	Deep seated fungus infection which often occurs at the site of a cut, usually on the legs. Fast growing bulbous mass of grayish-pink tissue which discharges infected material.

Botulism

What is botulism?

Botulism is a form of food poisoning caused by the bacterium, Clostridium botulinum, commonly found in the soil and in the environment of decaying plant or animal matter. The toxins formed by these bacteria are the most potent poisons known.

What is the effect of Cl. Botulinum?

Botulism toxins act on the peripheral nervous system by preventing transmission of nervous impulses, thus causing a limp paralysis. It is not certain if the toxins prevent the release of a transmission chemical at the nerve junctions or if they bind with it, preventing transmission of the nerve impulses.

What is the source of infection for Cl. Botulinum?

The environment is most frequently present in decaying plant matter or animal tissue of dead or live animals. On open range, animal carcasses may be chewed or eaten by animals with phosphorus or protein deficiencies. An animal carcass may have large numbers of Cl. Botulinum in it. Horses or donkeys may also be fed hay or grain contaminated by dead rats or other animals. The conditions for botulism is favorable for mold growth, so that incriminated hay or grain may also be visibly moldy. Poorly maintained stock tanks are also a source of infection.

What are the signs of botulism?

Botulism occurs most commonly in foals 2 to 8 weeks, but up to 8 months of age. Affected foals are often found laying on their side unable to rise or occasionally dead. If seen earlier, they may lie down more than normal and usually with their head laying on the ground. It may be difficult for them to walk, usually dragging their legs. It is difficult for them to swallow so often you'll see milk dripping from their mouths. Up to 90% of foals affected die.

In adults, following access to the toxic material, the poisoned animal may develop signs within three to seven days. Signs include lack of fever and progressive difficulty in biting, chewing and swallowing food. The tongue and pharynx become completely paralyzed so that swallowing is impossible. Generalized weakness, depression, muscle tremors, and a reluctance to move. Overall paralysis follows but death results from paralysis of the respiratory muscles. Some animals die quickly without prior signs of illness, others may not eat or drink for a day or two.

Botulism may be mistaken for equine encephalomyelitis or ragwort poisoning. In equine, botulism is rather rare, but it is usually fatal. *(We at MDT have heard of two possible cases of botulism in donkeys in the past.)*

How is it diagnosed?

A presumptive diagnosis of botulism can be made upon finding clostridium botulinum spores in colonic contents, feed, wounds, or the feces. Spores can be found in the feces of 20 to 30% of affected adults and about 80% of affected foals, whereas they are rarely present in non-affected equine.

What is the treatment for botulism?

General supportive treatment is indicated, but no antitoxin has been found that is economically practical. Purgatives to remove toxic material may be administered and animals may be fed by stomach tube. Treatment is usually attempted in cases where the signs develop slowly and some hope for recovery may be held.

Can botulism be prevented?

The best method of preventing botulism lies in careful inspection of hay and grain and proper storage conditions. Patrol of range areas to remove dead animals can prevent accidental poisoning of water sources. *(We know of a girl who lost her horse due to botulism after it drank from a puddle in the pasture, which contained a deal bird.)*

Vaccination is available from a veterinarian for the strain of Cl. Botulinum found in the area's soil. In areas and especially on farms where botulism has occurred, vaccination may be indicated but because it is uncommon otherwise, vaccination is not indicated. If you've had a case of botulism on your farm, you need to immediately find the source of it.

The Obese Donkey

It is very common is this country and Canada to see overweight donkeys. It is rarely encountered in other countries where donkeys are used as work animals. The usual site for a large fat deposit in donkeys is the neck, otherwise referred to as a fat *roll*. You'll also see fat deposits around the buttocks and abdomen.

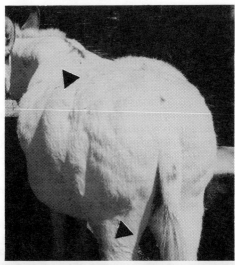

In some horse breeds, fat is a very common site in halter classes. Most notorious are Quarter Horse and Appaloosa horse shows. Unfortunately the desire for a 50 cent ribbon overrides the health of the horse. But then again, excessive fat can hide faults so judges should be giving preference to the horse in good weight and not the horse that borders on obesity.

Excess fat in older donkeys results in stress with a capital "S". The heart has to work harder in order to pump blood through the added bulk. Lungs also function overtime to move oxygen through the extra body mass and fat also has an affect on the kidneys. Feet are called on to carry the extra weight. Keep in mind how small donkey's feet are compared to their even normal weight.

Obesity causes a general lack of well-being in the donkey just as it does in humans. The donkey doesn't feel as well as he should. Overweight animals have problems with anesthesia and surgery if they are ever sick or injured. Fat holds anesthetic agents, thus it takes a greater quantity of the drug to anesthetize an overweight animal. This leaves a greater quantity of anesthetic in the body to be detoxified. The animal is down longer and has less chance for recovery. There is a greater probability of complications. Surgery itself is more complicated due to fat in the surgical area.

**Broken Crest
(fat roll hanging on neck)**

Jennets who are too fat often do not come into heat properly or may not cycle at all. It is a known fact that fat jennets may take four or five months longer to conceive than a jennet in good weight. Breeding jacks who are overweight may show lessened interest in breeding due to being overweight and in poor physical condition. Extra fat in the scrotum insulates the testicles and raises their temperature, often leading to lessened fertility and viability of the sperm.

Hyperlipaemia is clinically described as follows: An abnormally high concentration of lipids (fats), in the blood. This is a very dangerous disease and there have been several confirmed cases of death due to Hyperlipaemia in Miniature Donkeys.

Prevention is better than cure and it is preferable to control a donkey's diet before it becomes overweight than to have to embark on a long, often unrewarding slimming regime. The fat crest on the neck is notoriously difficult to remove and it is possible to have an otherwise very thin donkey that has retained its fat neck.

Donkeys are 'easy keepers', meaning they utilize all their food very efficiently. Few Miniature Donkeys are worked in this country with close to 90% being nothing more than outside pets. While you are feeding, those calories are turning into fat with little exercise to deplete them. Most people I talk to -- even the ones that complain about their donkeys being too *fat* - feed grain. We have covered this many times in MDT.

The majority of all Miniature Donkeys do not need grain. I am estimating that less than 50% of nursing jennets really need grain. Just because a jennet is pregnant does not mean that she automatically needs grain. A great deal of this depends on what type of pasture you have and what type of hay you are feeding.

If your donkey is too fat, cut out the grain completely. If you are feeding a mixed hay that has alfalfa in it, change to a lower calorie hay such a grass hay. Take your donkey for a walk once a day. It will make both you and him healthier.

The Death of... or the Euthanasia of...
One of our Beloved Pets
by Jim Ensten and Bonnie Gross

Jim

This article is not about "The Lighter Side of Miniature Donkeys." It deals with a tough, sobering subject that sooner or later affects all of us with our animals. Writing about the sober topic of death is a difficult task for me. I don't particularly enjoy writing a serious commentary on any subject. It is much easier hiding behind a mask of a little humor. Very few reports in today's modern magazines and periodicals have dealt with "death." The theme is just not politically correct, nowadays. The poets of a hundred years ago had no such problem. Poe, Shelley, Keats, Shakespeare, wrote and almost seemed fascinated with the concept. Death was an inescapable and an entirely natural aspect of reality. People seemed less given to suppose they would live forever then, than we are now. For they were reminded of the contrary every day. Doctors were few and medicines were herbalist. Old age meant fifty-ish, however, times have changed. So maybe you and I can look at death dispassionately for just a moment. Not a cold clinicians view, but a sensitive understanding of the eventual demise of our friends.

I spoke to many people about the loss of their companions. I decided not to refer to any specific incident, but to examine the common threads in their examples. Everyone was willing to talk about his or her particular occurrence. Most recalled every minute detail as though it had happened yesterday. Oddly, I found that children adjust to an animal's death easier than the adults. A simple "he has gone away" or "he is in heaven" placates the youngest. The realization of the finality of death comes with aging. Men, with their chink proof machismo armor, openly cry like babies when Old Duke is lowered into the ground. The women seem to adjust better and grieve quietly. The variety of pets ranged from mice and guinea pigs to dogs and equine, (yes, one was a donkey). "He was the best," "They broke the mold," "There will never be another as good as," "The kindest, the gentlest"; these are the verbal epitaphs usually lamented. "No more ___s, I just can't go through this again!" This is said immediately after a loss, but after an appropriate "grieving period." There appears to be enough love left in their hearts for a new friend.

Natural Death

We know it is going to happen, whether a gerbil with a life span of two or three years or a dog that expires after ten. When it happens, very few can keep the achy loneliness in check without support form family or friends. It is interesting that some people just can't deal with your loss. You ask for support, and get a cold "pull yourself together" rejection is an intuitive human's dread of death. A mask, a denial of the passage of time. "He was 15 years old"... in our grief, all too often there is a shutting down. A closing off of feelings, due to the very natural fear of loving and losing again.

Euthanasia

This is the toughest one of all. This animal is alive, and you have decided to end its life. It didn't die of "old age." It wasn't an accident, hit by a car and killed instantly. You have made "the" decision and will have to bear the guilt that you are going to kill this animal. You now have a tiny glimpse of the sorrow people have, when agonizingly, they "pull the plug" in a hospital. You do a lot of soul searching. You rationalize, "put him out of his misery", "for his own good", "he'll be better off". Yes, I have said them all! You mean of course, "I can't cope with this any longer, I have to call for help." The help you look for is usually the veterinarian. You look to him for two reasons: One, to confirm, relieve, or absolve yourself of "your" diagnosis, and second, to handle the "messy" business. The veterinarian is usually highly skilled in handling both aspects of your dilemma. The veterinarians, I know, are warm, caring, and compassionate people. They deal with animals' lives from the alpha to the omega. Thus, this aspect of their profession goes with the territory. He is your strongest psychological ally at this time. He will lift the heavy weight from your shoulders, probably placing it upon his own, for he has emotions also.

This is a traumatic time in our life. We all react a little differently. We usually build a monument. Some make it out of a stone and mark a grave. Others keep a photo or a small lock of hair. Those less demonstrative can carry a lump in the throat and a painful memory for weeks. I have a letter written form a friend from the fairgrounds race track in New Orleans, upon the euthanasia death of his fine colt, that he raised from a bottle. ...."Max stood quietly behind the barn... and as if raising a building with dynamite, it hangs for a moment in its original magnificence, then lists a little, and finally crashes to the ground with incredible violence." This letter was his ... Max's monument.

From an Appalachian folk song... Old Blue... Remember this one...
Mike...

When Old Blue died,
He died so hard.
It shook the ground
In my back yard....
So I dug his grave
With a silver spade
And lowered him down
On a golden chain.

Bonnie

I've had my share of phone calls over the years from people who have
just lost a donkey. Many times it is the loss of a newborn foal. Not an
animal that they grew to love, or watched a personality develop, but what
saddens them is that they never got the chance to love this animal.
Others have been adult animals with unexplained deaths and yet others
have been donkeys they loved but could not afford the expensive care or
were given little hope of survival.

When dealing with an illness or injury there are two things we generally
follow. One is our heart, the other is the knowledge and advice of a
trusted veterinarian. What are the chances of recovery? Will the animal
get progressively worse and be subjected to a great deal of pain? If the
animal is repairable, how much will it cost. Can you not only afford the
expense, if you work, can you take the time off work to properly care for
the animal? What are you going to have if you save the animal? How
about a jennet that can no longer be bred or a jack who cannot breed
because of a leg injury. Donkeys are very very inexpensive animals to
maintain so keeping one as a pet will not be a financial burden to anyone.
What kind of patient is the donkey. A donkey that has spent most of his
life in a field and is not used to much human attention can be very difficult
to treat - and after the daily fight - will the donkey be for the worse or for
the better.

"Donkey People" are not like "Horse People." I believe we have a closer
bond to our animals. MDT surveys show that 90% of donkey owners do
not show their donkeys and have no desire to show their donkeys. Most
owners, have their donkeys just to love for they are as much of a

companion as are dogs. This makes it very difficult for us when *the time comes.*

The loss of a newborn foal can be very difficult, especially after a year anticipation. Through the years, and after talking with many, many people, I have determined that donkeys will carry a defective foal much longer than a horse will - and sometimes to full term. Horse mares will usually abort a defective foal before three months gestation and in most cases the fetus is never found. Unfortunately, donkey jennets just don't want to give that baby up. So if you have a late term abortion, or a stillborn, consider that it was not a viable foal to begin with, let your heart heal and begin to look forward to the next baby.

Ashley and A.J. Schappacher of Ohio with their friend Bandit

Chapter 6

Vaccinations and Medication

The *Ins* & *Outs* of Antibiotics

Antibiotics are a class of drugs extracted from cultures of certain soil and airborne molds. Their mode of action varies from one type to another. Some, like penicillin, actually kill the bacteria, while others merely slow them down so that the body's defenses can attack and kill them more readily.

Here are two important rules for antibiotic treatment:

RULE #1 - Always give an adequate dosage
of whatever drug you are using.

Using less than this amount only gets rid of part of the bacteria, allowing the infection to continue, and is likely to leave the rest of the bacteria in better shape than ever, possibly even resistant to the drug. You may end up having to switch to another drug to get the desired effect, which costs both extra time and money, and leaves the possibility that the bacteria may gain enough resistance to overwhelm the animal and kill him. ALWAYS use the recommended amount of antibiotics. If you aren't getting the result you think you should, check with your veterinarian about a possible change to another antibiotic or a change in dosage.

RULE #2 - Anything worth treating is worth
treating for at least three days.

If you give only one or two injections, there is a good chance that the harmful bacterial haven't been killed off, and the ones which survive the treatment may have become resistant to the drug. Then you really DO have a problem. So, if you feel that you only need a day or two of treatment, don't bother to give antibiotics at all. The animal will get well without them. Then, you don't help build up resistant bacteria which will cause problems later. Often it is necessary to treat for two or three days *beyond* the time when the animal appears well. This allows the drug to finish getting rid of the bacteria. Follow your vet's advice on how long to treat.

One of the first questions to ask is if the animal really *needs* antibiotics. If a virus is causing the problem and there are no complications from accompanying bacteria, using an antibiotic will do no good, and may do harm.

The next question is **which** antibiotic to use. Some are more effective than others for a given infection. This even varies from one area of the country to another. Often, a drug which is effective against one type of bacteria in one area will be ineffective against it elsewhere. It is usually best to rely on your veterinarian's advice on antibiotic selection. Do not pour penicillin or another antibiotic into an animal on a random basis and expect good results.

Do not give two antibiotics at the same time unless instructed to do so by your veterinarian. Some combinations of antibiotics - penicillin and streptomycin is one - give better results when used together than either one used alone. Other antibiotics have differing modes of action, and can actually cancel each other out, leaving the animal in worse shape than if he had no medication at all. An example of this is the use of penicillin and tetracycline together. Do not mix antibiotics with other medication unless you have veterinary advice to do so. The other medication may neutralize the antibiotic, again resulting in no action. As with any medication, give antibiotics only by the route recommended by your veterinarian or the product label.

If no improvement is seen after 48 hours of treatment, consult your veterinarian. He may wish to change the dosage you are using, or switch to a different drug.

PENICILLIN
For Use In Antibiotic Therapy

Penicillin was the first antibiotic discovered. While Penicillin is far from new, it is by no means outdated. It remains perhaps the most commonly used antibiotic for treatment of infection in both humans and animals.

Penicillin is generally very safe, and does not cause problems even when given at many times the normal dosage rate; however, allergic reactions may be seen. *Epinephrine* (adrenaline) should be handy when ever you give an injection of this drug to an animal, so that it can be given if anaphylactic shock occurs. *(Owners who give their own vaccinations or injections should always have Epinephrine on hand. You can buy it through drug catalogs, your vet or feed stores that carry antibiotics.)* Although these reactions are rare, I just had my first one happen so it can also happen to you.

Penicillin is used in donkeys and horses in several forms. The one most commonly used is in combination with another antibiotic. Penicillin-streptomycin combination, is used in most instances where penicillin treatment is required. The two drugs attack different types of bacteria, complimenting each other to give far more benefit than either one alone.

The general dosage for adult Miniature Donkeys would be between 6cc and 10cc. A good sized 35-36" donkey would receive the 10cc dosage.

The drug combination can be used for up to five to seven days. After that, the streptomycin portion can cause damage to the animal's inner ear. For this reason, when animals need a longer course of therapy, we usually switch them to procaine penicillin without the streptomycin.

Procaine penicillin, whether by itself or in combination with dihydrostreptomycin, gives a good blood level of antibiotic for only about 12 hours. For this reason, it is best to split the total daily dosage and give half in the morning and half in the evening. Give the two doses as close to 12 hours apart as you can.

We at MDT probably get well over 100 calls per year on how to treat respiratory disease in donkeys. Around 25 of these calls are from veterinarians asking our opinion on how to proceed after they've had no improvement from conventional treatment. By this time, the donkey is usually very sick.

Clinical signs of respiratory disease can encompass all or some of the following: Crusty eyes, thin or thick nasal discharge, coughing, a fever ranging from 102 to 105, not eating normally and in more severe cases, rapid shallow breathing. By far the sickest donkeys we hear about are those under one year of age. For donkeys purchased at sales, the incubation period for upper respiratory disease varies from 1 to 10 days. In the beginning you will notice a slight fever, a somewhat depressed animal, and a thin, clear nasal discharge which may later change to thick. Donkeys purchased at sales should always be quarantined or you risk infecting your entire herd.

Step 1 - Call your veterinarian to determine what type of disease you are dealing with.

Respiratory and/or severe colds can be caused by either a viral or a bacterial infection. Your veterinarian needs to draw blood to determine the difference. Your vet also needs to know of current vaccinations and dewormings and how long the donkey has been sick plus what treatment you have administered to date.

Step 2 - Your donkey should be made comfortable.

In summer months the donkey should be put in a shaded, fly-free environment. In winter months, he should be stalled in a very clean, dust-free, dry stall. If chilled, hang up one or two heat lamps in the stall (5 feet above stall bedding) or cover the donkey in a pony blanket.

Donkeys are such social animals in that they sometimes have a best friend that they-cannot be separated from. If this is the case, and when separated the donkey either becomes severely depressed or starts pacing the stall, you may have no choice but to put the friend in with the sick donkey. Obviously you risk the other donkey becoming sick also. This decision will have to be made in each individual case.

He should have unlimited access to clean water and a good quality of hay to help encourage him to eat. Years ago I purchased a young jennet at a sale that became very sick. She had no interest in eating hay or grain. The farm land that surrounds us was planted in winter wheat. I would go in the field several times a day and grab several handfuls. It was soft, green and tender and was encouraging enough that the jennet ate two or three handfuls a day.

Step 3 - Fevers are not always bad.

A fever is one of the body's mechanisms to help deal with the invading viruses and should be allowed to run its course. If the veterinarian concludes that it is a viral infection, and the animal is not deathly ill, he may advise not to treat with antibiotics. (Remember, in humans, there is no cure for the common cold and most must simply run their course.) In mild viral infections, the body's own immune system will fight the disease. This obviously, is the most important reason for vaccinations. In more severe cases, antibiotics to lower a fever will make the animal feel better, therefore will encourage the donkey to eat.

Step 4 - In cases where a donkey has stopped eating for more than 36 hours, a veterinarian must be called in.

The donkey is at risk of dehydrating, compounding the problem. In this case, intravenous fluids will be administered.

Step 5 - Most antibiotics will bring down a fever.

Most people automatically assume that the donkey is well, because they are no longer running a fever and stop giving antibiotics. After 24 hours when the antibiotics have worn off, the fever has returned. *Remember, anything worth treating is worth treating for at least three days!*

Several years ago, some type of respiratory disease made its rounds at all the exotic animal sales and severely affected many donkeys. I worked very closely with Dr. Christopher Brown, BVSc, PhD, Professor of Equine Medicine of Michigan State University. The drug, Azimycin, was discovered to be the drug of choice when treating for severe respiratory illness in Miniature Donkeys. Azimycin was a prescription drug (no longer on the market) and was obtained through a veterinarian. I personally, used Azimycin, instead of penicillin, several times since then, with fantastic results. Azimycin contained the following ingredients and your vet may be able to mix something up that closely resembles it: 0.5 mg dexamethasone; 10 mg chlorpheniramine maleate; 10 mg sodium citrate; 20 mg procaine hydrochloride; 250 mg dihydrostreptomycin (as sulfate); 200,000 units penicillin G, 1 mg lecithin (with 2% tricalcium phosphate); 1 mg propylparaben sodium as preservative, water.

> **WARNING:** ALWAYS consult your veterinarian before giving ANY type of drug to your donkey. Each animal will display different symptoms and should be treated accordingly, on the advice and knowledge of a licensed veterinarian.

Another drug I have found to work very well on Miniature Donkeys is Tribrissen, also a prescription drug. I use this on milder cases of respiratory infections and colds or influenza. It comes in both paste form and tablet. The paste form has weight indications on the tube which you give accordingly. If using tablets, I give 1/2 tablet twice per day. I take 1/2 tablet and crunch it down to powder form. I put it in a 12cc syringe (without the needle) and cut off the tip of the syringe, at the same time making the out-coming hole a little larger. I then mix in a little corn syrup to make a paste. I insert the syringe and squeeze out the mixture on the backside of the donkey's tongue. The corn syrup not only makes it taste better, but stops the donkey from spitting it out.

NOTE: The above is *only* a guide to suggested dosages and should not be taken as advice on how to treat a sick donkey. Again, each donkey *must* be treated as an *individual* according to that particular animal's illness.

Remember, many youngsters between the ages of 4 months and one year go through stages commonly known as "the snots". It's a time when these young animals come in contact with mild viruses and bacterial infections and their body's immune systems are not yet developed enough to totally fight off the disease.

In mild cases, most of these donkeys do not need to be treated. In fact, if treated with antibiotics, their own immune systems shut down to let the antibiotics work, instead of building up the way they should. If unsure whether your weanling is going through one of these "growing stages" or is sick with a viral or bacterial infection, consult your veterinarian. You will find that if you vaccinate your weanlings against Rhino, you'll virtually eliminate these sort of respiratory problems.

Buffington Farm's Marcus owned by Karen Buffington of Ohio

Do Mini Donkeys Get Mini Vaccinations?

Many people ask me if a Miniature Donkey should get a lesser dose of vaccine than the manufacturer recommends for a full-sized horse. Below we quote from a letter written by David Hustead, DVM of Fort Dodge Laboratories when he was asked the same question regarding a miniature horse, and as you know, we vaccinate our mini donkeys the same as horses.

"The immune system of all horses is controlled by its genetic coding. This coding is almost exactly the same in all horses, regardless of size. The immune system in a tiny horse does not know that its body is only the size of a large dog. For all the immune system knows, it could just as easily be in a 1500 pound Shire draft horse.

The currently held theory for vaccine function is that an individual immune system is stimulated by what we call antigenic mass.

The antigenic mass can be compared to the number of BB's in a shot gun shell. If we have enough BB's we can kill our game. If we have enough antigenic mass in a vaccine, then the immune system is stimulated. If not enough antigenic mass is present, then we get no response from the animal in response to our vaccine.

Since the immune system in a 350 pound horse is the same immune system that is found in a 1500 pound horse, they both require the same antigenic mass to be stimulated by a vaccine. So, while you are correct that the dose to weight ratio is very high in your miniatures, you can see this is not the important issue as far as we can tell.

Until better scientific information is available, I would recommend your miniature get the same dose as vaccine as any other horse."

(Please take notice that this only applies to vaccines such as flu, rhino, tetanus, etc. It does not apply to other drugs such as pain killers, antibiotics, prostaglandin's, etc. These drugs are given by weight. A miniature could easily be killed by giving too much of these drugs.)

The facts about Vaccine Products

Just how safe and effective are equine vaccines? How long are they truly effective and what if your donkey's yearly booster is a week or two late? What accounts for the differences in vaccine prices? Why do some products seem expensive while others are less costly?

How Are Vaccines Developed?

Most vaccine research is done by biological research companies - the firms that manufacture the vaccines. After initial laboratory work, efficacy tests begin in-house with clinical trials. The safety and effectiveness is under the authority of the USDA which grants or denies licenses to companies to produce the vaccines.

Research is as follows: They grow the medium, harvest the vaccine, inject the result, challenge it with the disease agent in two weeks, repeat the above, send it out to vets in the field, then the findings are sent to the government for approval.

Not all that long ago, they developed combination vaccines to reduce the number of injections, which ultimately reduces the incidence of reactions.

Once field data is compiled it goes to the USDA's Animal and Plant Health Inspection Service to begin its own testing at the National Veterinary Services Lab in Iowa. If a license is granted to a vaccine, the USDA continues to monitor the manufacturer. In addition to ensuring that all biologics on the market are pure, safe, potent and effective, APHIS also investigates consumer complaints.

How Do Vaccines Protect The Donkey?

Most vaccines are formulated by taking a small amount of disease causing virus or bacteria and blending it with a compound that assists with the proper absorption of the substance. When the vaccine is injected, the immune system produces antibodies that reject the attack. The donkey is left with a reserve of antibodies so that when the donkey is exposed to the same type of invader, the body calls up the reserve of antibodies and triggers the development of even more antibodies.

The way in which the immune response is developed allows a limited amount of leeway in scheduling the donkey's annual injections. Re-exposure is critical to developing and maintaining immunity. Annual vaccinations should be given within a two week time frame of the previous year.

How Should You Handle Vaccines?

Careful storage and handling of vaccines is critical to successfully protecting your donkey from disease. The manufacturer's instructions on expiration and storage conditions ***must be followed to the letter.*** A syringe or bottle of vaccine being frozen or left out in the heat can alter the formulation of the vaccine. This could actually create something harmful to the donkey. If you mistakenly left the bottle of vaccine out on the kitchen counter overnight, call the manufacturer and ask if it's still usable. If in doubt, throw it away.

How Do I Administer Vaccines?

Whatever dosage the manufacturer recommends for horses, is the same dosage that should be given to Miniature Donkeys. Most vaccinations are given intramuscularly. The donkey's muscle tissue can accept and dissipate drugs. Administering drugs into a blood vein is very risky. Injecting a drug in a blood vein that shouldn't be can damage the vein or even kill the animal under the right circumstances. Always read the manufacturer's directions.

How Well Will My Donkey Be Protected?

Some vaccines work better than others. Some are more effective and longer lasting. An example is the influenza vaccine. It's terrible in both humans and equine simply because immunity properties last such a short time. The flu antigen can be cleaned out of the system in as fast as two months.

Other reasons can be behind a vaccine failing to prevent a disease. Some of the simplest things - like stress, pre-existing conditions, concurrent drug therapies and improper administration or handling - can be critical to the way the animal reacts to a vaccine.

What Factors Influence Cost?

Research and development costs obviously affect what the consumer pays for vaccines. Some vaccines are derived through tissue culture, which often means manufacturers have to put in lots of expensive stuff to make the virus grow.

Beware of discount drug companies. Many are not under any regulations on how they must handle drugs. Others buy quantity discounted drugs that are very close to the expiration date. We recently heard of a large booth a lady set up at a horse show which carried all sorts of equine medical supplies along with vaccines. A suspicious person reported her and it was found that the vaccine containers were filled with plain water. If you come across a discount drug catalog and the vaccine prices seem *too low*, it would be wise not to buy from them.

Vaccinating your Miniature Donkeys is one of the smartest decisions you can make. The loss of a donkey or the veterinarian costs resulting from a sick donkey, will more than make up for the cost of vaccinating.

Miniature Donkey Vaccinations

Some vaccinations such as Strangles, Potomac Horse Fever and Rabies may not be needed in your particular area. Always check with a local veterinarian to find out what vaccinations are needed and what diseases you need to protect against.

There is a controversy as to when foals should get their first vaccinations. Some veterinarians argue that before the age of 4 months, a foal's immune system is not developed enough to properly break down the vaccine and provide immunity. However, others will argue that vaccinations should be given at three months of age if a jennet is not current on HER vaccinations. To my knowledge, there is no scientific evidence to support either argument, although the latest research is leaning more toward waiting until the age of 4 months before vaccinating. Again, discuss this with your personal veterinarian and make the wisest choice. Note: Some vaccine labels will state that they are not to be given to any animals under the age of three months. Read the labels!

At *Pheasant Meadow Farm*, they vaccinate between the age of 4 and 5 months. They use a 5-way vaccination that incorporates immunities for five diseases: Tetanus, Eastern and Western Encephlomyelitis, and A1 and A2 Influenza. They also give a Rhino vaccination to foals, however, wait at least two weeks after they give the 5-way vaccination. They have found in the past that smaller foals do not tolerate giving the Rhino and 5-way on the same day very well and have shown severe signs of depression. They vaccinated pregnant jennets with Rhino in their 5th, 7th, 9th and 11th month of gestation.

Tetanus

Otherwise known as "lockjaw" is a bacteria found in all soils. Tetanus vaccination should be given on a preventative basis and also be part of the treatment following surgery or injuries that result from cuts and abrasions. Few animals are as susceptible to this disease as the equine and they must be managed accordingly. Tetanus Toxoid is used as a preventative whereas Tetanus Antitoxin is given after potential exposure to the disease.

Strangles (Equine Distemper)

Strangles is also caused by bacteria and is extremely contagious. It is transmitted from equine to equine via feed bunks, water, buckets, brushes, etc. Although death results in only a small percentage of the equine it affects, it is not uncommon for nearly 100% of the animals on a farm to contract the infection and display signs associated with the disease. After they first show signs, animals are a source of the infection to others for up to four weeks. As with most serious diseases, the goal is always aimed at prevention. Strangles bacteria can live in the soil indefinitely and once your farm contracts it, you must forever vaccinate every animal against it.

***Miniature Donkeys are much more susceptible
to respiratory disease than are horses.***

Influenza

This is a highly contagious disease that can be caused by either of two viruses known as Equine A-1 and Equine A-2. Entire herds can be infected in a few days. Striking after an incubation period of 1-7 days, infected donkeys quickly develop high fevers, nasal discharge, swollen lymph nodes, muscle fatigue, swollen limbs, become depressed and go off food and water. Most donkeys recover in 2-3 weeks but some will show signs for several months.

Potomac Horse Fever

I do not know if there has ever been a case of Potomac Horse Fever found in a donkey, however, if in an area known for the disease, don't take a chance on being the first case. Horses experience severe diarrhea and fever and death is common.

Encephalomyelitis (Blind Staggers, Sleeping Sickness)

Two different strains are found in the U.S. - Eastern and Western, however, there is also a Venezuelan strain that has not been diagnosed in the U.S. for many years. The Venezuelan strain HAS been found in Mexico so states bordering should check with their local veterinarians. The disease is transmitted by biting insects, especially mosquitoes. In those that do recover from the disease, mental impairment is often permanent.

Rhinopneumonitis

This disease is known to cause abortions in jennets and donkeys under the age of one year have been known to die from it. We do know of two breeding farms that lost all their foals due to Rhino. The problem is compounded by the fact that the virus can live outside of the body for up to seven weeks. In areas where donkeys are not vaccinated, this disease returns year after year as recovered animals have no long acting immunity. Modern vaccinations against the disease are reliable and provide excellent protection. It is extremely important in Miniature Donkeys, that weanlings be vaccinated against Rhino.

What Vaccinations Do I Really Need?

Does geographical location make a difference?

Yes, it can along with what you use your donkey for and the age of your donkey. Maternal antibodies which the foal receives from his <u>vaccinated</u> mother will protect the foal for the first months of its life. Some new interesting studies have just been completed regarding influenza and the foal. These studies have indicated that colostral antibodies that pass through the milk can block the vaccine up until six months of age. Some veterinarians are now suggesting that you do not vaccinate a foal for influenza until it is at least four months old and you may have to vaccinate monthly because you do not know when the maternal antibody block drops off. Studies continue in this area.

The following is what veterinarians are recommending for different parts of the U.S.

West Coast

Tetanus, Influenza, Rhino and Sleeping Sickness. You should check with your local vet to see if there have been any localized outbreaks of Potomac Horse Fever or Strangles. Northern California owners be aware of rabies and if any cases have been reported in your area.

Colorado Area

Eastern/Western Encephalomyelitis, Tetanus, Influenza, Rhino. Check with local vets regarding Potomac Horse Fever and Strangles. Some vets are suggesting that jennets get Rhino every two months maximum.

Texas Area

There's a lot of tetanus in the soil so this is a concern in this area. Also, the mosquito population caused an outbreak of eastern encephalomyelitis several years ago. Tetanus and enceph is generally given twice a year. Normal vaccinations will include influenza and Rhino. Check with local vet regarding rabies.

Southern United States

Because of warm temperatures, equine diseases tend to thrive. Botulism is a real concern and should be discussed with your vet. Encephalitis and rhino are also high on the list. Kentucky has a high skunk population so donkeys should be vaccinated for rabies.

Florida

May through October is a peak time for encephalomyelitis. University of Florida advises pet owners to vaccinate twice per year. Check with local vet regarding rabies.

East Coast

Potomac Horse Fever is a threat to *horse* owners but it is not known if it even affects donkeys. Discuss it with your vet. Five in one all-around vaccinations are generally given. Botulism can be a threat in certain states. Rabies vaccines are highly recommended in New England and Pennsylvania - other areas should check with local vet.

The very minimum a donkey should receive, no matter what the locality, is a 5 in 1 vaccination which consists of E/W Enceph, A1 and A2 Influenza, and Tetanus. With the donkey virus that continues to show up at many donkey shows and sales, it is of the utmost importance that you give Influenza and Rhino 30 days in advance, if you go anywhere near these events.

Respiratory Infections

A common problem in weanlings and yearlings and
something you need to keep up to date on

Your donkeys are up to date on their vaccinations, yet one day you walk out and you hear a cough. Taking a second look, you see one donkey with a slight clear discharge from the nose. Grabbing a thermometer, your donkey comes up with a 104 temperature.

Respiratory infections are common in cold weather. Respiratory infections can occur almost weekly in an unvaccinated herd. The symptoms can range from a slight cold (low fever, runny nose, mild cough) to the severe depression and massive can-be-fatal lung-chest infections of pneumonia and pleurisy.

Respiratory infection *bugs* are everywhere. They are generally airborne particles that are released when a sick donkey breathes or coughs. Whenever your donkey mingles with other donkeys, such as at a show, fair, when bringing a new unvaccinated donkey home or even your own pasture, he may be exposed, despite their owners' precautions. Young donkeys (under 2 years old) are especially prone to attack. Think of them as kids going off to first grade, going away from home for the first time. They get together and pass the viruses back and forth because they have not been exposed to these viruses before and do not have sufficient immunities to fight the disease.

Stress from showing or travel can decrease an immune system's ability to fend off respiratory system attack. Can you give your donkey a cold by bathing him in cold weather? No, but you can stress him out to the point that his immune defenses are lowered making him susceptible to infection.

Vaccinating your donkeys against respiratory infections can certainly minimize the severity of the disease, however, may not prevent the donkey from contracting the disease. An unvaccinated donkey may very well die from respiratory disease, but a vaccinated donkey may only show mild to semi-severe signs of the disease.

The second problem with a virus is that once it attacks the weaken respiratory system, it allows bacteria to also invade, making the donkey even sicker. Fortunately, bacteria lives outside the cells, rather than hiding within cells like a virus, therefore making bacteria easier to battle with antibiotics.

Equine Herpes Virus - Influenza

The two most common respiratory disease viruses are equine herpes virus and influenza.

Equine Herpes Virus is the most common respiratory virus. It is known commonly as "Rhino". It not only causes cold-like symptoms but can also cause abortion in jennets. Rhino is highly contagious, but rarely fatal, in older animals.

There has been a lot of discussion of late regarding Rhino and the sub types of the disease which are EHV-1 and EHV-4. It can be very confusing as to just what you are suppose to vaccinate against and what causes what to happen. Some vaccines only target one or the other and other vaccines target both EHV-1 and EHV-4. And which one causes abortion?

Influenza virus, just as in people, constantly changes. There are so many forms of the disease that it is difficult to vaccinate against all strains. There are however, two primary subtypes which are A1 and A2. Make sure the vaccine you purchase covers both of these.

Both Influenza and Rhino vaccines are very short lived in producing high immunities. If you show your donkeys or otherwise expose your animals to a lot of new animals with unknown vaccination histories, both Rhino and Influenza should be given as often as every 2-3 months.

Fact List

- ♦ **FACT**: EHV-1 is the subtype known to cause abortion
- ♦ **FACT**: EHV-4 is the subtype that is likely to be the common cause of respiratory disease
- ♦ **FACT**: New discoveries show that both EHV-1 and EHV-4 can cause respiratory infections, however, EHV-1 may cause a more severe infection than EHV-4, but, EHV-4 is the one your donkey is most likely to encounter.
- ♦ **FACT**: In the past, vaccines generally targeted one or the other. Now newer vaccines target both sub types. Check the label!
- ♦ **FACT**: Research shows your donkey's immune response against one form will provide a certain amount of protection against the other form.
- ♦ **FACT**: It would be preferable to purchase vaccines that fight both EHV-1 and EHV-4. If this is not possible, young non-pregnant donkeys should be vaccinated against EHV-4.

Management

Good farm management practices can certainly help in avoiding and/or cutting down on the severity of respiratory infections. Keep your barn clean and dust free. Constant exposure to dust can irritate the respiratory tract and break down its barriers.

Most people do not realize how damaging urine odors are. The ammonia can damage the lining of sensitive upper airways. After digging out wet spots, sprinkling lime over them can help cut down on ammonia odors. (We would also like to hear from anyone who has found other products that cut down ammonia odors.)

It almost goes without saying how important a regular deworming program is to keep donkeys healthy.

Quarantine all new donkeys coming into your barn. Ideally they should have their own separate pasture area and their own stall area and have no direct contact with your other donkeys. A 10 day quarantine is usually adequate if within that time frame you see no signs of illness.

Recently on the market are equine immune stimulants. There of course are no studies on these as to how they affect donkeys. When equine receive an immune stimulant, it supposedly activates his own immune system to more quickly combat a virus. When do you give an immune stimulant? During the very first stages of sickness. Your veterinarian must administer these immune stimulants, and they are expensive - $40 to $75 per injection and the animal may need several injections. *(Update: My research veterinarian clinic advises that they have injected over 200 horses at race tracks with immune stimulants and have seen little to no improvement in response time for horses recovering from respiratory disease.)*

Symptoms and Treatment

■ Mild Viral Infections

Temperature of 103 to 105 for several days. Mild depression. Clear nasal discharge. Some coughing.

Treatment: You may not need to treat the donkey with any antibiotics, instead, let his own immunities fight the disease. Remember, when you give an antibiotic you are basically shutting down the donkey's immune system and letting the antibiotic fight the disease. Keep the donkey out of bad weather and take temperature twice daily. Consult with your vet.

■ Prolonged Viral Infection

Temperature at 103 or higher for longer than 3 days. Loss of appetite for more than one day. Clear or thick nasal discharge. Persistent coughing.

Treatment: It's time to call the vet. He may pull blood to see if bacteria is also involved and may want to start on antibiotics specific to the disease, along with cough relievers. Keep donkey stalled with dust free hay, dust free bedding such as sprinkled down straw and clean fresh water.

■ Virus plus Severe Secondary Bacterial Infection

Temperature greater than 103. Severe depression and refuses to eat. Thick nasal discharge. Coughing every few minutes. Difficulty in breathing to the point where the donkey's sides are heaving in and out.

Treatment: This is an emergency. Your vet will administer specific antibiotics. Your vet will recommend prolonged rest and may even want to hospitalize the donkey. Don't take the cheap, easy way out or you may very well lose your donkey! Follow the vet's advice to a T. Constantly monitor the donkey and don't be afraid to call your vet daily with questions.

When purchasing a new donkey, make certain you get vaccination records. We constantly hear, "the seller told me she was vaccinated but couldn't give me dates". If a seller can't or won't give you exact dates, assume that the donkey has never been vaccinated. If you have other animals at home, you may very well insist that a veterinarian vaccinate your new donkey before it leaves the seller's property, to protect your own donkeys.

Donkeys at play at Precious Acres, Ft. Lauderdale, Florida

Injections: What You Should Know

Not all medications, drugs, tranquilizers or even vitamins may be safely injected intramuscularly. Some must go intravenously (in the vein) due to their acidity, potential for irritation, or preponderance to development of abscesses so you must be sure that your veterinarian has stated specifically which medications you may inject into muscle.

The reverse is also true. Some drugs may not be injected into the vein. An example of this is the commonly used antibiotic, procaine penicillin G. Reactions such as convulsions can occur due to the procaine carrier. Penicillin in another form, i.e., sodium or potassium penicillin, is suitable for intravenous administration. Some drugs are so irritating to soft tissue, such as phenylbutazone, that they must be given into a vein and no leakage into surrounding tissue can occur or the tissue may necrose and slough.

Also, there are drugs such as aceptromazine or Rompun which may be given intravenously or intramuscularly, *but* should they accidentally be injected into an artery instead of a vein, convulsions and possibly death may occur.   For this reason, it is best recommended for the non-veterinarian or those not highly familiar with injection techniques and the drugs being injected, to forego attempting intravenous injections.

When injecting medications into the muscle, a 22 gauge, 1" needle should be used for adult Miniature Donkeys. A new sterile needle should be used each time. With the availability of disposable needles now, it is best to purchase these in leu of purchasing reusable needles that you have to sterilize after each use. Syringes may be used over for short periods, but their sterility should be maintained by *not* washing them out with tap water and never touching the exposed tip or inside. Use the same medication in the same syringe each time and refrigerate the syringes between use with a new needle placed on the tip. If blood has been aspirated into the syringe, do not use again.

The sites for intramuscular injection include the neck, hindquarters, and pectoral muscles. There is a triangle area on both sides of the neck which is safe for injection. The outer boundaries of the triangle are 1) the slope of the shoulder, 2) the ligamentum nuchae, and 3) the cervical (neck) vertebrae. The ligamentum nuchae is a ligament running along the top of the neck to the skull to help support it. Thus, the base of the triangle is in front of the shoulder and the apex or extent of the triangle is not more than halfway forward up the neck.

The area for intramuscular injection in the hindquarters is in the muscle bundles at the very back of the hindlimbs and a few inches below the tailhead. The lower limit is a line even with the bottom of the flank.

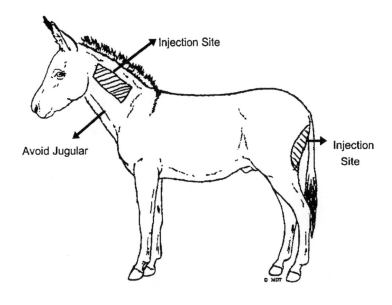

Injection Sites

Needle Sizes: Adult donkeys 22g X 1, Weanling donkeys, 22g X 3/4, Newborn Foals 25g X 5/8

The third site for i.m. injection is the pectoral muscle between the front legs. This is reserved for medications with a high tendency for abscess development as drainage would be good. Do not routinely use this site unless directed.

When multiple injections are to be given, the sites should be rotated. Also, no more than 20 cc should be injected into any one specific spot.

In the past, it was always advised to take cotton with alcohol and clean the injection site. Studies in recent years now conclude that alcohol should **not** be used. Alcohol or disinfectants might kill or inactivate the virus particles in the vaccines. Research has shown that infections are more likely to develop when injections are given through wet skin than when they are given through dry - even somewhat dirty - skin. Research has also shown that it takes 15 minutes for alcohol to destroy bacteria.

To administer the medication, remove the needle from the syringe and insert it straight in and deeply to the hub. Attach the syringe and then aspirate (pull back on the plunger) to check if any blood comes into the tip. If blood does appear, then pull the needle out *slightly,* change the angle of direction, push the needle back into a new area and aspirate again. If no blood, then inject up to 20 ml. If you have a larger amount to give, rather than sticking the donkey again, just pull the needle out slightly, redirect, push into a new area, aspirate again, and inject. Any time the donkey moves or you move the needle, aspirate to be sure that the tip of the needle hasn't inserted itself into a blood vessel.

By having the needle unattached to the syringe when you insert it, should the donkey jump or shy, the needle will likely stay in place. However, if you try to stab the needle in with the syringe attached, the syringe and needle may both end up in the straw if the equine jumps at the wrong time.

Try to keep the donkey still. If he's walking around while you have a needle inserted, it is more irritating to the muscle tissue. If slight swelling or soreness occurs at injection sites, apply hot compresses. If the site is very painful to the touch and/or hot, or the donkey develops a fever, call your vet.

Intramuscular injections in foals should be given in the hindend because if their neck gets sore, they become unwilling to nurse and can rapidly dehydrate.

It is wise to learn how to give your own injections. A sick donkey may need injections of antibiotic every 12 hours. A donkey who has been operated on could need injections every six hours. Veterinarians generally charge between $20 and $30 just to come to your farm and this could get very expensive. If you are breeding donkeys, your jennets need to be vaccinated against Rhino every two months.

Cost difference between purchasing your own vaccines verses having a veterinarian give them.

Veterinarian Giving Vaccinations:

Farm Call Fee		$25.00
Rhino		$15.00
5-Way (E/W Enceph, A1 & A2		
Flu and Tetanus)		$30.00
Single Tetanus		$12.00
Rabies		$20.00
	Total	$102.00

Purchasing Your Own Vaccinations:

Farm Call Fee		$ 00
Rhino		$8.80
5-Way		$6.85
Single Tetanus		$2.85
Rabies		$2.25
	Total	$20.75

As we have stated before, in some states it is unlawful for you to give your own rabies vaccinations and vaccine companies will not sell the rabies vaccine to a lot of states. You also should have certification from a veterinarian that they gave the rabies vaccine in case your animal comes in contact with a rabid animal. If your state health department did not believe your animal was vaccinated by yourself, and a rabid animal is found on your property, they could insist that your donkey be destroyed and also place your entire farm on a six month quarantine. To make matters worse, the equine rabies vaccine has never been approved for donkeys so you may still be quarantined.

Some rules of thumb:

1. Be sure the vaccine comes from a reliable manufacturer or major drug company. Modified live virus vaccines are particularly susceptible to mishandling and heat damage.

2. Always read the product insert carefully. It will tell you how the product is to be given and how often.
3. Always give the full dose. Miniature Donkeys DO NOT get half dozes of vaccines!! Antibiotics and other products given by *weight* should be given accordingly.
4. Never mix medicines or vaccines until you are ready to use it.
5. Always give the vaccine by the proper route and with a clean syringe and needle.
6. Never use a vaccine past the expiration date.
7. You can give multiple vaccinations at the same time. Some weanlings will have a reaction such as running a fever that you will have to keep an eye on. If you do decide to spread vaccinations out, says G. L. Hoeppner, DVM, be sure to wait at least two weeks between vaccinations. For about two weeks after a vaccination, the body produces interferon which can interfere with subsequent vaccinations given in that two-week period.

10 Vaccination Tips

1. Only vaccinate healthy animals. *Never* vaccinate an animal who is running a fever or one who appears to be ill. Good response to vaccines depends on a healthy, properly functioning immune system. Avoid vaccinating stressed animals and do NOT vaccinate a donkey that has just been shipped. Allow those donkeys to rest a few days and this also allows you time to make sure the donkey is not getting sick from being shipped. Giving an influenza vaccine to a donkey that is coming down with the flu may make the donkey twice as sick.

2. Use only quality vaccines obtained from your veterinarian or a reputable vaccine company. Never purchase bargain priced vaccines. Never purchase vaccines from a fly-by-night vaccine catalog that you get in the mail and never heard of before. If you intend to penny-pinch in this area, you would do better not to vaccinate at all than to take a chance on injecting your donkey with a product that may be useless or harmful.

3. Never use out-dated vaccines. Out-dated vaccines will not produce the immunity responses your donkey needs.

4. Read labels! Store the vaccine the way it is suppose to be stored. Never let a vaccine freeze or sit out in the heat. Inject the total recommended amount (exactly what it says to give horses). DO NOT give Miniature Donkeys one half the dose recommended for horses.

5. Never mix two vaccines in the same syringe.

6. Keep syringes and needles clean. If you are using a modified live vaccine, cleaning needles or the injection site with alcohol can inactivate the vaccine. If the site you plan to inject the vaccine is dirty, clean it with water, not alcohol. Use disposable syringes one time only and throw them away.

7. Never inject two different vaccines in the same area. Too many different vaccines given at the same time can overload the immune system and result in decreased response. Some veterinarians will tell you not to inject more than one vaccine per week. This topic is debatable depending on which veterinarian you ask.

8. Make sure your donkey is properly restrained. If a donkey is jumping around, you may inject into a blood vessel, you may accidentally squirt out some of the vaccine before it is injected. The more trauma you cause to the tissue from a donkey that is moving around, the more chance you get of a reaction to the drug in the form of an abscess.

9. Keep accurate records! You should keep a chart of each donkey, what they were vaccinated with, and when they were vaccinated.

10. If you purchase a donkey and you cannot get the owner to give you exact vaccination dates, assume the donkey is not vaccinated, wait several days and then vaccinate.

A good series of vaccinations for an open jennet or jacks is a 5 in 1 vaccine consisting of: Eastern & Western Encephalomyelitis, A1 and A2 Influenza and Tetanus along with a separate vaccination of Rhinopneumonitis. The 5 in 1 is one injection and the Rhino is another injection. Give on opposite sides of the neck. Only one injection of each per year is needed. Such a small amount of money and time spent to save yourself the worry and expense of disease. It is recommended that bred jennets be vaccinated 30 to 40 days before foaling to give the foal very high immunities.

We are indicating giving first vaccinations to foals at 4 months of age. Ongoing studies suggest that immune systems are not developed enough to process vaccines at 3 months. This is something you need to discuss with your veterinarian and decide together what is best for your donkeys.

Biologicals	Foals	Yearlings	Brood Jennets	Mature
Tetanus Antitoxin	At birth if dam not vaccinated and/or not there to iodine navel	Give in case of injury if vacc history is unknown or vacc was in excess of 30 days	Give in case of injury if vacc history is unknown or vacc was in excess of 30 days	Give in case of injury if vacc history is unknown or vacc was in excess of 30 days
Tetanus Toxoid	1st dose – 4 mths 2nd dose – 5 mths	Booster at 12 months after initial dose	Booster Annually, 30 days prior to foaling	Booster Annually
Influenza	1st dose – 4 mths 2nd dose – 5 mths	Booster Annually	Booster Annually, 30 days prior to foaling	Booster Annually
Rhinopneumonitis (Rhino)	1st dose – 4-1/2 mths 2nd dose – 5-1/2 mths	Booster Annually	Start at 5 months of pregnancy, 7th, 9th, 11th month	Booster Annually
Eastern/Western Encephalomyetis	1st dose – 4 mths 2nd dose – 5 mths	Booster Annually	Booster Annually	Booster Annually
Venezuelan Encephalomyetis	Discuss with your veterinarian			
Rabies	Administer to all donkeys in areas where rabies is a problem			
Strangles	Discuss with veterinarian		Do not give to pregnant jennets	

Important Notes About Administering Medications!

Medications should NEVER be administered without the advice and direction of a licensed veterinarian!

A common cause of disasters related to medication administration is giving the wrong dose. We must remember that our society stalled out trying to adopt the metric system, and this fact gives many of us difficulty. The common units used for many of the typical medications administered to horses are the milligram (mg) and the milliliter (ml). A liquid drug will generally have a drug concentration reported in milligrams/milliliter (mg/ml). The milligram is 1/1000 of a gram and the milliliter is 1/1000 of a liter. Another unit that often confuses people is the CC. The abbreviation CC stands for cubic centimeter and is the same unit of volume as a milliliter: l ml = 1 cc.

I might be a bit hard-line, but I am generally of the opinion that no medications or combinations thereof should be administered to your animal without some form of consultation with your veterinarian. All drugs have the potential to be toxic if used in an indiscriminate manner. There are drugs that can be toxic at the therapeutic doses if predisposing factors exist, and it is necessary to know what side effects to look for in case there is a reaction. This includes vaccines.

On the antibiotic front there also are some concerns. The indiscriminate or improper use of antibiotics is a very serious problem in both people and animals. The number of bacteria that are developing resistance to many-if not all-antibiotics is growing at an alarming rate. The emergence of bacteria that are highly resistant to antibiotics is frightening and in many cases related to poor judgment in antibiotic use. If antibiotics are used, we have a high level of responsibility to ensure that 1) the use of antibiotics is really warranted; 2) if antibiotics are warranted, an appropriate one is selected; and 3) if antibiotics are warranted, they are administered by the appropriate route, at the appropriate dose, frequency, and duration.

Intravenous (IV)

I am reluctant to talk about intravenous injections in any great detail as I feel very strongly that unless you experience significant training and direction, these should be left for a veterinarian or qualified technician. I have several reasons that I'll elaborate on.

The main place for intravenous injection is the jugular vein coursing down either side of the neck. One of the reasons that untrained intravenous injection is dangerous is the proximity of the carotid artery (a little finger size artery that takes blood straight to the brain) to the jugular vein. It's right underneath it! There is not much room for error when giving intravenous injections, and the risk of accidentally injecting a drug into the carotid artery can be great for the inexperienced.

If a drug is inadvertently injected into the carotid artery, the reactions are a little different depending on the drug, but at the very least the animal will flip over backwards and seizure, and, many times, the animal will die. This is the number one reason for leaving intravenous injections to those who are properly trained.

Another reason for staying away from intravenous injections is that some drugs (phenylbutazone being at the top of the list) cannot be administered outside of the vein without causing severe irritation. If you want to see a large portion of your animal's neck slough away, just get some phenylbutazone outside of the vein or accidentally administer it in the muscle. Yet another reason to stay out of the vein is the fact that many drugs cannot be administered into the blood (for example, procaine penicillin) without doing great harm or actually killing the horse.

Should your horse require a drug that only can be given intravenously and your situation will require you to perform these injections, you should discuss this seriously with your veterinarian. You should never attempt this without appropriate training.

Reference: Small portion of a large article written by Michael A. Ball, DVM entitled Administering Medications

Most Commonly Used Medicines

There are an enormous number of drugs available to veterinarians, many of which are also easily obtained by owners, for treatment of disease and injury in equine. However, although you as a donkey owner should be familiar with the use and effects of the most commonly used medicines, it is unwise to undertake treatment with unprescribed drugs without consulting your vet.

The following notes are not inclusive but serve as a guide to the most commonly used and/or readily available medicines.

Acepromazine   This is one of a group of antihistamines used as tranquilizers and sedatives in the equine.   The group also includes Chlorpromazine and promethazine.   The animal must still be handled quietly after tranquilization because over-stimulation will result in the donkey overcoming the calming effects of the drug.   These drugs also have an analgesic effect and may help to reduce muscle spasm and pain.

Adrenaline   Is commonly found in solutions of local anesthetic agents where it helps to prolong the effect of the anesthetic.   It may be used on its own to control minor hemorrhage when applied topically to a wound.

Aloes   Aloes is one of a group of substances -the anthracenes - used as purgatives.   Other related drugs include Altan and Danthron.   They have an irritant and stimulatory effect on the large intestine and aid passage of material through the gut.   These substances are most often used as laxatives or in the treatment of colic associated with impaction of food material or straw in the large intestine.   Overdose can cause severe diarrhea or death.

Ammonia   Is applied to minor sprains or injuries as a liniment.   Inhalation of ammonia vapor stimulates respiration and the circulatory system when these are depressed.

Anabolic Steroids   This is a group of substances which effect the acceleration of recovery of weight loss due to debility or under-nutrition; an increase in muscular development and tone; the speeding up of tissue regeneration to help in bone and tissue injuries and assisting in recovery from infectious diseases.

Anodynes (colic mixtures)   These are medicines which relieve pain in colic (abdomen).

Antibacterial and Antibiotics   These substances are used to destroy or inhibit the growth of bacteria and other disease causing organisms. Needless to say, there are a large number of these agents.   Drugs are constantly being developed and others which were previously only available to doctors are being made available to veterinarians. Many of them are unsuitable for use in the equine because of their side effect and consequently we often fall back on the basics such as penicillin and sulphonamides. The main group of antibiotics and antibacterial agents include: The penicillin's (benzyl penicillin, ampicillin, carbenicillin, amoxycillin). Penicillin is the most commonly used antibiotic in equine veterinary practice. Other antibiotics include: Gentamicin, Streptomycin and Neomycin, Tetracyclines, and Sulfonamides.

Combinations of drugs are often used either to broaden the range of treatment or to enhance the effectiveness of one or other of the constituents. The effective combinations are fairly standardized and random mixing should not be undertaken. The choice of antibiotic or antibacterial agent is essentially based on culturing the infecting organism and observing its susceptibility to various drugs in the lab. Antibiotics can be administered by injection, by mouth or topically, the route depending on the drug used and the nature of the infection.

Antihistamines This is a class of drugs which interfere with the action of histamine, a substance released in the body which causes itchiness, rash, or narrowing of the smaller airways.
Aspirin This drug is used as an anti-inflammatory analgesic agent in the treatment of muscle or joint injury and arthritis. It is used to decrease fever however, long term use is risky because of stomach irritation and hemorrhage.
Atropine Used topically in eye preparations to relieve pain and spasm of the iris by dilating the pupil. It has a long action of several days. Occasionally used prior to general anesthetic. It causes a slowing of intestinal motility and reduces the production of saliva and digestive enzymes.
Boric Acid Is used as a wound dressing either alone, as a 4 percent solution, or combined with zinc oxide for application to wounds.
Caustics These are substances which destroy excess granulation tissue and minor superficial tumors. The cause of death of cells and accelerate protein to form a scab. The skin surrounding the excess granulation tissue should be protected by a covering of Vaseline and the caustic carefully applied to the lesion only.
Chalk Prepared chalk is a valuable antacid and protectant in the treatment of diarrhea. It is usually combined with kaolin.
Chloramphenicol Is a potent antibiotic which can cure many bacterial problems that are resistant to the more common antibiotics. It can only

be used for a short time and is also incorporated into many eye ointments.

Codeine Is used as a cough suppressant in animals with respiratory disease and as a constipant and analgesic in equine with diarrhea. Can be given orally or by stomach tube.

Corticosteroids Cortisone is a steroid hormone produced by the adrenal gland. It is used in the control and reduction of inflammation associated with skin, muscle and joint conditions. Can cause side effects influencing tissue healing and hormonal balances.

Electrolytes Are salts of various kinds and are used in therapy for diarrhea, excessive sweating, exhaustion and dehydration. Most are added to drinking water but in severe cases, can be administered by a veterinarian through a stomach tube.

Epinephrine Also called adrenalin, it primarily affects the heart, blood vessels, blood flow and circulation. It is used to treat anaphylactic shock which may follow injection of vaccines or antibiotics. Miniature donkeys would receive 2 to 3 cc dosage depending on body weight of donkey.

Iodine Has antiseptic and irritant actions. Weaker forms are used for cleansing and antibacterial, pre-surgical skin preparation, and cleansing of wounds.

Magnesium Sulphate Is commonly used as a laxative and at higher doses, a purgative in equine. It acts to increase the amount of water in the food material passing through the intestine, thus increasing the fluidity and volume of the intestinal contents.

Oxytocin A hormone produced by the pituitary gland. Given to jennets who fail to pass their afterbirth. Also used on jennets/mares to stimulate milk production if given within the first few days of birthing.

Pen Strep A broad-spectrum antibiotic solution indicated for a wide range of conditions as an aid in the treatment of shipping fever, infectious diarrhea, pneumonia, foot rot, mastitis and in small animals, wound infections.

Phenylbutazone Is one of the most frequently used and abused drugs available for equine. Used widely for reducing pain and inflammation in the treatment of traumatic or inflammatory musculoskeletal disorders, lameness, reduce post-operative swelling and pain. Injectable phenylbutazone *must* be given intravenously and it can cause severe reaction if some gets outside the vein. Long term use causes irritation of lining of the stomach and intestine.

Poultices Are valuable soothing applications and for cleansing wounds, and should be combined with a mild antiseptic. Applied to the feet with the aid of a boot or bandage. Poultices have a drawing action on wounds and are most useful in cases of puncture or infected wounds.

Sulfa Drugs   Were the first class of drugs able to attack and retard growth of bacteria.   The effect allowed the body to overcome the bacteria and survive the infection.   They are used often to remove debris from the surface of old, contaminated wounds.

Sulphonamides   Are antibacterial compounds used both topically and internally for the prevention and treatment of non-specific infections. Sulphonamides are bacteriostatic, that is, they prevent the multiplication of some bacteria but do not destroy them.

Sulfur   Has for many years been used as a treatment for skin diseases of bacterial and parasitic origin.   Frequently found in shampoos.

Terramycin   Sterile injectable aqueous solution for the treatment of enteritis, metritis, shipping fever, etc.

Tetracyclines   Are mostly given intravenously and are a major class of antibiotic.   Some Tetracyclines are given intramuscularly but they cause severe tissue reaction and damage.   Tetracyclines are a useful class of antibiotics having a different spectrum of action than penicillin.   They are often used in cases where penicillin administration does not get any response.

Tribrissen   A trimethoprim and sulfa diazine combination which is highly effective in combating a wide spectrum of bacterial pathogens.   An excellent drug to use on weanling and yearling donkeys for cases of mild to semi-severe cases of influenza.

Chapter 7

Worms and Parasites

The Worm War

Parasites have no respect for your donkeys whether they are weanlings or senior citizens. If you are going to own donkeys, then you must have a deworming program. No matter how clean you keep your barns and paddocks, worms are a fact of life. Donkeys fall under the equine category therefore you would follow the same deworming program established for horses in your area.

There are six major equine internal parasites that you must be concerned with: large and small strongyles, ascarids, tapeworms, pinworms and bots. All donkeys have some degree of worm infestation but you need to control them so that they do not affect the health of your animal.

Internal parasites are host-specific meaning equine parasites can only exist in horses and donkeys. Do not use cattle dewormers on donkeys as donkeys do not get cattle worms.

Large and small strongyles, or bloodworms, are the most damaging of all equine parasites. They attach themselves to the intestinal wall and live off the donkey's blood. They will also travel throughout the body and can affect the heart, liver, and lungs as they destroy tissue.

Bot fly's are very annoying as they buzz around your donkey. They land on your donkey's forelegs, shoulders and flanks. They don't bite the donkey but what they do is lay tiny yellow eggs on the hair. The eggs enter the donkey through the mouth as the donkey licks his coat. They attach to the stomach lining and do their damage. Not all dewormers are effective against bots so you must make sure when you deworm for bot larvae (in the fall) you must use a dewormer that specifically states that it is effective against bots.

Ascarids, when mature, are 6 to 15" long and resemble an earthworm. They are rarely found in adult donkeys over the age of five years but can do much damage to young foals and weanlings. They not only attach to the intestinal wall but will also make their way to the lungs where they contribute to respiratory diseases.

Tapeworms are usually associated with digestive disturbances and are found in the small intestine.

Pinworms will cause severe anal itching. The main characteristic of pinworm infection occurs when a donkey rubs the tail area and causes hair loss. Pinworms are less damaging than other worms but can cause unsightly hair loss and skin irritations as the donkeys rub up against fences and trees.

All equine parasites threaten the health of an animal and rob the donkey of needed nutrients. Thin donkeys with a rough, dull hair coat are a sure sign of parasites. Other health problems include, diarrhea, overall listless appearance and weanling and yearling donkeys who stand around a lot instead of running and playing quite often. Worm infestation weakens the immune system so if a donkey comes in contact with a bug, they are more likely to get seriously ill than would a donkey in good worm-free health.

How often you deworm your donkeys depends a lot of their housing arrangements. Donkeys exposed to manure in paddocks and stalls need to be dewormed more often than donkeys whose owners pick up on a daily basis. The life cycle of worm eggs inside the donkey varies. On average it is 8 weeks. Therefore, it is not practical to deworm more often than that and plus you take the chance of the worms becoming resistant to dewormers. Donkeys whose owners clean up after them two or three times a day can go as long as 4 months between dewormings. Always deworm new donkeys in the quarantine pasture before they are turned out with your other donkeys.

Prevention and Management Tips

Prevention of parasite infestation is far better and more efficient than having donkeys infected with worms and trying to remove them. The following management practices help reduce the number of parasite eggs or larvae available to infect donkeys:

1. Feed donkeys from mangers or racks rather than on the ground where they can easily ingest worm eggs.

2. Fence off or drain manure-contaminated water sources such as ponds and streams.

3. Compost manure before spreading it on pastures. The heat generated by manure decomposition helps kill worm eggs.

4. Remove feces from stalls and paddocks frequently.

5. Drag pastures weekly or monthly to break up manure piles and expose parasite eggs to the sun. If possible, remove manure droppings from pasture.

6. If possible, rotate pastures. It is possible to reduce pasture contamination through interruption of the parasite's life cycle.

The most important thing to remember in your deworming program is that you must not only rotate dewormers, you must rotate <u>classes</u> of dewormers

Until further studies are completed, worms can become resistant to dewormer products. You need to switch classes of dewormers so that you are administering <u>different ingredients</u>. You should alternate dewormers every other time. i.e. use Zimecterin or Eqvalan one time and the next time use Strongid.

If you have a "herd" of donkeys, all donkeys on the premises should be treated when deworming is performed. It does little good to intensively treat some animals while leaving others untreated. The unwormed donkey can shed large numbers of eggs, quickly reinfecting the others.

Foals are born free of worms but begin to pick up infective larvae within the first few days. The worms then go through their migration and return to the foal's intestine where they begin to lay eggs. Worm eggs may be seen in the foal's feces between 8 and 11 weeks of age. Foals should receive their first worming at between 6 and 8 weeks of age. Six weeks if you have a large population of donkeys in a small area such as 4 donkeys on a half acre of ground. Deworm monthly thereafter until they are six months of age and then you can go to every two months.

Should you *Really* be using Ivomec® on your Donkeys?
(The answer is NO)

It has come to my attention that there are a number of breeders using Ivomec - cattle wormer - on their donkeys.

I personally have purchased several donkeys over the years whose records indicated that they were "dewormed" with Ivomec. Most of the weanlings had rough, dull coats, large bellies, and were somewhat depressed. They did not act or play like weanlings their ages should. Upon arrival here, they were wormed with either Zimecterin or Strongid equine paste wormer. Normally within two weeks, their hair coats improved and they began to look and act healthier.

Several years ago, Ivomec developed an injectable equine wormer. It was an oil base and veterinarians reported numerous severe abscesses at the injection sites, therefore the product was taken off the market.

Miniature Donkey Talk Magazine consulting veterinarians tell us that there have been no studies done on giving Ivomec cattle wormer, orally to equine. Why? Because it was developed for cattle, *not* equine.

The insert that the distributor, Merck & Co,. puts inside each box of Ivomec states as follows:

"Ivomec injection is indicated for the effective treatment and control of the following harmful species of gastrointestinal roundworms, lungworm, grubs, sucking lice and mange mites **in cattle. CAUTION:** Ivomec Injection for Cattle has been developed specifically for use in cattle and reindeer **ONLY.** This product should not be used in other animal species as severe adverse reactions, including fatalities in dogs, may result."

When the distributor warns against using this product on animals other than cattle and reindeer, why is it that some donkey breeders are using it? My number one guess is that they feel it is cost effective. Although a small bottle of wormer cost around $32.00, it would last a very long time. Because of this, I also suspect that people are not paying attention to the expiration date on the bottle, making the product even more useless on donkeys.

Since my personal experience of purchasing donkeys who have been given Ivomec has been so negative, I am wondering the effectiveness of this drug on donkeys. If no studies have been done on the effectiveness of its use on equine parasites, my guess is that this drug is not effective on all parasites that are harmful to equine. With the numerous deworming products on the market specifically made for use in equine, why would anyone use a dewormer specifically made for cattle? If cost effectiveness is the reason, resulting veterinarian bills due to internal parasite damage will surely override the savings of using an ineffective dewormer.

Most equine dewormers state on their packaging whether they are safe for pregnant or very young equine. Some are not. Since Ivomec warns against using on any animals other than cattle and reindeer, who is foolish enough to risk using it on very young donkeys or bred jennets?

We advocate the use of equine dewormers *only* on your donkeys. There are numerous equine dewormers on the market which can readily be found in any part of the country.

Read your deworming paste labels carefully.

Safe-Guard and **Panacur** - Both safe for foals under the age of 4 months.
Zimecterin or **Eqvalan** are good for use between the months of December and March to rid your donkeys of bots. (We recommend not using on foals under 4 months of age as several breeders have reported diarrhea in their foals after use.)
Strongid, Telmin B, Cutter are all good equine dewormers to use on adult donkeys.

Don't risk your donkeys very life on cheap deworming agents. It simply isn't worth it.

It always amazes me the number of health problems that are attributed to worms. They can range from skin ailments to the death of an animal.

Donkeys act as a host to many different types of internal parasites. The most important group of worms are known as strongyles. Both large and small strongyles are usually present in the large intestine. These worms spend a portion of their life cycle traveling through other parts of the donkey's body, especially the lining of the major abdominal blood vessels. Small strongyles are usually confined to the intestinal lining and heavy infections are most common in young animals, especially those under two years of age. Severely infested animals may show a poor growth rate or loss of weight, rough hair coat and anemia.

Drugs used to reduce the worm population in the donkey's intestine are call anthelmintics or dewormers. Unfortunately worms keep changing in response to being attacked by the deworming medications. What happens is the worms which are susceptible are killed off by the dewormers. Worms who are resistant and who have survived the medication multiply.

One method used to monitor the effectiveness of horse dewormers is the fecal egg count. The count measures the number of eggs in a certain amount of manure. The number of eggs present in the feces may vary from one time of day to another, as worms lay eggs in cycles. Doing a fecal egg count at a time of low egg production could lead to a false impression of low numbers of parasites.

Types of Worms

Large Strongyles

The sexually mature worms are attached to the large intestine where they lay eggs that pass out of the donkey in the feces. These larvae can become infective in less than a week. Infective larvae travel up stems and blades of grass where they are ingested by grazing donkeys. The ingested larvae then begin their various migrations through the host until they mature and repeat the cycle.

Small Strongyles

Small strongyles encompass some 40 different species of parasites. They penetrate the intestinal lining in their larval stage. Here they form small cysts. The size of the cyst increases as the larval worm grows and escapes into the intestine. A severe inflammatory response may occur in the intestinal lining.

Strongyloides

Also called threadworms, these are common in foals. The infective larvae are passed in the jennet's milk for a period of time after foaling, beginning about the fourth day after the foal is born. Many farms routinely worm the jennet the day the foal is born to help reduce the numbers of these worms that she will pass on to the foal. Diarrhea is the most common sign of strongyloides infestation in foals.

Ascarids

Ascarids are seen in young foals. Ascarid eggs are ingested in contaminated feed or water. These eggs pass to the intestine where they hatch. From the intestine, larvae penetrate the intestinal wall and migrate through the veins to the liver and the lungs. The damage caused in the lungs by the larval migration may result in pneumonia. After a period of growth and development causing destruction in these organs, larvae invade the respiratory passage and are coughed up and swallowed. When the larvae reach the intestines again, they mature and remain in the small intestine. Often the young donkey will have a rough hair coat and severe potbelly. At this point, these donkeys should be wormed once a month for three months.

Bots

Bots are another of the common donkey parasites in the U.S.. Bots are insects; bot flies look much like bees and may be seen buzzing around the donkey, especially around the front legs in the knee area. They lay small, yellow eggs on the hairs. When the donkey licks his legs, the larvae hatch and are ingested.

Eventually, the bots reach the stomach where they attach themselves to the stomach lining with their biting mouthparts. A portion of the stomach may be solidly lined with attached bots, so that none of the lining is visible between them. Another species of bots has larvae which attach to the terminal part of the intestine just inside the rectum and may occasionally be seen protruding from this area.

These parasites may perforate the stomach wall, producing an ulcer and subsequent peritonitis. Occasionally they may cause colic. Bots are not diagnosed on fecal examination used for other parasites unless one of the larvae happens to be present in the sample. Animals who have bot eggs present on their hair can be presumed to be infected with bots.

Dewormers that kill strongyles do not necessarily also kill bots. Special products must be used to remove them from the digestive tract. Directions on the dewormer must specifically say that they kill bots.

Pinworms

These worms live in the rectum of the donkey. The worms are more common in young donkeys. The donkey may rub all the hair from the head of the tail. In some cases the entire tail may be rubbed bare.

Lungworm

Lungworms breed in the lungs of the donkey. They live without causing much harm and lay large numbers of eggs which contaminate the pasture. Horses grazing this pasture eat the eggs which hatch out in the intestine. They migrate to the lungs where, with few exceptions, they remain as infertile worms unable to complete their life cycle, but they cause a chronic cough in horses.

Donkeys seldom show clinical signs of infection but horses do. General body condition of the horse along with appetite and temperature are not affected but respiratory rates may be elevated and coughing may become more apparent when the horse is exercised.

Diagnosis is difficult since the parasites have developed only to immature adults therefore eggs will not be passed in the manure. Treatment is very simple. All donkeys and horses sharing the same pasture should be wormed at least every six months with ivermectin. This chemical class can be found in two very popular dewormers, *Zimecterin* or *Eqvalan*.

NOTE: You'll still find many uninformed horse owners telling people to never put a horse in the same pasture with a donkey because of lung worms. This is a not-to-worry if you deworm your horse at least twice a year with Ivermectin which will eliminate the lungworms from your horse.

Worming Methods

Several methods are used to deworm donkeys. The most convenient and safe method is by using an equine paste dewormer. For adult donkeys, we take a half piece of bread, apply the correct amount of paste, fold the bread and feed it to the donkey. Most never know they were dewormed.

Foals and weanlings generally do not acquire a taste for bread until they are yearlings therefore you will have to set the correct weight on the paste tube and apply to the side and back of the tongue. Whenever deworming a donkey, make sure they do not have hay or grass in their mouth or they will spit it out.

There are new deworming agents on the market that you mix in the grain on a daily basis. Obviously, you cannot use them if you do not feed grain. Also there is the concern that worms will become resistant to a dewormer that is fed daily.

Depending on the agent used, there are two things that happen to the worms. One is that the product kills the worms so that they are digested before they are passed. Other products make the worms disoriented and they lose their grip on the intestinal wall. In this case, large numbers of live worms will be passed and may infect your pasture before they die. This is why in small areas, it would be best to remove the manure.

Chapter 8

Reproduction, Breeding, Foaling

Prostaglandins
Their Use and Function

These are the new wonder drugs of the last few years in equine reproduction. Prostaglandin F2 alpha is used for treating dysfunctions of the reproductive cycle in mares and jennets.

The drug is given to mares and jennets who do not come into visible heat and are not pregnant or who come into heat erratically. It can be used to bring a jennet in shortly after she has gone out of foal heat so that instead of waiting 21 to 25 days for the second heat, she may be bred about 15 days after she foals. This allows her reproductive tract a bit more time to rest and get ready for pregnancy, but still brings her in earlier than she would come in by herself. It can be used to shorten the time between heat cycles when a jennet is missed or too many jennets are booked to the jack at the same time.

Prostaglandins are used in jennets who have too long a time between heat cycles. They bring the jennet back into heat and allow her to be bred sooner than her own hormones allow. They may be given for diagnostic purposes to problem jennets to see if they can be stimulated to come into a normal heat at all.

These drugs can also be used to synchronize heat cycles among a number of jennets so that they will foal within a short period (for management reasons).

These drugs may also be used to abort early pregnancies, such as a jennet who is bred who should not have been covered or her pregnancy has been diagnosed as being twins. One dose may not do the job; it may be necessary to give it two or three days in a row. When abortion is produced in this way, the jennet may not come into a normal heat for several months.

Prostin is one of the drugs most commonly used and it should be used in accordance with the label directions.

Prostaglandins only work on about 3/4 of the mares and jennets to whom they are given. The others often have hormone imbalances or an ovarian dysfunction so that they cannot respond. Most mares show signs of heat within 3 to 7 days after treatment. This is generally a fertile heat and the mare or jennet can be bred at this time. Mild, transient side effects may occur with the drug. These are generally not severe enough to be treated. Most jennets will show signs of sweating and general nervousness. Most jennets show signs of heat with one treatment. A few will require two or three treatments.

While these drugs can work wonders in some cases, they are by no means a cure-all. If the jennet does not have the ability to ovulate or has other abnormalities, they will not work at all.

Jennets who will not come into heat should be checked by your veterinarian to determine if they are doing so silently or if their ovaries are simply not functioning so that they cannot respond to the prostaglandin. Many jennets will have "silent heats", or show no signs of heat towards a jack, until their foals are several months old.

Prostaglandins are potent hormones. The reality of the changing hormonal concentrations in the body of an equine relative to changes in her sexual behavior during the estrous cycle is a complex interaction, not just a simple relationship of cause and effect. Changing the level of hormones in the body by artificial means can never, therefore, be simplistic. Administering one hormone at any given time may be likened to increasing one ingredient of a cake without reference to the other ingredients. When we give hormones to an equine much of the effect depends on the makeup or state of the jennet at the start of the treatment.

Since prostaglandins are potent hormones, they are not to be spilled on your skin while giving injections. Some labeling also advises against their being handled by pregnant women or people with asthma. They are not terribly dangerous drugs, but should be handled with respect.

UPDATE: One of my vets who is the reproduction specialist, has advised me of a relatively new drug on the market called *Estrumate*. It works the same as *Prostin* however does not cause the sweating and general signs of colic that *Prostin* does. **Important Note:** You must wait 7 days AFTER you feel the jennet has had a heat cycle before giving *Estrumate* or *Prostin*, or your jennet will not have an egg to be fertilized.

Cryptorchidism

There's been a lot of talk about cryptorchidism (retained testicle) within the Miniature Donkey industry. Speculations, rumors and incorrect information has been distributed so we wanted to get the most up-to-date and correct information straight from the horse's mouth. With the help of my equine surgeon, I interviewed Dr. John Hurtgen, DVM, President of the American College of Theriogenology (the study of animal reproductive diseases).

MDT Editor: Please tell me something about cryptorchidism.

Dr. Hurtgen: Cryptorchidism is a hereditary trait. The problem comes in that, and I can't tell you off hand, what the mode of inheritance is, but it's not a straight forward dominant type of inheritance. In other words, it's not so much that the stallion is a cryptorchid he needs to carry the gene for cryptorchidism.

He may or may not in fact be a cryptorchid and the mother of the resulting foal also has to have some combination of genes also and then you will produce a high incidence of cryptorchidism. There's one farm in Texas that has two stallions that they stand at stud. One is a cryptorchid and one is not. About half of the colts out of the normal stallion are cryptorchid and about a fourth of the colts out of the cryptorchid stallion turn out to be cryptorchid. Both of his stallions carry the gene for cryptorchidism and both of his stallions are abnormal. Again, cryptorchidism is hereditary but many cryptorchid stallions that are at stud are bred to mares that don't have that gene in their background, may never produce resulting foals, but if the resulting offspring then somewhere down the line are then bred to a horse with the cryptorchid gene then you are likely to see a slew of them.

MDT Editor: If you breed a cryptorchid jack, mainly because you are trying to reproduce a certain color, to his daughters, is the cryptorchid gene then doubled?

Dr. Hurtgen: Yes, a lot of their male offspring will be cryptorchid.

MDT Editor: If a son out of a cryptorchid jack has both testicles, what are the chances of his producing cryptorchid sons of his own? Then again, I suppose it would depend on if the jennet carried the cryptorchid gene wouldn't it.

Dr. Hurtgen: Yes, that's correct. Just because the sire is cryptorchid doesn't mean he will pass the cryptorchidism condition to his son. Let me see if I can give you an example.

Say you have a male red rose and a female white rose and you breed them four times. You will end up with one red rose, two pink roses and one white rose.

Cryptorchid Male   **Female**
Red Rose   BRED TO   White Rose
RR   rr

      Produces
      Rr (Pink)

Breed Two Pink Roses (Rr, Rr) – 4 times

      Produces
RR   rr   Rr   rR
Red   White   Pink   Pink

If the jack you want to breed to happens to have the genes of the white rose (rr) and another white rose (rr) even though it resulted from two pink breedings, you would have no chance of producing a Red (RR) rose. IF the colt you want to breed to happens to have the genes of Rr so to speak and you mated them to another Rr maybe you would end up one fourth of the time having a normal colt with two testicles, half the time you'd have a colt with two testicles but he'd carry the genetic factor for cryptorchidism, so when you subsequently bred that jack that has two testicles but really he's carrying gene for cryptorchidism, half of his resulting offspring would be carriers, one fourth would actually be cryptorchid and one fourth would be okay and not have the gene. That's a lot.

The genetics for cryptorchidism isn't quite that simple. It's two or three gene combinations that produce cryptorchidism.

MDT Editor: How do you feel about people using cryptorchid stallions as sires?

Dr. Hurtgen: Well, I don't know about the miniature donkey industry but you see the horse industry is not driven by economics. It's driven by non-economic factors therefore it is very difficult for a breed association to do anything about somebody who wants to stand a horse that carries a genetic defect, other than education. Of course the genes get spread within the gene pool. In the Quarter Horse for example there are certain sire lines that are pretty popular in which we see a fair number of cryptorchid foals every year and we see a lot of umbilical hernias in certain sire lines so umbilical hernias are also hereditary. Parrot mouth and offset knees are also hereditary.

MDT Editor: This is the problem with miniature donkeys because my guess is that there are under 10,000 (1995) miniature donkeys in the U.S. and Canada. I know of one jack who has produced quite a number of cryptorchid sons that people purchased as babies and didn't know that the weanling was carrying this defect.

Dr. Hurtgen: Well, these people didn't have to buy them, they could have had the jack examined.

MDT Editor: Well, how would they know if they purchased them as weanlings?

Dr. Hurtgen: Well, a normal colt has two testicles at birth. Now there are times when a colt is born with only one testicle but by the time he's six months old the second testicle will descend. I have had a few horses as old as 4 years old drop the second testicle even though he had just one up until that time. In a horse that drops that second testicle at the age of 2, 3, 4 years of age that horse may be carrying exactly the same gene as the horse with one testicle and always has one testicle. However, the normal situation, is for a foal at birth - at one day of age - to have two fully descended testicles. That's what is considered normal. There are supposedly horses that have two descended testicles, let's say until they are six months or a year old then all of a sudden a two years old, boom, they're gone. Now, the documentation of that is kind of difficult to come by. When a horse turns out to be a cryptorchid as a two year old and then you go back to the guy who owned the horse when he was a foal and say "hey, do you remember if this horse had two testicles when he was a baby?" Oh sure, he had two testicles. Well, see the horse may or may not have been specifically checked for two normal testicles in his scrotum.

It's a shame to have these genes continue to be bred into the miniature donkeys since you have such a small gene pool to begin with. In mammoth jacks there has been the importation of semen from Spain,

Poland, etc into the United States to introduce totally different genetics but apparently you don't have that option.

Castration

This is the name given to the surgery which changes a stallion into a gelding and renders him unreproductive by removal of the testicles. The procedure is also referred to as "gelding".

Donkey and horses are castrated for several reasons. Removing the testicles eliminates the source of male hormones in the body. This takes away the animal's sex drive, resulting in an animal who acts more like a mare than like a stallion. This allows the gelding, as the resulting animal is called, to be used around jennets/mares [usually] without undesirable breeding behavior. It also makes the animal much safer to handle and to be around.

A gelding usually has a more consistent disposition. Another very important reason for castration is to keep inferior animals from reproducing; this is important to the improvement of all breeds of animals, not just horses.

As with many other types of surgery, the earlier it is done, the easier it is on the animal. Donkeys and horses may be castrated at a few weeks of age. There is a problem with this procedure at such an early age. The resulting gelding sometimes has thin poorly developed front quarters, neck, and head. For this reason, most people wait until the animal is at least a year of age.

Most miniature jack donkeys usually start feeling their oats at around one year of age and some sooner. Most people have their jacks gelded at this age.

Many ranchers castrate their own horse colts. This is generally a rough-and-ready rodeo, with the animals roped and tied down and some cowboy wielding a sharp knife. My opinion is that this is a rather barbaric way to do a major operation on an animal as sensitive as a horse. For that reason, this article does not include a description on how to castrate your own animal. It is worth the price to most owners to have the surgery done under anesthesia to lessen the animal's suffering. A final word on this point - the shock resulting from the excitement combined with the pain of the surgery can kill a horse. That makes a veterinary bill look small in comparison.

THE OPERATION

The animal should be in good health when the surgery is done. He should not be recently recovered from any serious disease, especially distemper. Be sure to tell your veterinarian if the animal has been on sweet clover pasture or has been fed sweet clover hay, as these feeds may make the animal more prone to bleeding. The animal should not have been recently wormed, especially not with organophosphate wormers; some of these make the animal more susceptible to some of the anesthetics that are used and may cause serious complications. If at all possible, surgery should be done in spring or fall, either before fly season, or after a frost has killed most of the flies. Most veterinarians do not like to castrate donkey and horses during cold, rainy weather. Not only is it miserable work, but it seems to me that animals have more complications if castrated during these periods.

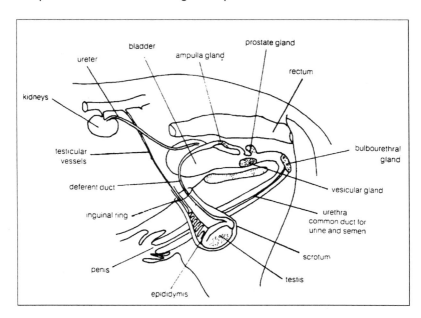

Veterinarians give some sort of anesthetic before starting to castrate. Your veterinarian has developed a routine which works for him. This may range from a small dose of tranquilizer and local anesthetic injected directly into the spermatic cords and nerves as he does surgery with the animal standing, to completely anesthetizing the donkey or horse until he is flat on the ground. He may or may not tie the animal up after it is asleep. He will then make incision - usually one over each testicle - and remove the testicles. He uses a clamp called an emasculator to crush the cords and blood vessels. This helps to prevent bleeding from the surgery site. After the testicles are removed, many veterinarians open the scrotal sack as far as they possibly can. This is to allow the area to drain well and to help prevent swelling and complications.

(Note: It has previously been reported to Miniature Donkey Talk that miniature donkeys have had a problem with excessive bleeding. The castration instrument, called an emasculator, has both a "crimper" and a "cutter". The crimper is ready-made for the large spermatic cord of the horse stallion. The spermatic cord of the miniature donkey, while not anatomically different, is smaller than the stallion. In some cases the crimper may not properly compress the cord, causing it to bleed when cut. The vet MUST be sure the cord is properly compressed, taking into account it's smaller size. DO NOT assume your vet is aware of this, so bring it to his attention.)

COMPLICATIONS AFTER CASTRATION

BLEEDING

Bleeding often occurs from the edges of the cut on the scrotum; it may also occur from a small artery in the spermatic cord. The donkey or horse may appear to bleed quite heavily, especially in warm weather. Untying the animal, if he has been restrained, and allowing him to relax will help reduce his blood pressure (which has been raised by the excitement and handling). This in itself helps the bleeding to stop. It rarely lasts more than 5 minutes. A small amount of dripping (a drop to a few drops at a time) beyond this time is not a problem. If the animal appears to be bleeding heavily more than an hour after surgery, consult your veterinarian and have him recheck the animal to make sure there are no problems or complications.

SWELLING

Swelling of the scrotal area may occur after castration, as well as swelling of the animal's penis, sheath, and hind legs. The animal may be reluctant to move; when forced to do so, he may move stiffly with a straddling gait. He may have an elevated temperature and little or no appetite. These complications can be almost entirely prevented by adequate exercise after castration to help keep the circulation moving in the area and to remove infected material.

If severe swelling occurs, call your veterinarian AT ONCE so that he may reopen the area, clean it out, and get it to draining adequately. He may wish to put the animal on antibiotics for a period of time. If he does use antibiotics, be sure to give the prescribed amount of medication for the correct length of time. Failure to dose may lengthen the animal's recovery time or result in his dying from infection. This problem can largely be prevented by adequate exercise after the surgery. If you have an animal swollen like this, it is probably your own fault. By trying to be "kind" to him, you have caused him a considerable amount of extra pain and discomfort and possibly endangered his life.

AFTERCARE

Some veterinarians administer penicillin after surgery; others do not. This is a matter of personal preference; a single dose probably does more for the owner's peace of mind than it does for the possibility of infection. If your donkey has not had a recent booster of tetanus toxoid, the veterinarian may administer either this or tetanus antitoxin, depending on the donkey's immunization history. If it is fly season, it will be necessary to spray the surgical area daily with a good fly spray. Don't spray it directly into the wound unless the flies are so bad that this is absolutely necessary. For most animals, spraying the vicinity is good enough.

Aftercare by the owner does more to prevent swelling and infection than anything the veterinarian can do. It is of the utmost importance to give the animal adequate exercise after surgery. This helps the opened area to rub together and drain out blood clots, as well as helping to remove infected material if there is any. It prevents swelling. If left to himself, the new gelding may stay in one place, nursing his sore spots. The worst possible thing that you as an owner can do is to just allow the animal to stand and become swollen. If a significant amount of swelling occurs, your veterinarian may have to re-anesthetize the animal and reopen and clean the wound. Some donkeys who have been allowed to stand will swell up to an enormous size. Needless to say, they will be in misery. The local swelling is usually accompanied by edema of the hind legs, often called "stocking" or "stocking up."

How much exercise should you give the animal? My personal policy is to let him rest on the day he is castrated. The day after, the owner is to exercise him 30 minutes to an hour. The second day after surgery, an hour is the absolute MINIMUM! Two hours are even better, continuing this amount of work DAILY until he is completely healed, which usually takes about two weeks. What kind of work? Spend that time walking him. Spending some of the time at a trot or a lope is even better.

Do NOT assume that since your donkey has been castrated, it is safe to turn him in with jennet and mares who are in heat. While sperm cells are no longer produced by the testicles, live semen may remain in some of the glands of the reproductive system for several weeks. Thus, the donkey or horse may be fertile enough to get a jennet or mare pregnant - usually the one you DIDN'T want bred. Assume an absolute MINIMUM of ten days for all fertile sperm to die. Two to three weeks are even better if you can allow that much time.

Also, it takes a period of time for the hormones to leave the animal's body. He may exhibit stallion-like behavior for a varying period of time, depending on how rapidly these are removed from the bloodstream. This usually requires a few days to a few weeks, depending on the individual. It also depends on how old he was when castrated. An older stallion may retain sexual behavior for a longer period of time than a younger animal would who was not fixed in this behavior pattern.

Reference: Ruth James, DVM, Bonnie Gross, Editor, MDT Magazine

Special Notes on castrating donkeys

All types of emasculators have been used on donkeys and mules and they do indeed, tend to bleed more following castration than do horses.

Relative to their size, the donkey has markedly larger testicles than the stallion. Many miniature jacks will have testicles equal in size or larger than those of a mature stallion. As one would expect, the larger testicles have larger blood vessels. Consequently, during castration, we are trying to crush larger vessels than when castrating the average horse. Thus a great chance for incomplete hemorrhage control.

In addition, the tunics and facia around the testicles of the jack seem to be more developed than in the horse. This further reduces the effectiveness of emasculation. In open castrations this toughness sometimes results in incomplete removal of the tunics.

Likewise the scrotum of the jack seems thicker than that of the stallion, due to increased presence of either the fascial or smooth muscle layer. There are also increased deposits of fatty tissue around the neck of the scrotum. As we would then expect, many times the post-castration hemorrhage is not always due to incomplete crushing or ligation of the vessels supplying the testicles.

Another consideration that may contribute to complications, including bleeding following castration, is the donkey and mules variable response to analgesics and anesthetics. Commonly used restraint drugs may not give as effective or as long a response in the donkey and mule as in the horse.

Elizabeth Kasnick's Emily with her companion goat

Caring For Your Miniature Donkey

Rectal Palpation

Are Broodmare Examinations As "Routine" As We Think?

(Ed Note: Anyone who has received MDT for any length of time knows that I am totally against rectal palpation of Miniature Donkeys to determine pregnancy. This article was written for LARGE HORSE MARES. Some people have stated that they use a tiny female veterinarian to palpate their mini's therefore, it is justified. This thought provoking article provides information on why palpation of a mini, by __any__ sized veterinarian is not rational.)

Palpation is a veterinary procedure which, although not complex in nature, requires tact and judgement. Almost every practicing equine veterinarian has had an experience where he has induced - probably through no fault of his own - at least a partial rectal tear. Given the high mortality rate associated with such injuries, the mere suspicion that a tear has occurred is cause for immediate concern. Rectal tears rank as one of the leading sources of veterinary malpractice lawsuits, according to statistics maintained by the American Veterinary Medical Association.

Is it the responsibility of the veterinarian to warn the owner and/or manager of the potential dangers involved each time a mare is examined? Is an annual review of the risks sufficient? Or is it a procedure so commonplace [in large horse mares] that the risk is understood and accepted by all parties?

The inner layer of the equine rectum is very fragile and can be easily damaged. The potential side effects - risk of infection, incoordination after use - limit its application. There are some mares in whom rectal palpation is simply not practical. The risk of injury is greater than the reward.

Although veterinarians palpate with their fingers as close together as possible, avoiding the use of a single pointed finger, the fingertips may cause some tears.

A veterinarian's suspicions of a tear will be confirmed by the presence of blood on his sleeve. Once the veterinarian acknowledges the fact that damage has occurred, he will proceed to discover how serious the problem might be. A first step is to examine the rectum using a glass or plastic vaginal speculum or a fibreoptic endoscope. After your veterinarian determines the extent of the damage, then the two of you must decide what medical steps are going to be taken. If the mare has suffered a complete rectal tear outside the peritoneal space, she is more likely to develop a massive abscess than deadly peritonitis, although both situations are life-threatening. If the perforation occurs in front of the area to which the peritoneum connects, it may only be a matter of hours before the mare dies an acutely painful death. At this point, there is no alternative except surgery: going in through the belly, flushing out whatever fecal material may be present, repairing the wound and administering high doses of antibiotics.

Anytime there appears to be even a remote possibility of damage, the prudent veterinarian immediately informs his client, then takes aggressive steps to either repair the damage or make some decisions about what to do.

When a complete rectal tear extends into the peritoneum, swift aggressive treatment is imperative, or death will surely follow. No matter how alarming the prospects, the potential for disaster is too great to ignore.

Reference: Portions of an article written by Bobbie Lieberman

Debbie Bradshaw in Kentucky supervising nap time

Udder Edema in the Miniature Jennet

Occasionally, the udder and the lower abdomen become engorged with fluid due to circulatory problems. When extreme, this udder edema is sometimes confused with an umbilical hernia, a blood-filled swelling (hematoma) or an abscess. Udder edema, however, is usually characterized by an accumulation of fluid within the mammary tissue and around the lymph vessels located along the jennet's belly.

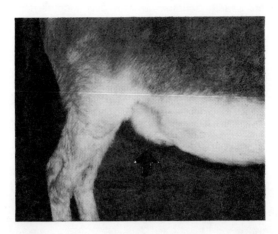

The condition, which occurs most frequently in heavy-milking jennets during early lactation and after weaning, can cause the udder to become warm and extremely painful. An emergency situation occurs when the udder is so painful that the jennet will not let her foal nurse. Severe edema predisposes the udder to infection and may prevent milk ejection.

You should call your veterinarian when you see an edema but first do a few things that your vet will surely ask about. Feel the edema, is it squashy or rock hard. Does the edema feel warm or hot to the touch? Take the jennet's temperature and report the reading to the vet.

Mild edemas will require no treatment other than exercise. Many jennets will develop a mild edema just days before she foals and it is a good indication that you can expect a baby soon. Many other jennets develop an edema within 12 to 24 hours after weaning a foal from her, and again the only treatment is exercise. It is rare, but it does happen, that a large edema will occur within two days of foaling, especially if the jennet is a heavy milk producer.

In severe cases, your veterinarian should see the jennet and he may advise massage, hand milking, cold and hot applications, and the use of mild counterirritants. He may administer diuretic drugs. Diuretics cause the shift of body waters into the urine. He may recommend lowering the jennet's salt intake in order to temporarily reduce fluid retention in body tissues. Reducing a jennet's grain intake may also help relieve swelling caused by fluid buildup within and around the mammary gland. Again, edemas are not usual]y serious, but they can become serious if you do not closely watch for changes.

Marty Wolfson enjoying a picnic lunch on Buckwheat's back

Early Embryo Loss

The term Early Embryo Loss means the pregnancy was terminated usually within the first 40 days of gestation. The exact cause is difficult to determine. The donkey's age can be a determining factor as jennets in their late teens have a slighter higher incidence of loss than younger animals. On the other hand, yearling jennets on up to two year olds have an even higher incidence of loss. This may be mother nature's way of preventing pregnancy in animals who cannot physically or mentally carry an embryo to full term.

A healthy inside layer of the uterus is crucial as this is where the embryo embeds as it starts to develop. Endometritis (inflammation or infection of the inside wall of the uterus) is a major reason for early embryo loss. The infection may kill the embryo outright or may cause decrease in progesterone, which is necessary for pregnancy. Progesterone is a hormone produced which quiets uterine muscle contractions. If the jennet conceives, her system will detect the baby and will continue to produce progesterone. *Note:* Once an equine aborts, the presence of a certain hormone can inhibit her ability to conceive again for up to four months. Ulcer-like structures, called endometrial cups, form in the uterus and begin manufacturing the hormone PMSG on about the 35th day of pregnancy, and continue to do so until about day 100. If an equine aborts any time after the 40th day, the cups continue to manufacture the hormone, and conception can become difficult until after the 100th day.

A healthy jennet has a much better chance of carrying the embryo through this first stage of gestation. Equines, which are very thin, carry a greater percentage of loosing the embryo. During breeding, the jennet should be at her ideal weight or <u>slightly</u> heavier. Dietary deficiencies are passed on to the foal making them weaker, have lower resistance to infection and often have defects in conformation.

Stress is an important factor in pregnancy loss and studies are currently under way in equines to determine just how much stress is harmful. It is thought that stress lowers progesterone levels, leading to embryo death. Stress also lowers the animal's resistance to disease.

Your jack should be a consideration in early embryo loss as he can transmit an infection from one jennet to another. Failure to get your jennets bred, should include an examination of him and his semen.

If a specific cause can be found for early embryo loss, prevention and treatment can be set in motion. In the case of progesterone deficiency, this can be provided either by injection or oral form. In the case of infection, lab tests can be done to find the specific antibiotic that will combat those specific bacteria, and infuse antibiotic in to the uterus.

In all cases, early embryo death should be investigated so that the cause can be eliminated. Sometimes no specific cause can be determined, in which case, the loss should be accepted and the jennet rebred.

Pheasant Meadow Farm's Precious

Causes of Abortion

The term abortion refers to the expulsion of the embryo or fetus between day 40 and 300 of pregnancy. Equine are much more susceptible to abortion than most other domestic animals. In the cow, the membranes surrounding the calf actually grow deeply into receptor sites in the uterine lining. By contrast, the membranes surrounding the equine foal only grow slightly into the mare's uterine lining. This makes disruption of the attachment much more likely.

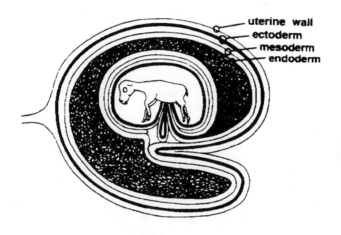

If the foal is delivered after a gestation of more than 335 days, it is designated as a stillborn, premature, or full term, depending on the circumstances of the delivery. Stillbirth, for example, is the expulsion of a dead fetus that has reached what would normally be considered a viable stage of development.

Hormone Imbalances, i.e. progesterone deficiencies can be an important cause of habitual abortion. This form of abortion usually occurs between the fourth and sixth months. Hormones must be produced by the body in the right sequence and amount in order to get and keep her pregnant. If anything goes wrong with this series of hormonal changes, the fetus will be aborted. Your vet may recommend progesterone injections to help maintain pregnancy.

Equine Viral Rhinopneumonitis is a highly contagious disease. The disease is seen in young donkeys as a respiratory disease then appears in older equine, often some months later, as the cause of abortions late in pregnancy although it can cause abortions as early as the fifth month. The jennet may show no signs of infection but the virus invades the placental membranes and attacks the fetus. The fetus is usually aborted in about 3-12 weeks when it is no longer able to function physiologically. Miniature Donkeys should be vaccinated with Equine Rhinopneumonitis Vaccine in their 5th, 7th, 9th and 11th months of pregnancy.

Bacterial Infections may cause the jennet to abort early in the pregnancy. Often no signs are noticed in connection with one of these early abortions. Bacteria such as Staph, Strep, and E. Coli are among those causing this type of problem.

Breeding the pregnant jennet can cause abortion in any month. Most jennets stop cycling once they have conceived but some continue to cycle for several months afterwards. If the pregnant jennet is bred, the cervical seal that maintains uterine stability will be disrupted and abortion occurs.

Rectal palpation to determine pregnancy has been documented as causing abortion in Miniature Donkeys for a variety of reasons.

Jennets carrying twins often abort after the 6th month of pregnancy, although there are a few documented cases of the delivery of twins. Twin abortion is often preceded by premature udder development and the jennet may drip or run milk beforehand. Apparently at around 6 months, the twins reach the limits of uterine stretch or capacity and abort for that reason.

Fescue toxicity is a more common reason for abortions in horse mares than it is in donkey jennets. I personally have never had a jennet abort due to fescue, HOWEVER, this may be due to the fact that our jennets get at least one flake of hay per day during summer months therefore they are not eating nothing but pure fescue. Fescue toxicity is caused by an alkaloid present in the grass during the lush stages of growth during the spring and early summer. I have heard of it causing placentas to become too thick for a foal to break through on their own. Fescue is seldom a problem on pastures that contain only a small percentage of fescue. The grass is less palatable than other grasses and equines usually refuse to eat it unless nothing else is available.

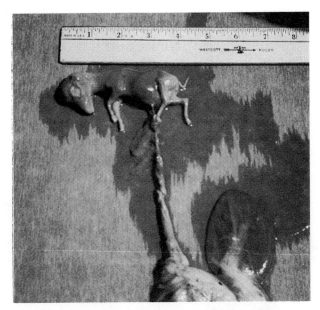

Aborted 58 day old miniature donkey fetus

Immature jennets may abort simply due to the fact that they cannot produce enough hormones and nutrients to produce a viable foal.

Trauma such as a kick, can cause abortion. The fetus is surrounded and protected by a cushion of fluid, however, a severe kick that hits the fetus directly may cause abortion. The aborted fetus usually displays a distinctive bruise at the site of injury. Severe stress due to overwork, fright or severe illness can also be responsible for abortion especially during the late stages of pregnancy.

Signs of abortion may be minimal, especially up through the 5th month. In early stages, you may happen to find a small, slippery sac and see a slight bleeding or dark brown discharge from the vulva or you may not see any discharge at all. If you are not in the right place at the right time, you might not see anything at all. In later months, you may notice a jennet has lost her pregnant look. I firmly believe that mother nature has a hand in some abortions to rid the body of a defective foal when no other causes can be found.

An aborted fetus is expelled wrapped in its membranes. If you wish to have it examined to try to determine the cause of abortion, be sure to save the membranes as well because they are often more informative than the fetus as to what caused the problem. If the jennet has aborted a fetus and the membranes have not followed, be certain to call your veterinarian.

Racing Donkeys?
Karla Wolfson's Cocoa in Florida

Helping To Avoid Foal Rejection

Sometimes after giving birth, a jennet will ignore or reject her newborn foal. Some will even viciously attack it. Some jennets seem confused and although express an interest in the foal, will not let it nurse and will kick it away.

There are a number of reasons why certain jennets balk at motherhood and can include hormone imbalances and physical problems that cause the jennet pain when the foal goes to nurse. Too much human interference during that critical time when mother and baby should be bonding, often causes many problems.

A nervous or insecure jennet may have her maternal instincts disrupted by too many, or too much, human handling at foaling. Some owners are too intent on making sure the baby gets up and starts to nurse. Their good intentions can often be the main cause of a jennet rejecting her foal.

The bonding between a jennet and her foal takes place - or is disrupted - during the first hour following birth. During this first hour, the jennet smells, nuzzles and licks her newborn and permanently identifies it as her baby. Too much human interference at this time can disrupt this bonding, especially if the jennet is a first time mother, timid or insecure. We have even heard of jennets who have had many foals, reject one that, because her owners did not give her time to bond with her foal, she no longer identified the foal as her own. Also, the placenta should not be immediately removed from the jennet as you will see her smell it then smell her foal which helps her identify the foal as her own. If you must dry the foal off, due to weather conditions, be certain to use a towel that has no odor, such as fabric softener on it, as this odor could get on the foal and also confuse the mother.

Too much human interference can also confuse the foal. The baby's natural instinct is to follow any large moving object - including people. Under natural conditions, the only large moving object is its mother as the jennet would leave the herd to give birth in a quiet place. If you enter the stall of an hour old foal, it will most likely follow you around as you move around the stall. This confuses the baby and doesn't make the mother any too happy either.

Immediately after birth and the breaking of the cord, the foal's navel should be dipped in iodine to prevent crippling joint ill or fatal infection.

This can be done in a matter of seconds. If no other life threatening situations develop, you should leave the stall and let mother and baby alone. The pair can be watched quietly from outside the stall or from a stall observation camera. Strange people especially tend to pose a threat to her newborn, in the jennet's mind, and cause her anxiety. If left alone, she will be more apt to concentrate her attentions on the new baby and begin her role as a mother.

Although donkeys are domesticated animals, a jennet's natural instinct at foaling time is to get away by herself and protect her newborn from predators. Even gentle laid-back jennets can become aggressively protective after she foals. When we have jennets act like this, we generally keep our distance for the first two days. Most will settle down, however, others remain overly aggressive and you may find yourself being kicked or run over when bending down to pet the foal. We deal with this situation by having one person that the jennet knows, halter and hold her while another person that the jennet knows, cuddles the foal at the same time petting the jennet. This shows the jennet that you have no intention of stealing or harming her baby. You may have to do this three or four times.

Newborn Miniature Donkey foals are generally on their feet within 30 minutes. Some take as long as an hour while others are scrambling to get on their feet within minutes. You should not help the foal stand up. (Remember, you aren't even supposed to be in the stall during this time!) With each unsuccessful try at arising, he gains coordination and strength naturally. The only exception would be if he has a physical problem, such as born very weak or has some other problem which needs veterinarian attention.

Be as patient as you can. Although the foal needs to absorb the colostrum antibodies in the mother's milk, his ability to absorb these antibodies remains very high for three hours. Don't feel like you have to push the foal to nurse as soon as possible, just because this is what YOU want.

Some jennets will not let a newborn nurse because their udder is extremely swollen and sore from milk. If you feel this is the problem, you will need yourself and one other person to help you. Halter the jennet and tie her to a post where she doesn't have much room to move. Scratch her chest and neck vigorously to help get her mind off the baby attempting to nurse. Have the other person put the foal in the nursing position - standing *along side* the jennet with head positioned near the udder. Put one hand on the foal's chest and the other on its hind end to hold it in place while it searches for its first meal. Do NOT hold the foal's head down to the udder. When you hold the head, all the foal does is concentrate on you holding his head - not where to find the udder. If you cannot hold the jennet still, you may have to resort to twitching her. (Twitching should be done by using a twitch on the upper lip. *Never ever* grab a donkey's ear and bend it!) Once the foal has nursed, it eases the soreness of the udder. Nursing also stimulates certain hormones and the "maternal instinct". Most jennets which initially reject their foals will eventually accept them if their owners go about every thing in the right way.

I hate it!

Unfortunately, there are always the rare few that viciously attack their newborn foals and in order to protect the babies, they must be removed from their mothers. Your veterinarian might want to try some tranquilizer on this jennet. If that doesn't work, the foal must be bottle fed or raised on a foster mother. We at Pheasant Meadow Farm had a foal rejection from a maiden jennet. We had just weaned another foal from its mother and this jennet gladly adopted this rejected baby and successfully raised him. We did manage to physically restrain the mother so that the foal could nurse from her eight times, and receive his colostrum, before he was taken from her.

The most common cause of foal rejection, is fear.

If one witnesses this kind of rejection, this is what happens: The jennet foals normally. When she gets to her feet, there is this strange little creature in the stall with her. Usually the foaling has occurred in a stall. They have spent their lives in a pampered, confined, artificial environment. They haven't grown up on a range or in a large-pasture environment, with donkeys or horses of different ages and genders and temperaments. They haven't witnessed birth and death like wild animals do in their normal environment. They react to the new foal with fear, just as they would if they have never seen a pig, or a cow, or a sheep.

If the afterbirth is hanging from their hindquarters, that panics them farther. They are already upset by the pangs of labor they have endured. Now a strange creature has suddenly appeared in their territory. Tie the afterbirth in a knot so that is it up off the ground.

When the foal starts to flop around, and struggles to his feet, that panics mother all the more. Then, when the foal approaches her, and she cannot escape, she freaks out and might defensively injure the foal.

If she knocks it down, or kicks it away, that reinforces that behavior and she will repeat it. Often, a painful udder complicates and worsens the situation.

Be very calm and reassuring with this mother. Talk to her, pet her, scratch her, and comfort her. Try to help her understand that this wet, little funny looking creature is not going to hurt her.

The most important trick-of-the-trade we can pass on to you is concerning maiden jennets (jennets who have never had a foal). These jennets have no idea what a foal is doing to her when it attempts to nurse for the first time. What we found is that if you start messaging her udder and touching her around her lower stomach, 3 to 4 weeks in advance of foaling, she begins to understand that this is not an off-limits area. She gets used to being touched in that area and will not be nearly as fearful of a foal approaching her there either.

We often hear of foal rejections but we honestly don't think there should be as many as we hear about. We at *Pheasant Meadow Farm* have had close to 300 miniature donkeys born yet have only had ONE complete foal rejection. That tells you how rare it SHOULD be.

We don't know all the reasons why some jennets reject or attack their newborns but we do know that human interference can be a factor in many of the cases.

St. Francis of Assisi administering a blessing upon Pine Grove Farm's Nestle and Buckwell Spent

Navel or Joint ILL

These are two disease problems seen in young foals, both of which result from infection entering through the umbilical cord (navel). In some instances, the bacteria causing the problem may enter through the digestive tract. They occur in foals from a few days to three or four months old.

An abscess at the stump of the umbilicus may be the first sign. The area becomes hot and swollen and may be discolored to bluish or purple. Sometimes, there may be no signs at the navel and the foal will be noticed to be severely lame. This may be bad enough that he is walking on three legs, and the owner immediately assumes that he has been kicked. Do NOT assume that he has been injured by the mare! Call your veterinarian immediately!

The lameness is generally accompanied by a fever (up to 101.5 degrees F or more (38.5 degrees C). The foal may be depressed. The pulse may be weak and rapid and the mucous membranes injected (reddened). Several joints may be swollen, showing that the bacterial infection has localized there. The fetlock, hip, stifle, and elbow joints are most commonly affected. The joints may feel hot to the touch and the foal may show severe pain if they are forcibly moved. The white blood count (W BC) is elevated. X-rays may be necessary to determine the extent of the damage to the joint. If left untreated, severe damage to the joint surface may occur and the animal may be permanently crippled.

Treatment includes antibiotics recommended by your veterinarian. These are usually administered for a MINIMUM of five to seven days. If treatment is started before damage to the joint cartilage has occurred, the foal may be much improved within 24 hours and will be nursing. The temperature will return to normal. Do NOT stop treatment at this time or the infection will come back. This time you will have pure pus in the joints. When the antibiotics are used for only three days, they will clear the bacteria from the blood stream (this is why the foal feels so much better). This length of time is inadequate to remove them from the joints.

Consult a veterinarian for a foal with joint or navel ill. Owner treatment, especially if inadequate in quantity or duration, may complicate the problem and lead to a joint ill that cannot be cured. Some foals may require surgery to help remove damaged tissue from the joint surface and bone. In some severe cases, the joint cartilage is damaged beyond repair and the foal will never be normal. In these cases, euthanasia is recommended for humane reasons.

In some cases, a procedure called joint lavage is used. This involves anesthetizing the foal and putting two large needles into opposite sides of an affected joint. Tubes are attached to the needles and a pump is used to flush antibiotic or other cleansing solutions through the joint cavity. Incidentally, the same procedure is sometimes used in older animals to remove cartilage debris and other material which is causing destruction within a joint.

If an abscess at the navel is the only problem, it may be necessary to open and drain it. Leave this to your veterinarian and follow his instructions for aftercare religiously.

Foal Septicemia

This is an infection which spreads throughout the foal's bloodstream. It may be due to bacteria, viruses, or a fungus. It may originate within the uterus before birth, or may enter the foal through the digestive tract, lungs, or umbilical cord.

It is most common in foals with poor immune systems, premature foals, or those less than two weeks old. A mare who drips milk prior to foaling may lose all her colostrum by the time the foal is born resulting in a lack of antibodies. It is also seen in foals who do not receive any colostrum.

Management problems, such as damp, drafty quarters, overcrowding, and filth, may make the foal more susceptible. However, it can occasionally occur under the best of conditions. A septicemia may result in an animal's death or leave it with a chronic infection, stunted, or a poor-doer.

The foal may be lethargic or depressed, even comatose. He may not be nursing, leaving the mare's udder bulging and painful. His mucous membranes may be bright red to purple. The foal may be in shock. He may be jaundiced (yellow). There may be small hemorrhages inside the mouth and ears. Nervous system signs may be seen, especially coma or convulsions. The foal may show dehydration. When the skin in pinched and released, it will stand up where it has been pinched together. Check the foal's umbilical cord for swelling or drainage of urine. He may or may not have diarrhea. Joint ill - with its hot, painful, swollen joints - may accompany the septicemia.

Foal septicemia is VERY serious and often fatal. Call your veterinarian immediately if you suspect this problem. Prompt, intensive treatment is the only thing that will save the foal. Even with the best of care, the problem is so intense that many foals are lost. Your veterinarian will treat for shock and for the organisms causing the disease.

Prevention involves management to reduce stress to the foal. Foaling quarters should be clean, warm, and dry. Make sure that the foal gets colostrum. If you have reason to suspect that the mare has none, try to get some from another mare or use some that you have frozen from a normal mare.

Foals from mares who have previously had problems may need preventive antibiotics for a few days. The mare should be kept up on her immunizations to keep up the degree of immunity that she passes on to her foal. The umbilical cord should be disinfected with iodine more than once. Do it right after the foal is born, and at least once or twice more, 12 to 24 hours later. On some premises, the umbilical stump is iodined daily for five to seven days.

Chapter 9

Behavior, Psychology
and Training

Wood Chewing

Wood chewing is one of the most common stable vices. Although pastured donkeys may occasionally chew wood, it is much more common in closely confined donkeys and those kept in stalls a lot. It is done at any age and by both jacks, jennets, and geldings. Foals as young as 1 month of age have been observed to mimic their wood-chewing mothers and herd mates. Breaking a wood-chewing habit by training would be time-consuming, frustrating, and probably fruitless.

Although all types of wood may be chewed, the vice appears to be greatest with softer woods, such as pine, aspen, and fir, and also plywood, particleboard and chipboard. Occasionally hardwoods, such as oak and locust, may be chewed, but they appear to be less attractive to the wood chewer.

Like many behavioral problems, wood chewing may to some extent be a normal behavior that becomes a problem only because it becomes an excessive or repetitious habit. However, any amount of wood chewing may be undesirable because of the damage it causes to facilities. The destruction of wood, and the expense of repairing stalls, fences, and barns destroyed by wood chewers may be second only to the cost of feed.

Generally, wood chewing doesn't harm the donkeys. Much of the wood chewed is dropped, although varying amounts may be ingested. Occasionally wood splinters may penetrate the mouth, causing infections. Wood chewing also increases dental wear. In addition, it may become such a fixation or habit with some animals that food and water intake is reduced. In some cases, wood chewing may lead to cribbing.

Although donkeys and horses by nature are primarily grazers, when they have access to brush and trees they may also occasionally browse, eating brush, very small trees, branches, leaves and bark, even when there is no scarcity of grass. Bark eating can lead to many trees being debarked from the ground to as high as the donkeys and horses can reach.

Many visitors who come here to our farm are pretty amazed that we have 4-board fencing, painted black, that is seldom chewed on and want to know my secret.

Although we have several pastures, we have one large pasture where most of the donkeys and horses are that has some woods in it. I'd say the donkeys and horses wipe out around 2 trees per year by chewing the bark off. I rarely see the donkeys chewing on trees but I do see the horses chewing on them, however, the donkeys will go after a downed tree like a kid in a candy shop.

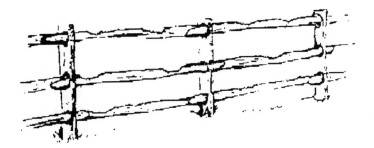

As for our fences, when we first purchased this acreage 12 years ago and put up part of our wood fencing, we painted it with creosote three times. At that time, creosote was still being sold as fence paint. Creosote used to be the anti-chew ingredient of choice. A pungent distillate of coal tar or wood tar, it was messy and smelly, but it worked. Several years ago the government severely restricted the use of creosote due to its carcinogenic properties. Our black fencing is attractive so we like to keep it painted. Since creosote is no longer available we've been using a black Asphalt Fence Paint obtained through a local paint dealer. Could it be that 12 year old creosote underneath about 6 layers of asphalt fence paint is still deterring the donkeys and horses from chewing on our fences? Don't think so. Why? Because we've also put in new pastures, with new fence, with only the Asphalt Fence Paint on it but no creosote.

The cause of wood chewing in confined donkeys may be a combination of any or all of the following: boredom, insufficient chewing or a desire for more chewing, mimicking others, or a liking for the taste of the wood.

We have seen an increase in the desire to chew wood when donkeys are fed pelleted feed or when donkeys are given grain and therefore less hay. Feeding pellets instead of long-stem hay increased the amount of wood chewed fourfold in one study, whereas there was no difference in wood chewing when hay was fed either loose or cubed. Wood chewing is also increased by decreased frequency of feeding.

A nutritional imbalance is often suspected, however, the only nutritional factors that have been associated with increased wood chewing are a protein deficiency and low dietary fiber, as in hay.

Like most stable vices, wood chewing should be prevented or stopped as quickly as possible before it becomes a fixation or habit, to prevent its detrimental effects, and to prevent it from spreading to other animals that might mimic those chewing wood.

To prevent, stop, or at least minimize wood chewing, decrease the animal's confinement and increase the animal's activity and companionship, ideally by putting the donkey on pasture with others, if possible. Feed less or no grain or pelleted feeds; feed more hay; and feed as frequently as practical. If a companion isn't provided, provide a toy such as a horse ball. If even with these procedures wood chewing occurs, large soft-wood tree trunks may be put in with the donkeys to chew on. Many people have stated that a large tree branch thrown in their paddock has stopped the fence chewing.

One option for protecting wooden facilities is to cover the areas, most likely to be chewed with a durable material. This can be an effective solution, but can require much time and expense. The most common materials used for protective edgings are plastic, sheet metal, and heavy screen. Wooden edges - horizontal, vertical, and every angle in between - are easy for a wood chewer to grab onto. Edges of square posts and boards can be protected using pre-bent 90-degree metal edging. Metal, 20-gauge or heavier and 1-1/2 inches wide on each side, provides adequate protection in most cases. Resist the temptation to use drywall edging made for home construction. Although readily available, they are much too flimsy and can easily tear off into pieces exposing dangerous sharp edges.

An electric wire, or covering wood surfaces with metal, creosote, or an unpleasant flavoring, may prevent wood chewing but doesn't provide what the donkey or horse wants or alleviate the frustration responsible for causing it to chew wood. As a result, the animal's frustration or unfulfilled need may be expressed in other ways that may be just as undesirable as wood chewing. Compounds put on wood to prevent wood chewing must be reapplied periodically, often stain anything that comes in contact with them, and often have an undesirable appearance.

Where it is not practical or desirable to cover wood with metal or plastic, the wood can be treated with an anti-chew substance. Home-made anti-chew concoctions include strange and diverse ingredients Aunt Tillie's Revenge hot sauce, used motor oil mixed with gasoline, etc. Many home remedies do nothing to deter chewing, however, and some even seem to encourage it.

Dyco-Sote smells and looks like creosote and seems to work as well for preserving wood and preventing chewing. Available in clear, brown, or black, nontoxic and non-carcinogenic Dyco-Sote is far safer to use than creosote. (Dyco Associates, Inc., 830 Hawthorne Ln, West Chicago, IL 60185 708-231-7000)

Although donkeys and horses are more likely to chew during cold, wet weather, only a few anti-chew products are recommended for application to wet wood. Chew Stop is a thin, clear liquid with a strong cinnamon aroma. Be careful Chew Stop may cause blistering if it contacts your skin. and it's extremely flammable.

Two other products suitable for application to wet wood are Raplast and Cayenne Hot Spray. Both contain a form of capsicum, an ingredient found in some personal defense sprays, which can be very irritating to the eyes, nose, mouth, and skin of people and animals.

Trees. Some horses and donkeys make beavers look like loafers when it comes to destroying trees. Once the bark is removed around a tree's circumference, the tree is as good as dead. Some home owners wrap chicken wire around the tree trunk. Others simply build a fence around each tree - far enough away so a horse/donkey can't reach the trunk. There are also several anti-chew products that can be safely applied to trees, including Bitr'Byte, Chew Stop, and Halt Cribbing.

References: Lon Lewis, DVM PhD; Richard Klimesh, Farrier, past issues of MDT Magazine

Twitching
The Oldest and most commonly used method of restraint

Most times, some form of restraint must be used to observe, manipulate or treat a part or the whole of the animal, even if it is done only by a halter. This not only applies to veterinary procedures, but also farrier or dentistry work. A twitch works by producing a certain amount of pressure on the sensitive nerves of the upper lip. This takes the animal's mind off a painful or annoying procedure being done elsewhere on his body.

It should be stated up front that your Editor, much prefers proper training and the application of patience, before the use of a twitch. However, there are times when a twitch is an absolute necessity, as the donkey simply cannot be worked on without it. As stated previously, some donkeys hate, and always will, having their hooves trimmed and the job cannot be done without the use of a twitch. When the only options you have are not trimming hooves, resulting in deformed legs and infected feet, or twitching, the answer is obvious.

As Dr. Robert Miller states, "To begin with, I'd like to make four statements that may be controversial. But they are based on experience, and I firmly believe they are accurate.

1.   The twitch is a perfectly legitimate and necessary device for doing certain procedures with equine.
2.   Like the bit, the twitch is grossly misused and excessively used, and is too often used abusively and unnecessarily.
3.   Nobody fully understands why and how the twitch works, although several theories exist.
4.   The twitch, used injudiciously, is probably the most frequent cause of injury to people working with horses on the ground.

The twitch remains an expedient and convenient method of restraint for the non-veterinary horseman.   But even the veterinarian will often choose to twitch an equine than sedate him, for a variety of reasons. For example, to do some brief procedures it may be quicker and simpler, and less expensive to the owner, to twitch rather than sedate. There may be less risk to the animal. Remember that *all* drugs, including tranquilizers, will sometimes have adverse side effects."

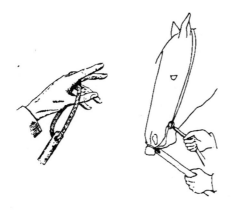

There are several methods in which to twitch a donkey, the most common being using a twitching instrument applied to the upper lip. The twitch, consisting of a length of smooth wood with a loop of rope or twine through a hole at one end, is a very useful tool when trying to restrain an equine physically. The loop of the twitch is passed over one of the operator's hands, while the handle of the twitch is held in the other hand or by the person holding the donkey's head. The donkey's lip is grasped in the hand with the loop. The loop is then passed over the hand and the twitch handle twisted to tighten the loop onto the lip. This will result in the donkey standing rigidly and any required procedure can then be carried out.

If the twitch is placed too high or twisted too tightly, it may interfere with the donkey's breathing and cause him to panic. Many people either apply a twitch too lightly or use excessive pressure. Too little pressure may cause the twitch to slip off at an inopportune time and too much pressure may injure a donkey by cutting it or simply making the animal explode in anger. It is also important to realize that a twitch will "wear off". Generally twitching will only restrain an animal for up to 10 minutes.

There are donkeys and horses who get mad and actually become harder to work on when they are twitched. These animals need to be tranquilized by your veterinarian.

A donkey can be twitched by hand; this is useful for short procedures when only a quick restraint is needed. You can either grab a handful of the end of the nose and twist or can just dig your fingernails in as you pinch from side to side. This procedure is also convenient when you don't have a twitch handy.

A popular sort of twitch is made like a nutcracker. It has a cord and can be snapped onto the animal's halter. This is useful when you have inexperienced help who can hold the animal by the lead rope, but cannot handle a twitch at the same time. It also works well when you are trying to do a procedure yourself.

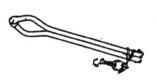 Pull the handles tightly together to put pressure on the animal's nose and get his attention. Then, wrap the cord around the handle one or more times to take up some of the extra cord and keep pressure on the nose. Drop the cord between the handles and proceed back to hook it on a convenient halter ring.

Many horse people, especially farrier's, believe in twitching by grabbing an animal's ear and twisting. Your Editor has a particular distaste for this method and would rather see a donkey chemically tranquilized, rather than having those precious - not to mention very sensitive - ears twisted.

To quote Dr. Ruth James, "Some people are in the habit of twitching an animal by the ear. This is not a good idea if you value your animal. The nerves around the base of the ear may be injured quite easily, resulting in an animal that is flop-eared for the remainder of his life. That's too high a price to pay for a few minutes of restraint. This procedure can also make a donkey extremely head-shy, only after one time.

I also do not like the use of stud chains on little donkeys. These are lead lines, usually made of leather that have about a foot of chain attached to the end. The procedure is to put the chain over the top gums inside the mouth. When the animal moves, severe pain occurs as the chain hits against the gums. It is my experience that 99.9% of anyone using a stud chain, does not have the experience to use it properly and are causing an animal unnecessary severe pain.

Recent studies have reported that twitching actually releases a natural chemical into the brain called endorphins. Endorphins are opiate-like painkilling chemicals, released by the brain in response to stress. Physical or mental stress can cause endorphin release. Endorphins have been found to be the cause of "runner's high," and the reason that some endurance athletes become literally addicted to their sport.

If done *correctly,* twitching can be a safe, humane procedure.

Reference: by Bonnie Gross, Horace Hayes, Veterinary Surgeon, Ruth B. James, DVM and Robert M. Miller, DVM

Donkey *ill-Manners*: The Biter

There are two major types of biters. The first is a young donkey (most common with intact jacks) that uses the nipping to release pent-up energy. This donkey is often fun and playful but tends to get very impatient. It is important to be firm with this young donkey and to "nip the problem in the bud," but you do not need to reprimand this donkey harshly. This form of nipping is actually "come on, let's play!" rather than "I'm going to get you."

The second type of donkey is usually more mature and has a history of being abused. He has turned to biting as a protective mechanism and cannot yet differentiate between friend and foe. He feels that all humans are out to hurt him, and he will try to get you before you can get him. This behavior cannot be permitted, yet it can be difficult to rid this donkey of the vice completely. Regardless, you should be patient and committed to bring about the maximum amount of reform possible.

Occasionally you will find a third type of biter. This donkey nipped as a youngster, and the previous trainer or handler smacked the donkey on the nose as a method of training. This donkey has turned biting into a game. He tries to get you as fast as possible, then sees how many ways he can find to avoid punishment. While not being mean, this type of biter can still be destructive. He will also tend to be head shy because of the hit-and-miss game that he has played in the past. Handling about the head and muzzle can be helpful in curbing this evasive response, but be careful that you are not bitten in the process.

Biting is fairly common among donkeys in the wild. Most donkeys can be broken of the habit, but others will be biters for life. The best solution is to prevent and catch the problem at a very early age. The motivation behind the biting and the current age of the donkey determine how much reform can occur. Even if you cannot completely break your donkey of this habit, you can take steps to reduce the problem. This will at least minimize the chance of injury to yourself or someone else.

When it comes to training your donkey not to bite, there are as many tricks of the trade as there are donkeys that bite. When working with your biter, you do not turn your back on him when you are within his reach, and never let him "play" with your zipper or the sleeve of your coat. More often than not, this is an entrée' to a nip. Also be careful when you are grooming any donkey that is known to bite. He may be waiting for you to turn your back and may get you where you least expect it.

When you are leading a donkey that bites, pay attention to where you place your lead-hand. Many biters will try to eat your hand as they walk. The biter has perfected the art of biting and then pulling away, and he is lightning fast. Keep your eyes open around this donkey or you may end up with less skin than you started with.

When you are training your biter, never hit him on the nose. This will inevitably lead to the head-shy problem described earlier. Smack him on the shoulder, on the rump, under the stomach, but not on the nose. It will solve nothing and will turn into a battle of the quickest. *(Note: You often see jennets correcting their very young foals by nipping them on the front legs in the forearm area. Considering that they are already used to being corrected in this area, you may also use this portion of the body to smack.)*

The best approach is to catch your donkey when he is thinking about it but has yet to strike. A sharp "no" or "quit" should make him think otherwise. If he does manage to get in a strike, slap him with the flat of your hand on the neck or shoulder (or on any large body part within reach). Repeat the command "no". Your donkey needs to know that you mean it when you warn him. You must be firm and consistent with this donkey. There is not room for "I'll let you get away with that one but don't do it again." Be vigilant and reprimand at each and every attempted bite. This especially holds true for the more mature donkey that has biting ingrained into his every thought. No matter where he is or who is handling him, do not allow him to bite or even attempt to bite.

Hand feeding your biter is also a no-no. Biting behavior can be exacerbated or even caused by hand feeding treats. We all know that a donkey is never satisfied by one treat alone, and his greed will usually lead to a certain amount of grabbiness. The more grabby he gets, the more he will reach for the hand. Out of frustration, he will grab at any hand, hoping that a treat is enveloped in it. If this happens enough, a biter is created. This is not to say that you have to withhold treats. Just be sure to place any and all treats for a biter in the donkey's feeder rather than feeding him by hand.

Handle your biter as much as possible around his nose and head. Be cautious, but rub his nose, chin, and jowl and let him know that handling can be a pleasurable experience. This will build trust with your donkey and will let him know that he doesn't have to be so self-protective around you.

In regards to biting jacks, much of it is instinctual. Jacks are born with strong herding and protective instincts. It was up to the jack to protect the members of his herd and to defend against intruders. Biting was an indispensable weapon in his arsenal.

Another training device that many donkey owners have used is holding a sharp object in your hand and letting the donkey *run into* it with his mouth as he goes to bite you. Do not jab at the donkey, as the idea is to let the donkey run into the object so that he gets the idea that attempting to bite *you* hurts *him*. The object should not be pointed enough where it would cut or puncture the donkey's skin.

Reference: This excellent article is from *Horse Training Basics*

The Elderly Donkey

When a donkey reaches the age of 10 years, it is termed "aged" even though 10 years is when a donkey is in the prime of life and perfect for all activities. It is not uncommon for a well cared for donkey to live well into their late 30's and for jennets to produce well into their 20's.

We purchased "Grandma" *(every large breeder I know owns at least one Grandma - and that's always her name!)* several years ago along with her daughter "Pebbles." We estimated Grandma to be in her early 30's. Grandma and Pebbles were usually inseparable up to the time that Pebbles had a foal at her side. At that time, Grandma respected Pebble's protectiveness for her foal and kept her distance. Once the foal was about a month old, they were again inseparable. We will refer to our personal experiences with her within this article.

Grandma at age 42

Most elderly donkeys suffer from some form of arthritis as does Grandma. Every year we noticed her becoming more cowhocked in her hind legs due to weakening of the joints. Cold weather certainly seems to bring on the signs of arthritis more so than warm weather. Older donkeys also cannot cope with temperature fluctuation the way younger animals can. It became apparent that "Grandma" could not tolerate severe cold and had to be kept in a stall as night along with heat lamps.

Every winter got a little more difficult for Granny until finally she developed arthritis in her back legs and as with people, she had a hard time during very cold weather. She went through a very difficult period where she couldn't get up on her own for several days without our help. Knowing how well she does in temperatures above 45 degrees we had to take several measures to help her get through the winter. For approximately 45 days we had her on 1 gram of bute a day. We squirted the paste on a half piece of bread along with Maalox® to ease the damage to her stomach lining from the bute. Being the little hoggett that she is, she gobbled it right up.

We also put her on a supplement called Syno-Flex which is a product that improves joint fluid. (These products can be expensive at $1.00 a day.) As shown in the photographs, we wanted to keep her arthritic legs warm so we bought heavy duty knee-highs that we cut the toes out of and put on her legs. At night, she was kept in a heated 50 degree stall and during the day she wore the knee highs. I'm not sure which procedure we did that had the best results or if it was a combination of everything, but as soon as the temperatures began to warm up and spring approached, you could find her trotting around on our lawn where she spent her days.

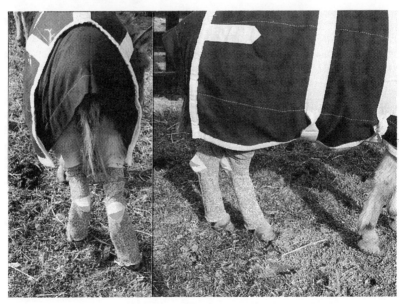

You will find that older donkeys will not shed winter coats as quickly as younger animals and sometimes do not shed winter coats at all. Because of this, summer temperatures can also cause heat stress problems.

The time comes, as it did with Granny, that older donkeys will not shed their winter coat's at all and must be clipped.

An older donkey must not be too fat or too thin. Once an elderly donkey has become thin, it is difficult to get their weight back up.

Teeth problems such as sharp points and missing teeth can make it difficult for a donkey to eat. In herd situations, older donkeys avoid confrontations so younger animals can stop them from consuming the amount of hay that they should. If you find this to be the case, feed your older donkey in a place off it itself. Also, if you find an older donkey with many missing or worn down teeth, you should buy a complete pelleted feed which consists of both hay and grain. On the other hand, many elderly donkeys will put on weight easily as they do not run and play like they used to. "Grandma" seemed to decline somewhat in winter even though she was getting plenty of excellent quality hay and otherwise appeared in good health. She could not afford any weight gain so we put her on a daily pelleted vitamin supplement.

A word of warning: Many of these vitamin supplements contain a high percentage of fat as they are normally given to hard keepers and/or under weight animals. Be sure the vitamin supplement you buy has a low fat content.

Exercise is very important for an elderly donkey. Plenty of exercise keeps arthritic joints pliable and is essential on a daily basis. It also should go without saying that vaccinations, especially influenza and rhino, along with worming schedules are kept up to date. Hoof care should be a regular routine as long, crooked hooves are painful and uncomfortable when they are on the end of arthritic legs.

An old faithful donkeys makes very little work for his owner, but it does need special consideration and attention. It is the responsibility of the owner to maintain his old donkey and adopt a common sense approach and routine to make the last few years of your friend as comfortable and happy as possible.

....On a sad note, we recently lost our old Granny donkey, estimated to be around 48 years of age. Many of you on visiting *Pheasant Meadow Farm* over the years met her as her and her elderly daughter, Pebbles, practically lived on our lawn.

We feared the end was near when we noticed in the fall that she couldn't handle even day time temperatures in the mid 40's. (She was put in a heated stall at night.) She would shiver with a heavy coat and knee-highs on. One night she went down and clearly indicated to us that she had no desire to continue. Things happened fast and her bodily functions quickly started to shut down. I said my good-byes, and she was humanely and painlessly put to sleep by our veterinarian with Mike at her side.

We rescued ol' Granny and Pebbles many a year ago, when both were near death due to starvation, and we brought them back to good health. Granny apparently never forgot that and lived for food. Because of being aged, she never became fat so we always had various goodies on hand for her. She had her share of special grain, bread, apples, carrots, and quality hay. She also apparently never forgot how people once treated her so she was never, shall we say, abundantly friendly with people. Maybe it was just her personality. She always did like bossing Pebbles around.

We remember the time about eight years ago, Pebbles foaled during the night and Granny promptly claimed the foal as her own as Pebbles stood patiently by, with a disgusted look on her face. No way was Granny giving up that baby. Every time Mike approached, Granny let out a snort and a kick. I finally said, "Granny you old fool, that baby's hungry now give 'er back to Pebbles" and she gave in.

Not long ago, we were outside trimming Granny's hooves. Mike would only pick them up a few inches off the ground because of her arthritic legs, otherwise she'd let out a loud grunt to warn you of her objections. That didn't stop her from raising her back legs plenty high enough to kick at Mike, occasionally landing a blow on his leg. The job always took longer than it should have because Mike could only work on her in between laughing at her spunk.

'Ol Granny was mean, ornery, ill-tempered, surly, grouchy, grumpy and just plain irritable most of the time. But, that's probably why we miss her so much.

A Little About Jacks

There are breeders with very mild mannered jacks who do have success running them with jennets and foals, etc. as a family group. However, I would venture to say these are in the minority and they certainly run a great risk depending on the jack never to change his behavior and become aggressive. In 21 years as a breeder, I have never run jacks with my jennets all the time. There are many reasons for my decision to segregate the sexes at Windy Ridge Farm, but the main ones are:

Many pasture bred jacks can be very rough on the jennets. Even when in standing heat, these jacks will often chase and bite jennets unmercifully. Maiden, new or visiting jennets can be quite terrorized and consequently driven to run into fences or jump them, in an effort to escape.

Mature jacks can become very aggressive and harass jennets almost continually whether they are bred or not. Such constant bullying and sometimes attempts at further breeding, can cause abortions to occur.

This same harassing behavior may also be seen if a jennet is left to foal in the same pasture as the jack (NEVER!). With the hormonal changes during the birth process, combined with other smells at foaling time, it is possible a jack may confuse the process with that of a jennet coming in season.

If left with the herd when the jennets are due to foal, some jacks will look upon the arrival of the foal, especially a jack foal, as an intruder. Not only will he then try to get at the foal, but he may kill it if he does reach it. *(Ed Note: We have heard of several jacks killing newborns.)*

If left with the herd when jennets foal, then the jack will likely rebreed the jennets when they come into foal heat (7-10 days after foaling). Equine research has shown that such early rebreeding is followed by a high abortion rate - the jennet's reproductive tract is simply not healed sufficiently to sustain another conception. It is preferable to wait for rebreeding until the second or third heat after foaling depending on the condition of mother and foal.

I have always preferred to keep my jennets, foals and youngstock entirely separate from my jacks. Pasture breeding may be the least labor intensive method, but involves the greatest risk, and I have always considered my donkeys to be too important to put them at such risk. Consequently our breeding is always in-hand breeding. Either way we have accurate, exact dates on which to predict foaling the following year. That does not however, mean that we isolate our jacks and treat them like lepers! Far from it, because such isolation only promotes the development of abnormal stallion behaviors.

Hand-Breeding

(*Ed Note*: We at *Pheasant Meadow Farm* always keep our jacks in their own corrals/pastures, each having access to their own stall inside the barn, from their enclosure. We never allow them in with the herd of jennets or around youngsters. When we are ready to breed, we **always** muzzle our jacks. The ritual of breeding always means jacks will run and bite jennets and we see absolutely no need for this torture. We muzzle the jack and usually put him in a large stall area or a small corral. We then bring the jennet to him – without her foal. We let the jennet loose in with the jack. Some jacks will breed a jennet within a matter of minutes and others will take as long as a hour. Regardless, the foal stays out of harms way and is only separated from its mother for an hour or less.)

In winter our jacks are kept in alternate large board fence corrals topped with hot wire. Each corral has a run-in box stall in the barn. The alternate corrals between the jacks are home to weanling jacks or jennets who are segregated by sex at the time of weaning (4 - 5 months). At no time are mature breeding jacks ever kept in corrals side by side!

In spring I always have one open jennet destined as companion for each jack, aside from the others he will breed. He will be allowed to hand breed her every second day then, as she is going out of heat, the pair will be put out in their pasture for the summer. I try very hard to chose a jennet that I know he likes and will not boss the jack around - some jennets can be VERY bossy. Some jacks have very definite preferences as to who they will or will not associate with!

Reference: by Sybil Sewell

The Donkey Guardian

I'm surprised in this day and age of excellent publications and instant communications to find the donkey's exceptional ability to be a flock guardian is still such a well-kept secret; or a concept fraught with misconceptions and misinformation.

In looking for a donkey guardian beware of the person who advertises "Weanling miniature donkey jack-good for sheep guard", or who tells you "just let this jack grow up with your sheep/goats/cows, etc." or "any donkey will do the job" or "get a jennet then you can have a foal every year."

For starters, "JACK DONKEY" and "GUARD" should never, ever be in the sentence. There are many nice Jacks out there who may never do one wrong thing but do you want to take the chance? <u>Intact jacks are for breeding, not for pets, not for guards.</u> That ol' testosterone can turn Dr. Jeckell into Mr. Hyde in a hurry with disastrous and heart-breaking results. **NO JACKS ALLOWED ON GUARD DUTY!**

Next, let's look at those weanlings, of any size. Would you let your 3 year old baby-sit your 2 year old? Of course not! You cannot expect a weanling, a baby, to take on the responsibility of a flock guardian. There are several outcomes to this scenario. Your "guard baby" can just as easily be killed by whatever is preying on your flocks as what he is supposed to be guarding. Your "guard baby" can easily be hurt or intimidated by an aggressive ram/ewe/doe etc. Especially if they are horned. Your "guard baby" needs to play. Donkey play is much too rough for sheep and goats or even calves. This is where some of that misinformation starts. Things like "Donkeys will kill your lambs, kids, etc. by ripping their necks off." Donkeys play by grabbing necks and walking each other around. Not appropriate and sometimes fatal treatment for kids and lambs.

Your "guard baby" is not really on duty so your flock is still in jeopardy from whatever predator started you looking for a donkey in the first place. Young donkeys need to play to develop strength and agility. They need to grow up and become mature enough to accept the responsibility of a guard. Maturity only comes with age. By 3 years of age, all of the play and silliness is over and a donkey is usually sensible enough to go to work. So, hopefully by now, you are looking for a 3 year old or older, standard gelding or tame jack **TO BE GELDED**!

Resist the urge to get a jennet just so you can get a foal every year or so. Some people say jennets don't make good guards. I don't find that to be so. Some of the best, most reliable and aggressive guard donkeys I have sold have been jennets. But, guard is all they do. Don't be greedy. In breeding your guard jennet you possibly will lose a lot more than you gain.

Towards the end of her gestation she will be heavy with foal and not very agile. There is a real good chance she will leave the flock/herd to foal alone. Then she, her foal and your flock/herd are all in jeopardy. She will, for a time, be more concerned with her baby than your flocks, and she should be. That's just natural. Then you have this high energy, rowdy baby running around looking for a play-mate, so we're back to that "baby" thing again. Baby donkey play translates into sheep and goat harassment.

So now you have eliminated babies, jacks and miniatures from your search. What are you looking for?

You are looking for a medium to large standard donkey gelding or jennet that is 42" to 54" tall at the withers. You are looking for something to run off, intimidate or kill those marauding dogs and coyotes, so get something big enough to be intimidating! ! !

Many miniature donkeys have the hearts of lions but can they back up the bark? Probably not. Many of the sheep and goat breeds today mature out bigger than the average miniature donkey. Any 2 dogs or 4 coyotes that can take down a large sheep or goat can take down your miniature donkey too.

Now that we have covered all of the "do-nots", lets start on the positive side. No, not all donkeys guard, but most donkeys will guard. You are taking advantage of two basic donkey traits. One, his or her need to be part of a herd, and two, his or her natural dislike of canines. Out of all of the donkeys we have trained in a guard capacity, only one failed goat guarding school. He was fine in the field with the goats but went ballistic when closed up in the barn with them. All of our guards are sold with a written money back 30 day guarantee. If the purchaser is unhappy with the donkey or it doesn't do its job, we, at the end of the month, will pick up the animal and return the full purchase price. Not one donkey out of 50 or more has ever been returned.

Any donkey, gelding or jennet that doesn't have an extremely shy or extremely aggressive temperament is a good candidate for a guard.

This is how you make it happen. First, find that donkey that is big enough and old enough to be a guard candidate. Bring him or her home and quarantine him/her, preferably in solitary confinement. Not only is this necessary for health reasons, but a little solitary confinement will speed up the bonding process with you and soon with your flock. Depending on where your new donkey comes from and whether you have any other equines, this phase can last from 1-2 weeks. Use this time to bond with your donkey. They love people and thrive on attention.

Brush up on or teach basic manners; grooming, leading, picking up or trimming hooves, update vaccinations and worm.

Your donkey will be very lonely and maybe a little depressed all by itself when you are not around. Sounds cruel, but this is what you want, a lonely, herd-less donkey. After quarantine is over move your donkey into a stall in your goat or sheep barn or an adjacent small corral where your donkey can see, smell, hear and get used to but not interact physically yet with it's new charges. Being herd-less, your donkey will be begging for interaction.

Turn your donkey out with the flock after a few days, in a small area so you can monitor its behavior. By this point, your donkey has been so starved for herd companionship he or she should bond easily (you will know fast if this is not the case,) and quickly with your flock and you can kiss your predator problems good-bye. Many donkeys have been trained to bring their charges back to the barn each evening saving their owners many steps.

One of the first jennets I ever tried to buy was owned by a little old mountain man who had a herd of cows out on about 500 mountain acres. This is long before I got into or really knew anything about donkeys. She was just about the sweetest thing I ever met and I didn't think Ol' Percy gave her enough attention. Little did I know! After repeatedly trying to buy this gal I finally asked Percy why he kept her. He went in the house and brought out an old hand-made goat horn. The old timers made them to call their hunting dogs in. He then told me whenever he needed to know where the cows were he'd holler for "Jenny" and she'd bray back.

He called and Jenny brayed. He said the cows were in such and such hollow. Then he blew the horn and said "Just wait." We did and in about 25 minutes Jenny came trotting up to the porch. For her reward she got lots of luvs and a big plug of chewing tobacco. This slick old man had her for 30 years as an integral part of his cow operation. Not only could he instantly find out where the herd was but if he wanted to see them he blew the horn for Jenny and would ride her back out. So Jenny not only watched over the cows, she would let him know where they were and then come and get him! She also plowed the garden and pulled a sled. Jenny died 27 years ago, one year before Percy died. That means Jenny went to work on Percy's farm 57 years ago so the donkey as guard and companion is not a new concept.

Reference: by Leslie Heulitt, from an article written for Miniature Donkey Talk Magazine

Guardian Donkey at Gate Farm Park, West Virginia

How to become Confident with your Donkey
(and how to make your donkey confident with you)

Most donkeys are by nature, very laid back and constantly seek people attention. There are a few, due to lack of handling when young, that are timid and show some fear of people. Likewise, people who have just purchased their first donkey may not have enough confidence or experience in how to form a relationship with this animal.)

A Lot of people become owners of donkeys because they do not feel very confident with horses. Horses seem large, unmanageable and rather frightening - but donkeys, because of their smaller size have the appearance of being much easier to get along with.

If you lack confidence with a larger animal, think very carefully whether you really want one at all. Yes? You really do? - well then the next essential step is choose your donkey with the greatest care, for the combination of a donkey without experience and an owner that is equally unsure, is not the most promising start to a happy association. Be prepared to spend a bit more on a donkey that has been well-handled and that is familiar and trusting with people.

Owning a donkey is a partnership where both of you have to make the relationship work. If you lack confidence you cannot hold up your side of the deal and both you and your donkey will suffer. If you are frightened of the donkey, he will be unsure and unhappy with you because you will be selfishly consumed with your own feelings and not considering his at all. Your donkey needs to be treated with understanding and respect.

When you approach your donkey, come from the side where he can see you easily. He cannot see directly behind him - this is not difficult to realize, but some folks do not understand that, unlike us, his vision in front is not very good either. Never approach the donkey from in front and never grab at his head. He will instinctively back away. Aim for his shoulder instead.

Always work with your donkey in a small yard, free from distractions and only when you have plenty of time and are in a relaxed mood. You can lure your donkey into the yard with feed, but otherwise be sparing with tidbits or you will be creating a spoiled, demanding donkey rather than a lovable one. And when you offer your donkey a tidbit, you will be standing in front of him instead the right place, by his shoulder.

Spend a lot of time with the donkey - take a chair and a book to the yard for a while. When he is used to your presence, walk up to him slowly and back away before he moves away from you. Talk to him while you are doing this so that he gets used to the sound of your voice.

You may be presented with his rump - he feels safer this way. If *you've owned donkeys any length of time at all, you know that the great majority of them love butt scratches! They walk up to you, turn around, and expect your fingernails to get to work.)* Don't worry, it is rare for a donkey to kick and he certainly won't if his tail is tucked in. When you get close enough stand still for a while, and then put out your arm slowly and touch him firmly on the rump - then move away again. Repeat the exercise. Take as much time as is needed, and then more, until you are able to walk up to the donkey, put your hand on his rump and move away again without his showing any disquiet.

When you are both confident about this, gradually work forwards until you can stand close by his shoulder with an arm around his neck. Scratch his neck, he enjoys this; don't pat. *Most people have a habit of patting a donkey on the forehead, the way you would a dog. Most donkeys hate this! Always pat or scratch on the neck.*

With a donkey that is used to being handled it will not take very long at all to get to this stage; he already knows all about it, its "old hat" to him and only you need to learn. If the donkey is nervous it could take a lot longer; take your time, as long as it needs (he has plenty of it!) and be patient.

When you are both happy with your position at his shoulder, introduce a halter. You will soon be able to slip it over his nose and buckle it up behind his ears. Then take it off again right away. Stand by his shoulder while you are doing this. This method of advance and retreat is applied to all your dealings with your donkey. Advance to where he is confident and retreat just before he objects or moves away.

Use it when you are grooming him; start by brushing around his withers and neck and work further and further away. If he objects return immediately to his shoulder and start again. Each time you will be able to reach more of him until there is no part of the donkey that you cannot touch. Work down the legs until you reach his hoofs; pick one up and put it down immediately.

The donkey has a big disadvantage in all of this for he is quite incapable of preventing himself from expressing his feelings - his ears give him away every time. When you are handling the donkey watch his ears constantly. They will let you know if he is tense or relaxed, anxious or confident, if he is bored or distracted, or listening to you. You will be able to anticipate every move he is going to make and keep one step ahead of him. And if you are really concentrating on his feelings and reactions, you will not be in the least concerned about your own.

Reference: written by Jennifer Simpson, Australia

Caring For Your Miniature Donkey

Hard to Catch Donkey

There are some donkeys that at times can be difficult to catch and some donkeys almost impossible to catch. If you have just acquired a new donkey and are having trouble catching it, it may just be that the donkey is not accustomed to you. This is particularly true with newly purchased weanlings. They have been taken from their mothers and the only homes they have known, and put in this strange place, no matter how nice it is or how nice you are. It's a big adjustment.

If you think the donkey is difficult to catch because of lack of confidence in people in general, you need to take a very relaxed approach to it. If the donkey is wild, you'll need to have it in a small paddock so that you can work with it. With very wild donkeys, you'll need to give that donkey some time to adjust to its surroundings and you. You should not trap it in a corner and man-handle it to get a halter on it. Give the donkey some grain in a feed pan or some hay and sit on a bucket yourself, some 10 feet from the feed. Do this for a week. Talk to the donkey in a very calm voice and don't make sudden moves.

We usually like to pair up a newly acquired donkey with a pal. Pick a suitable friend that is very laid back and willingly comes to you. This is helpful in showing the new donkey that there is nothing to be afraid of. Don't pick a pal who wants to crave all of the attention and kick at the other donkey to keep it away from you.

Once you catch the donkey, put on a halter and lead rope. Rub the neck and scratch the chest area. Most donkeys love to have their chests scratched. Don't immediately start pulling the donkey towards some place to tie it up. Just stand with the donkey, talk softly and rub its chest for a few minutes than let the donkey go.

If you are trying to catch a nervous donkey, it is important to do it in a quiet manner. If the donkey is in a corner, walk up to it slowly. It will generally have its back to you. Most of the time, a donkey is not inclined to kick you. Most scared donkeys will run from you, not kick. Be cautious, as there is the possibility that you have purchased an abused donkey that will kick you. If the donkey takes off running, don't go running after it, chasing it all over the paddock as you are defeating the purpose. Never, ever lose your temper and throw a halter or anything else at the donkey. If the donkey keeps running around the small paddock area that you are in, walk - don't run - up to the donkey. If you are walking and the donkey is running, the donkey is going to get tired before you do. Once the donkey is tired, you might be able to walk up to it.

Some donkeys are easy to approach until they notice you are carrying a halter. If you have a donkey like this, hide the halter behind your back. After the donkey gets used to you, you can also walk up to the donkey with the halter in your hand but never put the halter on the donkey. Just pet him and walk away.

Never keep a halter on a donkey that you are not working with. This is true whether the donkey is confident with you or one that runs from you. When a donkey wants to scratch its head, it usually does it by turning around and lifting its back leg and scratching with the hoof. It is so very easy for and hoof to get caught up in the halter and you have a real disaster on your hands.

There are some breeders who do not spend a lot of time with their weanlings and that is why these weanlings are frightened of people. I personally can't seem to stay away from our weanlings, so this is a practice I don't completely understand. If you purchase a weanling like this, spend as much time with it as you possibly can. These weanlings are easy to turn around. Adult donkeys can be another story. If you have a lot of spare time that you can spend with this donkey, you can accomplish a lot. Most often, these adults will never fully trust people, and will never be an overly affectionate donkey, (although this is not an impossibility as I have seen it done) but you can certainly improve on its present state of mind. Kindness is the key word.

Dale Haworth from Tennessee with friend

Teaching a Young Donkey to Lead

One of the kindest things you can do for your donkey is to teach him or her to lead properly from the beginning. For your donkey's sake and the safety of those who will care for him during his long lifetime, let's give him a solid foundation on which to build.

__Our Goal__ is to teach the young donkey to lead without crowding, scaring, or forcing him. This approach makes his life easier and certainly ours!

With horses, I believe most trailer loading problems are actually leading problems. If your donkey won't jump a little branch next to you, it is probably a leading problem. We all want willing animals, and we all like nice obedient human children too. Seems to me, all we have to do is teach them correctly from the beginning.

Keep in mind, donkeys vary in learning speed. Time is not important. Some are just smarter, earlier than others, but once they get it right, it is forever. So keep your cues simple, and your hands kind!

__To Begin__, you need to set aside a quiet time when you can be totally alone with your student. No distractions. If you have a round pen, that is ideal, but any quiet spot will do.

If your donkey has never had a halter on at all, he should first be able to accept you as a human creature. Touch him, rub him, talk to him sweetly. Before the halter you need to address these questions with him: move for me - go left, go right. Accomplish this by presenting your body language to him. Good Boy! Always talk to him with praise and acceptance. Control his direction by where you step. Move away from me, you might ask, when I step behind you. Stop, when I am in front. WATCH ME - be attentive to me. Make eye contact, you are asking for a bonding. I am your friend, don't be frightened. STOP. STAND. Let me approach you. Let me pet you. Don't be scared. RELAX. Rub his head, stand on his right side - stand on his left. Let his eyes follow you, as if to ask *who are you*. Rub him all over. Now, touch his legs, when he picks them up - don't grab them, that will scare him and he will feel trapped, and then he won't be sure about you. Just like a cat he will give you one chance before he becomes concerned. Let the donkey place his legs naturally. Give and take. Look him in the eyes! You always want his attention. That will come through quietly talking to him and by moving around him. He will watch you, he doesn't know you yet. But, when he knows you, you need him to trust you totally!

When you ask your donkey to jump a jump, or walk into a trailer, or walk over a bridge, he MUST trust you.

Haltering

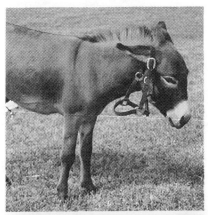

To get your little one used to the halter at first, SHOW it to him. Let him smell it, put his nose on it, you might hang it on his ear, he shouldn't balk. Then quietly and very nicely place it on his head. This shouldn't be a big deal. Never restrain him while doing this. Take it off, put it on, take it off. Goodboy! Lots of talking. He's getting to know you and your voice, as well, all the while. They learn fast. Rub him all over and pet him. He will say, in his own style, "oh, that feels good, yeah, I like that halter thing."

Lesson #2 - Next, quietly show him a burlap sack or a towel. Put a hole in one end of the towel and fold the towel length-wise in 1/3. Place it around his neck. Just the towel (or burlap), no halter yet.

Tie the towel around his neck by placing a hole at one end, put a rope through the hole and tie the ends together with a knot that won't tighten the sack or strangle the donkey. This method is better than a halter at first because any pain on his sensitive poll will lessen learning. The towel hurts - not at all, by spreading pressure over a larger area. This lessens pain - thus fear and quickens learning.

- Now, ask your donkey to feel the pressure of the towel. Use a long rope so that if he reacts sharply. You can still move slowly.

- Ask him to bend his neck, by letting him walk into the pressure, or by pulling him gently. Very important here. <u>His reward is a release of pressure</u>. Release the pressure once he has done what you have asked. "Good boy!" He will be happy with your praise and willing to do it again.

- Ask him to bend his neck and leave it bent, when he moves his feet and turns toward you. Reward him by giving him slack. Simple but true, that is how they learn.

- Now, put the halter on.

- Thread the rope through the halter. Repeat the above. This way he will feel some pressure and he will already understand the lessons.

- Gradually, use just the halter. Always use soft pressure and remember to reward with slack - not food! Food is a temporary fix, does not teach, and will encourage biting and chasing. Cocoa taught me this 1-2-3!

Your lessons should last only as long as you have his attention. Remember to be patient and kind or you will loose his attention in a

second. All the while you are really asking him to accept this concept: <u>Follow</u> the pull rather than being pulled by the rope.

- Go side to side, asking him to move, one step in your direction. Release the rope, give him slack. Teach him not to resist.

- With a baby it is tempting to "teach him who's boss". That is <u>always</u> the wrong approach. Someone will get hurt that way. Take time to <u>teach</u> him. You don't want your donkey to grow up having learned from you - how to resist.

- Still with just the sack or towel and long rope, after he moves forward a few steps, walk behind him and ask him to drive forward, as he does, give him slack. Discourage dragging by driving him way in front, gradually, reduce the distance as he walks and he understands he must stay in front.

You should now have an excellent beginning for your donkey to lead.

I admit to being no expert where donkey's are concerned. What you have read applies to what I know about horses. Both being of the equine species, it seems fitting however, what I have learned from *Cocoa* and *Buckwheat Too* in the short period of time is important, as well.

#1 If the donkey does not feel it is <u>safe</u>, forget it, unless you force him, thus scaring him, he will not lead where you want him to.

You must be *more* patient and understanding with a donkey. It seems they are smarter and more cautious than horses in general.

#2 If they move their feet, only then can you direct them. I have found it builds trust to let the donkey tell you sometimes. Give and take. You

might want to go right, he wants to go left. Okay, go left, then go right - as long as he's moving and not planting his feet - stubbornly.
Be his companion - not his boss!

Reference: written by Karla Wolfson for Miniature Donkey Talk Magazine

Jack Daniel of Short ASSets Ranch in Texas

How to teach a donkey to lead...... Quick

Unlike the previously article which shows you the PROPER way to teach a donkey to lead, here's a quick cowboy way.

Put halter and lead rope on the donkey. Position yourself on the donkey's left side. You face straight forward - do not look at donkey. Pull on the lead line and say "walk". Have someone in back of donkey with 6 foot driving whip. While you pull, have the person in back make a "SHUUSH" sound (donkeys don't like that sound) and lightly tap on back legs. Keep tapping on the legs with the whip. DO NOT HIT THE DONKEY WITH THE WHIP!!! THE KEY WORD HERE IS "TAP".

The donkey will want to move forward - away from the 'irritating' tapping on the back legs. Keep stopping and starting this. Keep saying "walk" - just before you pull lightly on the lead line. When you stop, say "stop". After 15 minutes or so (whenever the donkey figures out and understands what is going on and what you are expecting him to do) you take whip in your left hand. As you say "walk" and pull forward on lead, also take the whip in your left hand, put your hand behind you and tap on the back legs. Do this without turning your body around - just turn your head around to see that you are tapping the back legs of the donkey.

Do this for 30 minutes every day for about 5 days so that donkey remembers. In all probability, you will not even need the driving whip after the second day.

Keith Whiteman of California with Murphy

Marsha Reed of Vermont

Fred Hartman of Nebraska with a team hitch

The Beginners Guide to Driving
by David N. Cox

Why Drive?

Driving and packing are two performance areas our miniatures can do with the best of them. Their loads have to be smaller and the speed is slower but the agility and heart are there. A well conditioned 34" to 36" Jack or gelding can easily pull a two wheel cart driven by a good sized adult. The joy of you and your little guy going down the road together is worth the work it takes to get there.

Stand Tied

I will move through the basics quickly. The animal you are going to train should be two years old and know the basics by now. Standing tied, a donkeys first lesson, is a good place to start his training as a harness donkey. Take him to a "training area" away from his stable mates. Tie him with a slip knot (in case he gets in trouble) and groom him. Up to this point grooming probably meant brushing his back and neck. You have to go farther than that now. As a harness donkey he will have straps put around his chest, girth and hindquarters. A crupper will be placed under his tail. His head and ears will be handled while putting on his bridle. His hooves must be handled for cleaning. The grooming you start each lesson with is to desensitize his body and smooth and clean the hair under his harness. He is not going to be too happy about you grooming areas he thought were private. Go slow, spread this over as many lessons as it takes. Talk to him, use "easy" or "steady" as you groom him and he settles down. This command will be used any time he gets nervous.

Keep your training time short. Fifteen to twenty minutes is about right. Train twice a day if your schedule permits. Always end on a high note - after he has done it right. You must show even temperament and patience. Never lose your temper or train when your mind is some where else.

You will find that your donkey will react to your praise and no other reward is needed. They also like to be scratched on their withers and upper shoulder, this is where "mom" would gently nip them when they were good. At the end of the training you may give him a treat, but not by hand. Get him a pan that is his and his alone. This oat pan will be used

later in training.

Leading

I hope your donkey already leads well - but in case he doesn't, here are a few tips. Lead from the left shoulder. Donkeys do not like anyone beside or in front of their eyes. Give the command "walk on", then step forward. If the does not move step back and tap him on the rump with a training whip held in your left hand. A donkey trained to lead this way will often move as soon as you start to step back.

Let's stop here and talk about two things I have mentioned. First, giving commands. You have to give commands like you mean it. You must always use the same command and give it before the physical cue. Second, the whip. A whip is a **training aid** and used to cue your donkey much like a rider does with his legs. To punish a donkey with a whip is a disgrace!! If you are to this point, have the donkey do some thing he knows and stop the lesson. The ideal whip to train and drive Miniature Donkeys is a 4 foot driving whip.

If he still won't move, have a helper make noise behind him when you give the "walk on" command. A plastic sack works good for this.

If he is still not going, loop a piece of bailing twine around his rump, tie the end together over his back. Clip the lead onto this loop then thread the lead through the ring under the halter. Give the command, then pull on the lead. If the donkey moves, even a little, heap on great praise and loving pats. Work on leading until he will willingly step out when you say "walk on".

"Whoa"

Of all the commands your donkey learns, "whoa" is the most important. This is your brakes when you are driving. This is the command you use when you sense or are in danger. When your donkey hears it he must automatically stop. As you are walking give the command "whoa" then pull back and down on the lead rope. If this doesn't work at first, walk him up to a wall or fence, then give the command.

The Neighborhood Walk

We have our donkey stepping out now at "walk on" and stopping for "whoa", and you are getting tired of walking around your training area.

4 Donkey Hitch

So, let's go for a walk. I feel this is very important basic training for a harness donkey. You know where you plan on driving your donkey, so you know what to introduce him to. Donkeys are very cautious, so introduce new things slowly. If he won't go near it today, try again tomorrow.

Take him out in the neighborhood. Walk on cement, blacktop and gravel. Walk across painted lines and railroad tracks. Don't try to walk across manhole covers and mudpuddles are not a must at this time. Walk where there are restrained dogs. Let him get used to the sound they make. If he is nervous, pet him and say "easy" or "steady". If you come across loose dogs, let them approach but protect your donkey with the training whip if they start to attack. Walk on the right side of the road and let cars pass. If cars or motorcycles seem to bother him, try to pasture him close to a busy road. He must also be exposed to bicycles, lawn sprinklers, lawn mowers and loud noises. Encourage people, especially children, to approach you on your walks. Give your donkey a "whoa" command, tell him to "stand". Tell them your donkeys name. Here is a good place to instruct your neighborhood children on approaching a donkey. Tell them to keep their hands low, talk softly and pet him on the shoulder not the ears.

These walks are good public relations in the neighborhood. They know you have donkeys and like to see them up close. If you have a donkey that brays a little too loud, they seem to be more tolerant of an animal their kids are on a first name bases with!

The Bit

When the walks are going well and he seems to be relaxed, it is time to introduce him to some of the harness he will be wearing.

Getting harness for Miniature Donkeys is difficult. If you are lucky you will know of a harness maker who will custom fit your donkey. If you have to order by mail, find a dealer who carries miniature horse harness and tell him it is for a donkey. If you are real handy, you can get a few books out of the library and figure out how to make your own harness.

It is assumed you now have your harness and are ready to start using it. We will start with the bit. You will need a 3" to 4" bit. A snaffle bit is best to start with.

Snaffle Bit   *Tie Bit To Halter*

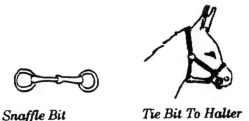

The bit should be touching the corners of the mouth, causing a slight wrinkle.

Introduce the bit at the start of one of the lessons. Gently slide it into his mouth. Using two small straps or heavy cord, secure the rings of the bit to the rings on the side of his halter. Don't get it too tight. Adjust it so there is one wrinkle at the corner of his mouth. Make sure the bit is on top of his tongue. *(Ed Note: Being that the people most interested in this article are true beginners and most having never owned a horse, I feel further explanation is needed here. Many times I have seen youngsters riding ponies with an improperly fitted bit. Usually, it hangs too loose in the pony's mouth. Unless the bit is in the proper place, your donkey will never get used to it. When the bit is in the proper position in the mouth, the corner of the mouth will have one slight wrinkle in it. If the bit hangs too loose, it will hit against the donkeys teeth and will cause him a great amount of discomfort. A properly fitted bit will rest on the gums, not the teeth.)* We will work on the bit with his mouth, but this will slow down as you get on with the lesson. After the lesson, remove the bit and rinse it in water. Keep the bit as clean as possible. Next time, leave the bit in his mouth while he eats. Build up the time he wears the bit until he is comfortable with it.

The Driving Bridle

Once he is used to the bit, place it back in the bridle. Loosen the adjustments on the bridle. Tie the donkey by his lead and halter. *(Ed Note: Never EVER tie a donkey up by his bridle reins with the bit in his mouth!)* Place the bit in his mouth then ease the bridle over his ears. Adjust the bridle so his eye is in the middle of the blinder, wrinkle at corner of the mouth and the strap under the neck is loose. The strap hanging down the back of his head is the overcheck and will be used later, for now roll it up and tie it out of the way.

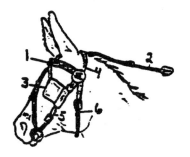

1. Browband
2. Overcheck
3. Blinder
4. Crown
5. Cheek Strap
6. Throatlatch

People often wonder why blinders are worn. The main reason is to prevent the donkey from seeing activity around him, especially behind him. Now untie the lead and take one of those neighborhood walks. You will find your donkey will get used to the driving bridle, and the fact he can only see forward, very quickly.

Ground Driving

The next step is to move from leading to driving your donkey. If we were training a horse we would have spent time longeing him before we got to this point. *(Ed Note: "longeing" is putting a horse on a lightweight 30 foot nylon line while you hold the other end and making him run around you in circles. It is a popular way of exercising horses without riding them.)* Most donkeys don't like to longe and get bored with it, so we will train him by leading.

Get out your harness. Remove the breeching from the rest of the harness, this is the wide strap that goes around the donkeys hindquarters. This will leave you with the backpad (it has two rings and a hook on it) and girth. Attach to the backpad is the backstrap and crupper. The crupper goes around the donkeys tail.

Ground Drive With Breeching Removed

Tie your donkey and lay the backpad on his back just behind his withers, do not connect the girth. Unbuckle one side of the crupper and place it under his tail. He will depress his tail as tight as he can. To get him to relax, rub along side his tail with your fingers. He will slowly lift his tail.

Place the crupper under his tail and buckle it. Now buckle the girth, but not too tight. This strap is never tightened as tight as the girth on a riding saddle. The extra straps you have from the girth are the wrap straps for the shafts. Run them through the leather shaft loops and buckle them to keep them out of the way. Place the driving bridle on over the halter. Hook the overcheck (the strap behind head) to the hook on the backpad. Run the driving reins through the terrets (rings) on the backpad. Have a helper untie the donkey and stand at the left shoulder. You take the driving reins and stand behind your donkey.

Let's talk about reins. When driving you must have constant mouth contact through the reins and bit. The contact is firm but smooth. Always imagine that bit in your mouth, and handle the reins accordingly. Don't jerk the reins, this is what happens if you slap your donkey on the top of the rump with the reins. This is a cruel habit that isn't helped much by the driving we see in movies. When you drive down the road, your voice and hands on the reins are your only contact, so keep them both firm but gentle.

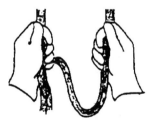

How To Hold The Reins

In this lesson, we want the donkey to get used to you giving commands while walking behind. Your helper is to say nothing, you give all the commands. Get your donkeys attention by saying his name, then give the command "walk on". Walk in a familiar area and don't try anything but "walk on" and stopping. When you stop, give the command "whoa" then gently pull on the reins. When he has stopped, relax on the reins. Work at this until he is used to you behind him and you don't need a helper.

The correct method of holding the reins is also the safest and easiest. Hold the reins properly from day one and it will feel natural by the time you get to the cart. Grasp the reins, one in each hand, between the first and second fingers, let the rein run on through the hand between palm and fingers. Press down with the thumbs. The reins should be buckled together and form a loop below your hands. This loop can be dangerous if it is too long and can get to the spokes or drag behind the cart, so it must be taken up and held between the third and little finger of your left hand. You must always drive with gloves, so get a well fitting pair and get used to wearing them while you handle the reins. You will also eventually hold a whip in your right hand, when first starting all of this seems a bit much, but you will get used to it.

When you and your donkey are used to the idea of you walking behind and giving commands, try some turns. Here again a verbal command followed by a physical cue is the best. The command for right is "Gee" or "Come". The command for left is "Haw" or "Git". Decide what command you want to use and always use it. When you start making turns, you may need your helper again. Give the command then gently pull on the appropriate rein. Do not keep a constant pressure on this rein. We are cueing him not pointing his head. Set up some obstacles to drive around and practice until you both feel comfortable.

Introduction Of Cart

Finding a cart the proper size for your Miniature Donkey may be difficult. Your best bet is to contact dealers who handle miniature horse tack and supplies.

The shafts of a properly fit cart will be level and form a straight line at the same height as the donkeys breast collar and breeching.

The cart should be well-sprung so it is comfortable for the driver and the donkey. It must be well balanced. There must not be any upward pull on the bellyband (overbalance to rear) or extreme weight on the backpad (overbalance to the front). A cart is in balance when there is just enough weight on the shafts to keep them steady in the shaft loops. Have the driver sit in the cart, and let someone lift the shafts. For a Miniature Donkey this weight should be 8 to 10 pounds. The shaft weight can be adjusted by moving the seat or axle forward or back. The easy entry cart by *Frontier* is an excellent cart for Miniature Donkeys. The shaft weight on this cart is set by moving the seat.

Park the cart in the training area and let the donkey get used to seeing it. Bring him up to it, let him smell it. Lift the shafts and drop them a few times so he can hear the noise, and be assured it won't hurt him. Ground drive the donkey by the cart a few times. Have a helper pull the cart behind the donkey so he gets used to the noise. It won't be long until the sight and sound of the cart won't bother him.

Hitching To The Cart

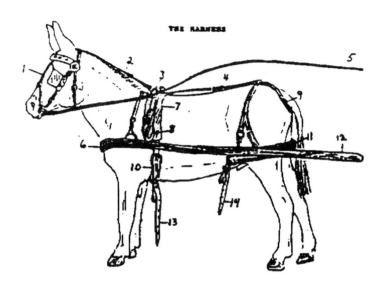

1. Bridle	6. Breast Collar	10. Girth
2. Check Rein	7. Backpad	11. Breeching
3. Rein Terrets	8. Shaft Loop	12. Trace
4. Backstrap	9. Crupper	13. Wrap Strap
5. Rein		14. Breeching Strap

Reattach the breeching to your harness. Adjust the breeching so it lays on the flat part of the donkeys rear flank. Place the breast collar and traces on your donkey. Adjust the strap that crosses over the neck so the breast collar is around the donkey's chest. Be careful here, too high and you are into the throat and restricting breathing, too low and you are on the shoulder and impairing movement. Cross the traces over the donkey's back, to keep them out of the way. Unbuckle the wrap straps from the shafts loops. You are now ready to hook up the cart. Have a helper hook a lead rope to the halter under the driving bridle and calm the donkey while you hitch the cart. Bring the cart up with the shafts held high. Lower the shafts and put them in the shafts loops. Connect the traces to the single-tree on the cart. Pull the cart back to tighten the traces and check shaft height and length. The shafts should be level and in line with the traces. The shaft can be raised or lowered by adjusting the shaft loop. The shaft ends must be at your donkey's shoulder. You can move the shafts forward or back by changing the trace ends on the single-tree. Bring the wrap strap up between the donkey and the trace. Wrap it around the shaft in front of the shaft loop, then behind the loop making a figure eight. Make sure you don't wrap the trace to the shaft. Take the end of the wrap strap down outside the trace and buckle it. The shaft loops hold up the shafts and the wrap straps hold them down, they have to be snug but not too tight.

Country Music Miniature Donkeys

Bring the breeching strap forward, between the donkey and the trace, wrap it through the "D" ring under the shaft. Bring the strap back outside the trace and buckle it at the end of the breeching. The breeching is what stops the cart when the donkey stops or holds it back when you go down hill, so its adjustment is very important. When the donkey is standing the breeching should be loose. When he is moving it should not rub or interfere with his movement. It should only come in solid contact when the donkey stops. If it is too loose the cart will roll forward a bit before it makes contact, this is hard on the harness and upsets the donkey. You are now hitched to the cart.

Pulling The Cart

Gather up your reins and stand behind the cart. With your helper holding onto the lead, give the "walk on" command. After you have walked a short distance give the "whoa" command, gently pull on the reins, let up when he stops and push the cart ahead with your leg. This will tighten the breeching and may frighten him. Make sure your helper knows this is coming and helps steady the donkey if he is upset. Work out of the cart until you both feel comfortable. Have your helper unsnap the lead. Work for a while and when you feel you are ready, get in the cart! You may want your helper on the lead for a while. Work slow and quiet with your donkey. I don't mean verbally quiet, talk to him just like you did in earlier training. Always give a verbal command before a physical cue. Work in your training area until you feel you are ready to go out into the neighborhood.

Donkeys seldom run away, but if they do, they don't run far. If you do have a run-away stay with your donkey and cart! Turn your donkey, not too sharp at first but as he slows tighten the turn until he stops. If you are in an arena or pasture, drive him into a corner. *(Ed Note: For those of you unclear about this, the point is to turn your donkey in a large circle the same as you would do with a run away horse, if you are not in a confined area. Eventually, they figure out that they aren't going anywhere and will get bored with it and stop.)*

Backing Up

After you have driven for a month or so it is time to work on backing. Backing is not a usual maneuver for a donkey. Backing is awkward and clumsy for him. Knowing this we have to use a lot of patience while teaching him to back. Start the lesson with your donkey in just a halter. Stand in front of him and say "back" while pushing on the shank. Soon he will associate the movement with the command. When you have him backing on command, with very little pressure on the halter, harness him for ground driving. Give him the command to "back" then pull and release the reins. When the donkey responds with a step to the rear, praise him and drive forward a short distance, stop and repeat the procedure. Gradually he will back up three or four steps, don't ask any more. Work at this until it is a willing movement. Make sure he always backs straight and drive him forward to where you started.

Now hitch him to the cart, and driving from the ground, drive him around a bit then stop and ask for a "back". If you only get one step, praise him and drive on. Repeat the lesson. You will see him improve with time, be patient. Remember, this is an awkward move for him.

The Trot

Work with your donkey at a walk until you both feel at home in the cart. You can train him to trot on a lead if you like. Set his oat pan on the ground and lead him away from it. Stop always out, turn, give the command "walk on" after you're moving say "trot" tap him with the whip and speed it up. You may not even need the whip, the oat pan will get him moving. Some drivers make a clicking sound with their mouth before the command "trot". Later just the clicking will make them speed up, even if they are in a trot.

When you first trot your donkey in the cart, trot him for a short distance then say "walk" and tighten the reins until he comes to a walk. Vary walk and trot and watch your donkey. The cart acts and sounds different at the trot, the shafts go up and down, he has to get used to this.

Harness Hints

After you have driven a while, you will not leave a halter under the driving bridle. Remember, this bridle is your control so never remove the bridle while your donkey is hooked to the cart. Never tie the donkey by the bridle. If on a drive, you stop for lunch, unhook the cart and tie your donkey using a halter.

Keep your harness clean and oiled. A good cleaner for removing dirt and sweat is a mix of one part vinegar to three parts water.

When you remove your harness, run the wrap straps and breeching straps backwards through their buckles. This keeps them up and out of the way the next time you put the harness on your donkey.

A Few Last Thoughts

All you and your donkey need now is lots of miles together.

Always groom him before and after a drive. This smoothes the hair under the harness, gets the dirt off him and gives you a chance to check for harness sores after the drive.

Inspect your harness and cart each time you use it. A lot of grief has been caused by broken harness or carts.

Make yourself visible to cars. Make sure you have a slow moving vehicle sign on the back of your cart (it's the law).

Drive on the right side and stop for stop signs. You will be surprised at how fast your donkey learns to stop.

Try to find others who drive small animals in your area and drive with them. Don't try to keep up with horses for any distance.

When you are ready, drive in parades and donkey shows.

I hope you agree that the joy of you and your Miniature Donkey going down the road together was worth the work you both put in. See you on a county road someday!

Madison Stocker of Alberta Canada and her friend Star

Chapter 10

Questions, Miscellaneous

Most Common Newbie Questions Regarding Donkeys

How much land do I need to keep a donkey on?

Donkeys should have a minimum of one acre of land. They need room to run and play and exercise. They also need shelter - preferably a darken barn in summer to get away from biting flies. One acre of land will not meet their nutritional requirements of course so you would need to feed them hay year 'round. You also need to check your zoning laws. Donkeys are livestock. Some localities require 3 acres for livestock, others one acre and still others 5 acres.

Can donkeys be housebroken?

No. Of course there may be a handful of people on this earth who claim they have a housebroken donkey and if you look hard enough, you may just find one that really is. Use your common sense here. Again, donkeys are livestock. How many housebroken horses have you heard of? How many housebroken cows? Goats? If you give it some thought, the concept of attempting to housebreak livestock is a silly one and should not be given serious thought.

Will donkeys get along with my dogs?

90% of all donkeys have a dislike of dogs. Most seem to really detest small dogs. HOWEVER, many many people who have donkeys also have dogs !! and if breeders raise newborn donkeys around dogs, there's an excellent chance that they can get along nicely. Mothers with foals can never be trusted around dogs even if they got along with them before they had their foal, simply because new mothers are so protective. My pastures that surround my yard are 4-board fencing and because we have small dogs, we lined the bottom of the fence with small gauge wire so that the dogs cannot get in the pastures, so there IS a workable solution.

Can you put donkeys in with horses?

Yes. Most of my donkeys are pastured with two horses. My gelding horse adores the donkeys and his greatest thrill is to lick a newborn donkey foal! The other horse is a mare and she would be happy never to see a donkey again. She would not hurt a donkey, but the donkeys know to give her plenty of room and to avoid close contact with her. Generally, donkeys and horses get along fine. Our barn is left open 24 hours a day so the donkeys and horses can enter and leave the barn at will. The donkey's section of the barn is cordoned off so that the horses cannot enter their section.

Will donkeys get along with my goats?

Sometimes. It has come to my attention over the years that a few breeders like to tell people that young jacks (males) make great companions for goats. FALSE! An ungelded young jack should never be pastured with goats. The main problem seems to be that young jacks like to play with goats the same way they play with each other - by grabbing the goat by the neck with their teeth. I lost count of how many phone calls I've gotten from grieving goat owners telling me how they found their goats dead from a broken neck. As a young jack comes of age, play turns to sexual aggression and the problem is worsened. So, can jennets (females) be pastured with goats? Possibly. Jennets do not play as aggressively as jacks so the chances of a jennet being pastured with goats has a better chance of working out. Some owners have told me that they give their goats an 'escape route' so if a jennet decides to play with or chase the goats, they can jump up on a large wooden box or have a small entrance into a separate barn that the donkey cannot get through.

Can I keep a jack and jennet together?

If the jack is not gelded, you've got a 50/50 chance whether they can be pastured together. See the chapter in this book, "A Little About Jacks" for more details.

Can I buy just one donkey?

Donkeys are herd animals. They love being with other donkeys. I personally will not sell one donkey to a person who has no other livestock such as a horse or pony. A lone donkey is a lonely donkey, a lonely donkey can be a stressed-out donkey, and a stressed-out donkey can end up being a sick donkey. It's always best to have two donkeys. They'll develop an extremely close friendship that will do your heart good.

Bonnie Gross

Miniature Donkey Foaling Manual

The ONLY Foaling Manual Available for Miniature Donkeys!

A MUST For Every Breeder!

Now in its 8th Printing! Written and Published by Bonnie Gross

Dedicated to all Miniature Donkeys in the hope that your human friends can assist in bringing your foals into the world healthier and happier

Partial List of Contents

What Does A Pedigree Mean
Causes of Abortion
Reproductive Complications
Barren/Repeat Breeder Jennet
Early Embryo Loss
The Older Jennet
Difficult births and how to Handle
Getting the Story Straight on Pregnancy Testing
Winter Care of the Pregnant Jennet
Feeding the Pregnant Jennet
Foaling Kit Checklist
When will that Foal Arrive? Helpful Hints
How Close to Foaling is She? What to look for
 Countdown to Foaling
Discharge in Pregnant Jennets
The Foaling Process in Photos
Trouble Signs during Foaling and What to do
CPR in the Newborn Foal
Newborn Umbilical Cord
Trouble Signs in the Newborn
Premature Foals

The Importance of Colostrum
Foal Rejection
What's Wrong with my Foal Chart - Detailed Analysis
Tetanus Antitoxin
Care of Jennet After Foaling
Is Your Newborn Really Nursing?
Testing for Newborn Antibodies
Foal Diarrhea
The Orphan Foal
Hemolytic Disease
Breeding in "Foal Heat"
Imprint Training the Newborn
Foal Nutrition, Worming, Vaccs
Foal Hoof Care
Training Foals
Biting Foals
Weaning Time Helpful Hints
Why Miniature Donkeys?
Buying Miniature Donkeys
But what do you do with 'em?
Miniature Donkey Facts
.... and much, much more!

$27.95 plus $5.95 s/h

Available From: **Miniature Donkey Talk Magazine**
1338 Hughes Shop Rd, Westminster, Md 21158
Telephone 410-875-0118 Fax 410-857-9145

I. M. D. R.

INTERNATIONAL
MINIATURE DONKEY REGISTRY, Inc.

The official Miniature Donkey Registry for today and the future.

For Miniature Donkeys 38" and under
Size Classification:
Class A: 36" and Under
Class B: 36.1" to 38" (Basically used for foundation stock)

Five easy steps to apply for Registration: You do not have to be a member of IMDR to register a donkey, however the registration fees are more expensive if you are not a member. See fee schedules below.

1. Call IMDR for Registration Applications.
2. Take pictures. The registry needs two photos of the left side, and two of the right side. These may be duplicates. One set goes on the back of the regisration certificate and the other set goes on file with the application. Take photographs in good light so all identifyable marks can be recognized.
3. Fill out the application form and all pedigree information. Pedigrees are not required for registration, but if they are known they should be indicated.
4. Complete the owner and breeder information on the form exactly as you want it to show on all registration certificates.
5. Enclose all with appropriate fees by check or enclosed credit card information.

IMDR Membership Information One Year Renewable Membership: $15.00
Five Year Renewable Membership: $60.00
Special Lifetime Memberships (reduced registration fees) are available on request.

Registrations and Transfer Fees: **Permanent**: Over 2 years of age $15 member; $18 non-member; **Temporary**: Under 2 years of age $10 member; $13 non-member
Pet or Gelding: $6 member; $8 non-member
Transfer from any other registry to IMDR: $5

Special IMDR Rating Program: IMDR has a special donkey rating program. This computer generated conformation grading system is unique and of great help to new buyers. When considering buying an adult donkey with IMDR registration papers, ask the seller what the IMDR Rating is on the donkey. Ratings are based strictly on conformation. A Two, Three or Four Star rating means that you are purchasing a quality animal. Write IMDR for details.

1338 Hughes Shop Rd Westminster, MD 21158
Tel 410-875-0118   24 Hr Fax 410-857-9145
(Office Hours 9AM-4PM EASTERN STANDARD TIME Mon-Fri)

Index

A

A & D Ointment 220
Aborted fetus photo 299
Abortion 297 149 151 187 248
    324
    from trauma 299
Abscess in chest 153
    draining 157
Abscess, hoof 98
Acepromazine 265
Acorns 121
Acreage needed 358
Administering Medications
    Important Notes 263
Adrenaline 238 265
Aged donkeys 320
Alfalfa 11 47 54 55 58 83
    161 208 231
Alkali disease 199
Allergic dermatitis 84
Allergies 138 84
Antibiotics 237 240
Antibodies from vaccines 152
Antihistamines 138 265 266
Appetite, normal 52
Arthritis 166 140
    from Lyme Disease 140
Arthroscopy 166
Ascarids 270 275
Asinine Herpesvirus 149
Aspirin 266
Automatic fly spray systems 86
Automatic waterers 47 49 50
Azimycin 241

B

Back legs locking up 183
Bacterial infection 239 242 254
    306

from Salmonella 188
Bastard strangles 157
Bedding 72
    disposal of 75 77
Behavior, normal 51
Behavioral problems,
    wood chewing 310
Biting 317
Bits 347
Blacksmiths 91
Bladder stones 203
Blister beetle poisoning 58
Blood chemistry counts 117
BO-SE 195
Botflies 84 86
Bots 276 86 87 270 274
Botulism 227
Bred jennets, moving 47
Breed Standards 13
Breeding the pregnant jennet 324
Broken Crest 230
Buyer information 27

C

Cancer 170
Carotid artery 264
Cart Training 343
Castration 285
Catching your donkey 333
Cattle wormers on donkeys 272
Chest, swelling in 153
Choke 173
Chronic pulmonary emphysema
    177
Coffin bone rotation 106 216
Coggins test 38 40 212
Cold Weather Care 79
    Weanlings 81
Colors 10

Commercial Haulers 38
Common donkey questions 358
Communication 11
Confidence and your donkey 330
Conformation 13
    Conformation charts 16 – 20
Conjunctivitis 136
Corneal Injuries 135
Corticosteroid 267
    corticosteroid ointments 110
Cortisone 138
Coughing 159 178 239 254
    55
Creosote 311
Cryosurgery 146 144 148 218
Cryptorchidism 282

D
Danby Farms 9
Death 232
Degenerative joint disease 166
Dehydration 188 207
    and foals 308
Dew poisoning 220
Deworming donkeys 277
    new donkey 46
Diarrhea 119 161 187 47
    52
    Diarrhea and viruses 187
    Diarrhea chronic 163
    Foal 164 308
    From antibiotics 165
Distemper 247 153 155 156
Dogs and donkeys 358
Donkey Drawings:
    Points of donkey 21
    Internal Organs 23
    Skeletal Frame 22
Donkey virus 149
Donkey Weight Condition
    Chart 213
Driving Bridle 348
Driving, Beginners Guide 343

Dryland Distemper 153
Dust and Heaves 177
    Dust, diseases from 180
    134 177

E
EHV1 & EHV4 149 153
EIA 167
Elderly donkeys 320
Embryo Loss 295
Emphysema 177
Encephalomyelitis vaccination
    261 83 228 248
Endorphins 316
Endotoxins 188
Epinephrine 267 238
Epsom Salts 98 119
Equine Distemper 156
Equine herpesvirus 149
Equine infectious anemia 167
E-SE 190
Estrumate 281
Euthanasia 232
Eye problems, treating 135
    tearing 134

F
Farriers 91
Fat donkeys 229 131 215
Fat deposit on neck 230 231
Feed composition 56
Feed tags, labels 59
Feeding Hay 11 54
    how much 55
    in winter 79
    the New Donkey 54
Feeding Grain 79 231 49 60
    80
Feeding treats 318
Fence chewing 310
Fences 62
    barb wire 69
    post and board 65

wire 66
pipe 67
Fencing, weanlings 82
Fescue toxicity 298
Fetlock skin inflammation 109
Fever 240 239
First Aid products 119
Flies 84
bots 276
Fly masks 84 85 134
Fly spray systems 86
Foal Diarrhea 162 163 164
Foal heat diarrhea 164 119
161
Foal lameness 306
Foal Rejection 301
Foal Septicemia 307
Foal Vaccinations 243 262
Foaling Manual 362
Foals, hot weather 162
Food Poisoning 227
Founder 215
Frog, diseased 101
Fungal diseases and flies 85
Fungal infections 220

G
Gelding 285
Goats and donkeys 326 359
Grass hay, 11 54 55 83 231
Grease heels 109
Ground Driving 349
Guardian donkeys 326

H
Hair loss 218 219 271 222
Haltering 331 334 337 341
49
Hand feeding 318
Hand-Breeding 325
Hard to catch donkey 333
Harness 343 344
Hauling 181

long distance 38 41
Hay 54
purchasing 57
Heads, conformation 13
Heat cycles missing 280
Heat exhaustion 181 182
Heat stress 181
Heaves 177
heave line 179
Hematology 117
Hematology Testing 117
Herd pecking orders 48
Herpesvirus 3, Asinine 149
History of miniature donkeys 9
Hives 218
Hoof abscess 98
Hoof care 92
Hoof diseases 98 101 103
107 109
Hoof Testers 99
Hooves, too long 98
hair loss around 109
lameness 101 108 306
trimming 92
Hormones 280
Hormone Imbalances 280 297
301
Horses and donkeys 358
Hot weather hauling 181
Household First Aid 119
Hyperlipaemia and Obese Donkeys
130
Hypothyroidism 175

I
Ichthammol 100 105
ill-Manners 317
Immune system 243 118 150
271
Infectious diarrhea 267
Influenza 247 252 41
vaccination 262 83
Injection sites 257

Injections: What You Should Know
    256
Insect bites 218
Insecticides 86   219
Internal parasites 270   274   78
    84   163   218
**International Miniature Donkey
    Registry** 13   363
Intestinal bacteria 162
Intramuscular injections 257
    in foals 258
Intravenous injections 263   256
Introduce the new donkey 46
Investment 11
Iodine 119   100   104   202   219
    223   267   301
Ivermectin 277   218
Ivomec 272

J
Jacks 324
Jack pastures 324
Jack with jennets 48   324
Jennets attacking foals 301
Joint ILL 306
Jugular vein 264

K
Kaopectate 119   162
Keratoma 107
Kopertox 101

L
Lameness 101   108   306
Laminitis 215   104   140
Lawn clippings 122
Lead training 336   341
Legs and Hooves, Handling 89
Legs, conformation 17
Legumes 55
Lice 219
Liver Disease 206

Lock-jaw 200
Lungs, diseases of 177
Lungworm 277
Lyme disease 140

M
Manure Management 77
Marketing Miniature Donkeys 30
Medial patellar desmotomy 183
Medicines, most commonly used
    265
Miniature Donkey Talk Magazine
    361
Mini Vaccinations? 243
Moldy corn poisoning 208
Muscle weakness 190
Mu-Se 195

N
Nasal duct 134
Nasogastric tube 173
National Animal Poison Control
    Centers 123
Navel 202   301   306
Neck conformation 14
Neck, fat roll 230
Needle size for mini's 257
Neomycin ointment 136
New Discoveries in Rhino Virus
    151
New donkey, introducing to herd 46
Nipping 317
Normal donkey behavior 51
Nutrition, winter 54

O
Obese Donkeys 229   130   214
Old donkeys 320
Oleander 121
Open Wound, Treating 210
Overweight jennets 130   214
    229
Oxytocin 267

P

Palpation 291
Panalog 110 148
Pastern area hair loss 219 109
Patella, Upward Fixation of 183
Pecking Order 48
Pelleted feed 179 311
Penicillin 238 237
    allergic reactions 256
    dosage 239
Pepto-Bismol 119 162 164
Peritonitis 276 292
Personality 11
Phenylbutazone 162 256 264
    267
Pigeon Fever 153
Pinworms 270 276
Poisonous plants 121
    Poisonous plants **charts** 124
    Poisonous weeds 62 124
Potomac Horse Fever vaccination
    246 247
Pregnancy and Hyperlipaemia
    130
Pricing donkeys 31
Prostaglandin 280
Prostin 281
Protein in feed 11 49 56
    Protein Requirements 11
Pulse, average count 118
Purpura hemorrhagica 157

Q

Quarantine 253 271

R

Radiation Therapy 171
Ragwort poisoning 208
Rainrot 219
Rasping and Trimming Donkey
    Hooves 92
Record keeping 51
Rectal palpation 291

Rectal tears 291
Registry ratings 29 27
Reproduction 10
Respiration, average count 118
Respiratory disease 41
Respiratory infections 251 254
    150 239 241 298
Restraint, methods of 314
Retained testicle 16 282
Rhino 298
Rhinopneumonitis 298 151
    149
    vaccination 80 262
Ringworm 222
Rompun 256
Rotavirus 163

S

Salivation, excessive 173
Salmonella Infection 187
Salmonellosis 187
Salt 61
    Salt starvation 61
Sarcoid 143
Sauerkraut wrap 110
Sawdust bedding 74
Scours 164
Scratches 109 219
Seedy Toe 103
Selenium Deficiency 190
Selenium intoxication 198
Selenium supplementation 192
    194
Selenium testing 194
Selling donkeys 30
Septicemia 307 188
Shipping donkeys 38
    Shipping stress 41
Sick donkeys, treating 237-239
    118 156 239
Skin conditions 218
Skin diseases 219
    Skin diseases charts 224
Skin Growths 143

Skin, hairless patches 222
Skylights in barn 85
Stable vices, wood chewing 310
Stall Bedding 72
Stallions 324
Stalls, locking donkeys in 177
180
Steroids 265 267
Stitches 210
Stone bruise 106 119
Strangles 156
    Strangles vaccination 246
    247
Straw bedding 73
Streptococcus equi 156
Streptomycin 238 239 266
Stress 212 216 260
    and abortion 295 299
    and hauling 181
    and hyperlipaemia 130
    obesity 230
Strongyles 270 274 275
Sutures 210
Swallowing, difficulty in 156 192
Sweet itch 219
Syno-Flex 321

T
T4 - T3 thyroid hormone 175
Taming your donkey 330
Tapeworms 270
Tear ducts 134
Tearing 134
Teeth 14 322
Temperature 42
    Temperature average 51
    118
Testicles, removing 285
Tetanus 200
    vaccination 247
    antitoxin 201 247 288
    toxoid 202 210 247

Tetracycline 105 142 201 238
    266 268
Throat obstruction 173 156
Thrush 101
Thyroid 175
Ticks, Lyme Disease 140
Trailers, home made 181
Tree eating 310 313
Tribissen 241 268
Triglycerides 117 130
Trimming Donkey Hooves 92
Trucking 38
    in hot weather 181
Tumor, cancer 143
Tumors 143
Twins 280
Twitching 314 303

U
Udder edema 293
Umbilical cord infections 306-308
Urinary stones 203

V
Vaccinations
    Chart 262
    costs 259
    dose for miniatures 243
    vaccination tips 260
    foal 246 262
    by geographical location 249
Vaccine Products 244
Vaccine research 244
Veterinarian, Tips on getting along
    with 115
    evaluating potential 114
    Veterinarians, choosing 113
Vices, wood chewing 310
Viral infections 160 240 254
Viruses 149
    Virus in donkeys 149 151
    and diarrhea 164

Vitamin E 190
Vitamin supplements 322

W
Warts 218
Weanlings
    cold weather care of 81
    feeding 49
    new 49
    respiratory infection 251
    training 50
Weeds, poisonous 121
Weight Loss 212   133   140
    208
White blood cell count 118
White Line Disease 103
White Muscle Disease 190
Winter care 81
Winter care, weanlings 81
Wood chewing 310
Wood shavings 74
Working with your donkey 330   314
Worming Methods 277
Worms 270
    dewormer pastes 277
    diarrhea 163

Z
Zimecterin paste 163   272   277
    87